Also available at all good book stores

9781785315688

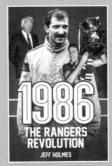

9781785311666

9781785314063

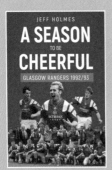

9781785313257

9781785311499

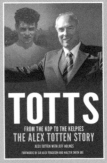

9781785310218

9781785312519

TORTURED

TORTURED

THE
SAM ENGLISH
STORY

JEFF HOLMES

First published by Pitch Publishing, 2020

Pitch Publishing
A2 Yeoman Gate
Yeoman Way
Worthing
Sussex
BN13 3QZ
www.pitchpublishing.co.uk
info@pitchpublishing.co.uk

A CIP catalogue record is available for this book
from the British Library.

ISBN 978 1 78531 725 5

Typesetting and origination by Pitch Publishing
Printed and bound in India by Replika Press Pvt. Ltd.

Contents

Introduction

IN AN era when many centre-forwards ploughed a self-regarding furrow up top, Sam English was the antithesis. So far removed from the role of maverick striker, he preferred instead to embrace combination – and it didn't stop the goals flowing.

Pulling his story together took around five or six years; a wee bit longer than normal but, as my granny often said, 'If you're going to do something, you might as well do it right.' When researching an era such as this, confirming data to be accurate can be a real issue. I like to find at least two sources which corroborate the information, but sometimes you don't have that luxury. You need to make a judgement call, especially on the few occasions where even verifying an interesting piece of information proves impossible. It's so frustrating when it's something that's far too good to chuck in the bin.

In the early days of my research, when a young colleague heard what I was working on, he asked, 'Sam English – isn't that the guy who killed John Thomson?'

Strangely enough, it's a 'line' I'd been brought up believing. Sam English played for Rangers long before I started going to

Ibrox, some 40 years or so, but it was a common misconception for those who didn't know any better, regardless of era. And it also illustrates to some extent what English must have been forced to endure throughout not just his career but most of his life. 'The guy who killed John Thomson,' regardless of the truth.

Thing is, he was no more to blame for the death of the young goalkeeper than any of the other players on the park that day. It was the most unfortunate of accidents, and while the Celtic goalkeeper tragically passed away a few hours after the match, it's no exaggeration to say that a big part of Sam English also died in the Glasgow hospital that night.

Sam's career had really taken off during his time at Yoker Athletic. The young man, born in the north of Ireland but brought up in Scotland from before the age of two, was the genuine article in front of goal and quickly became the hero of Holm Park. Due to a split within the structure of Junior football, Senior clubs were prohibited from signing players from the Intermediate ranks, and the Yoker committee took full advantage of the situation to assemble a thoroughly decent side – spearheaded by 20-year-old English – that were regularly in the hunt for top honours.

In his three seasons at Yoker, he scored more than 250 goals, an incredible haul which marked him down as a wanted man once the Intermediate dispute was over. When the time came, a glorious line of top clubs were queuing up to sign the young shipyard worker with magic in his boots. Arsenal and Rangers were at the front of the queue, but there were many others. Legendary Gunners boss Herbert Chapman had personally travelled north – just days after an operation – in an attempt to secure Sam's signature. In a face-to-face with the player, in a twilight rendezvous at a Glasgow hotel, he would say, 'I'll admit I don't know much about you, but as every other club seems to want your signature, I would be foolish not to join the queue!'

Of course, Bill Struth – who had been slipping Sam regular 'bungs' during the Intermediate period – won the race to sign English and the talented centre-forward had the most sensational debut campaign. I offer up 44 league goals as proof; an Ibrox record which still stands today, 88 years after it was set. A first-year rookie knocking it out the park was real-life Roy of the Rovers stuff, but there was certainly more to this young man than goals.

He had the lot. His control of the ball was top-drawer, he could shoot with both feet, he possessed near-Olympic style speed over the necessary distance, and his ability to link up play from middle to front was positively revolutionary.

And for a man a shade under 5ft 8in, he could head the ball with a technical accuracy that was anything but an integral part of the game in the 1930s. Dixie Dean, of Everton, is frequently held up as the perfect centre-forward; the best in the history of British football, but the late, great Bob McPhail – no slouch in front of goal himself – once said, 'Though I never played with the great Dixie Dean, I did play against him. I would have taken English before him.'

The revered right-half, Chic Geatons, who played for Celtic from 1927 to 1941, said, 'Sam English was quickly becoming one of the best centre-forwards of his time. He was not a rough player; he was a cultured footballer, and I know that if anyone could have avoided that impact [with John Thomson] it would have been Sam.'

While English played for Liverpool it was suggested that he led the Anfield line in a way no one had done previously. He was a team player, had a devotion to combination and always put the good of the team before his own interests.

English would also play for Queen of the South and Hartlepools United, but by that time he was going through the motions and playing merely for a wage. Any love he'd once had for the beautiful game had long since dissipated, which was no surprise as on arriving home one day, after playing a round of golf on a rare day off, he was greeted by the sight of his three little girls waiting patiently in the driveway of his Dalmuir home. 'Daddy, did you kill a man?' asked Eleanor, his youngest. While playing in the local park, a boy of primary school age had asked young Eleanor that very question. This was a few years after the incident. At that moment, it was clear there would be no rest for Sam; a tragic accident in a football match would define him for the rest of his life.

When he finished playing he went back to work in the shipyards, and even when ill health forced him to give up work, the odd Saturday afternoon outing to the football would be met with the type of stares normally reserved for a grotesque peep show.

As much as the kind words from fellow professionals and team-mates were welcome at the time of the accident, these were soon vastly overshadowed by the terracing taunts, shouts in the street and the sick comments from fellow pros on the park. No matter how much he tried to get on with his life, and career, the events of Saturday, 5 September 1931 refused to conform, and followed him around like a recurring nightmare.

The bright light which had once illuminated this young, talented footballer was slowly dimming, and despite finding some form of solace on the football field for a time after the accident, at the end of that season the light had not only dimmed quite considerably, it had all but gone out. Try as he might – and boy did he try to keep his career illuminated via several fresh starts – it was more or less over. Not even the comforting words of John Thomson's parents, who said that they truly hoped he could overcome the events of that horrific day, were enough to give him the strength to continue to do what he had been doing so well. As the light faded, so too did the soul of Sam English.

Seven joyless years of sport indeed.

One

IF EVER one could choose their birthplace, the tranquillity, beauty and lush, rolling hills of Crevolea would be an excellent place to start. The slow pace of life and natural splendour entranced both Richard English and his wife, Jane Milliken, just like their parents before them, so it was no great surprise when they chose to raise their family in the small townland they called home.

Crevolea is one of more than 60 such townlands in the parish of Aghadowey, which is situated in the vast county of Londonderry, in the north of Ireland, just slightly east of centre. The town closest to Crevolea is Coleraine, just eight miles to the north, while the village of Garvagh is less than five miles away in the opposite direction.

The birthplace of Sam English takes in an area of around half a mile and has just a single street. You can hear a pin drop as you walk along the narrow, but deserted pavements in the picture-postcard hamlet. Time has stood still in Crevolea, where a couple of dozen houses are protected from the outside world by rows of carefully planted trees, standing guard jealously in perfect formation, just 40 minutes – but a world away – from the nearby city of Londonderry.

Our story starts a few hundred yards from the main Drumcroon Road on the morning of Saturday, 8 August 1908, when Richard and Jane English introduced Samuel as their tenth child. When the fair-haired baby was settling down to life in the brood, he had nine sets of sibling eyes trained upon his tiny frame, as well as those of his proud parents. William, who was 18, Robert (17), James (15), Bessie (13), Annie (11), Ellen (eight), David (six), Jane (four) and Richard (16 months) were more than happy to welcome this new life into the family. One more child, Mary, would come along a little more than four years later, once the family had moved away from Crevolea. Only then would there be enough children to complete Richard's very own football team! So how appropriate that young Samuel was born on a Saturday.

For now, though, home was Crevolea, a Presbyterian stronghold where all but one of the 62 residents practised this faith. In fact, in 1908, the vast majority – around 90 per cent – of those living in the northern part of the country were Presbyterian.

Life in Crevolea, while undertaken at a slower pace than any of the main towns or ports in the north of Ireland, was still tough, and it was becoming increasingly harder for Richard to eke out a living on his small farm and provide for his burgeoning family.

Although born in the United States, Richard came from strong Aghadowey stock. His mother and father, James English and Elizabeth Gresham, had married in 1865 in Aghadowey Parish Church, and left shortly after the wedding to start a new life in America, as James had family there. The American Civil War hadn't long ended, and even though the effects of the four-year conflict were still being felt from north to south, the English family pressed on with their plans. Richard was born in 1867, and his father had still hoped to make a go of it in the new world, but Elizabeth longed for home and so the family made the decision to return to their roots and re-settle in Ireland, where they would raise their children in Aghadowey.

After meeting and marrying local lass Jane Milliken, Richard had taken on the smallholding at number nine Crevolea Road, which was situated just a few hundred yards from the main street. The three bedrooms in the pretty grey-brick house with low-slung thatched roof provided adequate accommodation for the family, and was one of just 11 dwellings in Crevolea. There were three windows to the front of the house, which meant stunning views of the sweeping countryside, which extended as far as the eye could see.

Richard's land included space for six outbuildings and, at the time, was the perfect place to bring up a large family with young children. The popular farmer kept cows and pigs and was helped with day-to-day chores by his brother, David, who lived close by at number 11. Their sister, Elizabeth, also lived at number 11, which was rented from the landholder.

But his main source of income, like many contemporary Irish farmers, was through the production of flax fibre, which was grown on the farm and then scutched, to separate the impurities from the raw material, such as straw and woody stem. Once scutched, the fibre would be bunched together – hence the saying 'flaxen hair' – and sold to agents. It was stronger than cotton fabric, but less pliable, and while the best grades were used for lace and damask, coarser cuts would generally be kept by the farmer and used to produce twine and rope. The linen industry was important to the Irish economy during the 18th and 19th centuries, and following the scutching process, many families would be employed by the agents to spin the flax into yarn, or bleach the linen. In the late 1800s and early 1900s, bleaching greens were a popular sight in Aghadowey.

Irish linen was world renowned, but while an abundance of flax had been growing in the country since the 11th century, by the end of the 1800s, countries in the north of Europe, such as Belgium and the Netherlands, had become the main centres of flax and linen, and as a consequence most of the trade in Ireland was lost to these countries.

Richard worked long hours to provide for his growing family, but as the focus of the flak trade shifted east, he was finding it increasingly difficult to make ends meet, and one spring evening, sat down with wife Jane to discuss their future. The majority of the children were fast asleep when their worried parents eventually came to a tough decision. They would leave behind the solitude of Crevolea in order to find the type of employment that would put food on the table and also provide a whole range of future opportunities for their children.

Richard and Jane realised that their children were growing up fast and that there wasn't sufficient job opportunities locally to satisfy everyone. The couple spoke of moving elsewhere within Ireland, but in the end somewhat reluctantly decided to let out the farm and head off to try their luck in Canada. It was a speculative and bold decision but one that was taken with their children foremost in their minds. No more would they open their front door to reveal some of the lushest grassy fields north of Belfast. The house, set back from the small through road which was just 15 yards from their front door, had been a good home to the English family for more than a decade, but it was time for a change and they began to make arrangements for their impending move across the Atlantic.

It was February 1910, and even though there was little interest in their property at first, they would sit it out and wait a few months before making any final decisions. Sadly, though, their plans were hampered by a general lack of interest in the farm, and without a tenant in place they were forced to abandon the notion of Canada in the short term. They resurrected the idea a few months later, although this time decided to put the farm up for sale.

But during the period between the English family putting their house on the market, and actually finding a buyer, Richard had been speaking to friends with family members who had made the move to Scotland, mostly to Greenock, and found employment. It wasn't nearly as far as Canada and there was the possibility of semi-regular trips home to consider. This curveball was a serious contender, so Richard and Jane gave their new option due consideration. Meanwhile, Richard learned of possible job opportunities at the growing John Brown shipyard, in the Clydebank area of Glasgow. It had become one of the most famous in the world through building and launching the likes of the RMS *Lusitania*, and he was tipped off that they were recruiting all manner of employees. The company had established a works in Coventry, and bought a stake in a Spanish naval yard, but it was the expansion to cover 80 acres at its Clydebank base which piqued his curiosity. It was boom time on the River Clyde; the ideal time, in fact, to make the move.

The sale of the farm was set for Monday, 29 August, and Richard was told by the auctioneers that it would be far easier to sell the property than find someone willing to take up the lease. Up for grabs was 15 acres of prime, arable land in the highest possible state of cultivation. There was easy access, and it was well fenced off and had good drainage.

Included in the sale was two good dairy cows, four young cattle and two fields of prime oats. The family house and offices were also part of the deal.

The sale took place on the farm and on the day, there was keen competition for No 9 Crevolea. After some frantic bidding, the winner was Mr John Kirkpatrick, from Dromore, which is south of Belfast. Mr Kirkpatrick paid a little over £237 for the property, and Richard was pleased with the price. It was a weight off his mind, and the handover was set for 1 November. However, in the middle of October, Richard held a sale of all household goods, including a grandfather clock, sewing machine and bicycle, and the family moved out of No 9 Crevolea later that day. They were ready to move to Scotland. They would be travelling light, with only one suitcase each of private possessions.

The family were ready to embark on a new adventure, with Richard, almost literally, at the helm of the ship. But even though their prospects were greater, it was still a tough decision to leave behind a home that had held so many special memories, but reality and necessity forced Richard's hand and as they filed dutifully on to the boat, they watched with tears in their eyes as the vessel left Belfast harbour and the city soon became a distant dot on the horizon. There were more tears on the three-hour journey to Scotland, but also hope.

And with every door that closes, a new one invariably opens, so Richard secured for the family a three-bedroom flat in Dalmuir, just a short bus ride from John Brown shipyard. Glenruther Terrace had rows of red sandstone tenement flats running the entire length of one side of the street, while on the other, tenement blocks stood either side of allotments, a park and a bowling green to offer much-needed green space. Thomas Lyle's popular restaurant was further down the terrace, closer to Dumbarton Road, while many 'delinquents' could often be found in the Clydesdale Billiard Saloon, which was run by James Brown.

Dalmuir was on the outskirts of Glasgow, roughly nine miles from the centre of the city. The bus journey could take around 40 minutes, but while the city was well within reach, Dalmuir was also far enough away to be referred to as 'out in the sticks' by Glaswegians, and while not on the same rural scale as Crevolea, there were still many parks for children to play happily in.

Within two years of the family's big move, Sam had enrolled at Dalmuir School, and his father was working as a labourer in the iron shop at John Brown shipyard, before becoming a storeman with the shipping giant. Despite being born in the US, he was able to work in Scotland as he was classed as a British subject, as his mother and father had been born in Ireland.

Both William and James worked as distillery clerks, like their mother, while Bessie was a machine needle worker in Singer's sewing machine factory in nearby Clydebank. Annie was a waitress in a fish restaurant, and Nellie was a message girl with a local grocery. The employment prospects of the family had indeed been greatly enhanced by the move to Scotland, and sufficient money was coming in to run the house comfortably, albeit with a degree of prudence.

But the family wasn't yet complete, and on 5 November 1912, child number 11, Mary, was introduced to the world and was born just round the corner from the family home in Dumbarton Road. By this time, David, Jane, Richard and Sam were all at school, but with a new life in the house there was always someone around to take care of babysitting duties.

At the start of the 1960s, Sam told the *Daily Express* newspaper of his earliest memories of living in Dalmuir, and his recollections of becoming interested in football. He said, 'There was never much money for buying footballs. Johnny Forsyth in the next close, I recall, had a number two bladder, or "blether" as we called it. But my brother Dick and I had to be content with an ordinary tanner ball.

'Even on the rainiest days we were off with it up to Somerville Park. Often just the two of us. On cold, damp grass we chased and trapped and punted through endless wet afternoons. And in the evenings our mother always had to call us up from the dirt yard beside the house, as we would have been out there practising into the wee, small hours.

'Dick excelled at wee headies against the wall. In fact, he had a brown scar on his forehead from it. He was always a better player than me. Perhaps I never would have been a great footballer. I was fit and fast – as quick over a two-yard burst as [former Rangers star] Torry Gillick, I'd like to think.

'We came from farming stock but my older brother, Bob, was also into football, and when we were in Dalmuir he would tell me of the games he played in the farmyard at our old home in Crevolea with other kids. They didn't have a ball so they would kick around a pig's bladder. Although I was too small to remember that, our place must have been good football country as nearby Coleraine bred the likes of Bertie Peacock, Billy Cook and Peter Doherty, all players of great quality, and all players who would sample life at some of the top clubs.'

Robert, the second-eldest of the English brood, was the only sibling not to travel to Scotland with the family, instead opting for a new start in the USA with relatives of his father. He would serve in the US Army during the First World War and eventually settled in Delaware, Pennsylvania. Older brother James also latterly crossed the Atlantic and remained in the United States for the rest of his life.

Two

IN THE 1920s there was a period of real upheaval in post-war Britain, and cities like Glasgow were still feeling the effects of First World War hardship. The economy was slow to recover after peace had been declared in Europe and the deterioration in living standards was something still being experienced by the majority of Glaswegians. This was the catalyst for the Labour Party's rise to prominence at the start of the 1920s (they were founded in 1900) as they promised to tackle the living conditions of the poor. Socialist visionaries like John Wheatley insisted that better housing conditions could only be achieved by voting in a Labour government and a political struggle between the main parties ensued. But it still wasn't anything like the struggle ordinary people were enduring on a day-to-day basis.

'Along Clydeside in the hungry 1920s there were two roads a youngster could take to free himself from the back streets. He could kick himself out, or he could deal himself out. There was football and there were cards.

'There wasn't much else. Work was short; leisure time ample. And in the shadow of the silent shipyards along the river we improved wonderfully at football and pontoon. It became a point of pride to leave no stone un-kicked. Every tin can lying in the street was reason enough for picking sides and having a game.'

The retrospective words of Sam English paint a vivid picture of how his life was, and life in general, in the early 20th century in the west of Scotland. The country was at the beginning of the Great Depression of the 1920s, and hardest hit were the industrial and mining areas of Scotland and the north of England. Unemployment reached 70 per cent in some areas and Clydeside, which relied heavily upon shipping for jobs, was particularly hard hit. The population of Scotland at the time was just shy of the five million mark, which meant a great deal of people were without a job, and living day-to-day was incredibly tough.

It was a far cry from just a decade earlier when the prospect of employment in the shipyards, and jobs for his growing brood, had led to Richard English abandoning his Canadian dream in favour of Scotland, and the lure of the shipyard. But nothing is for ever.

In late spring/early summer, 1923, a teenage Sam was among the latest crop of youngsters to emerge from Dalmuir School. How to find a job was the big question. He was eager to work, which was half the battle, and was fortunate enough to secure a position as a grocer's boy in a shop close to his home. He was 14 years old and would be in the shop early in the morning to help the shop assistants prepare the store for opening time. He would then spend the next few hours on his bike delivering groceries to customers in the Dalmuir area. With so many children in the family, and employment at a premium, every penny was a prisoner and the money Sam earned went straight into the pot to help with the household bills and upkeep.

But it wasn't too long before the youngster was facing a dilemma. His interest in football had grown steadily and it was becoming more and more apparent that he had something special about him. He had performed admirably for his school team, which had gained notable success with Sam leading the line. Local youth and amateur teams were starting to take notice, and he regularly had representatives of clubs on his doorstep. The only trouble was, these clubs played on either a Saturday morning or afternoon, and the first day of the weekend was one of the busiest of the week in the grocer's shop.

Sam sought the advice of his father, a quietly spoken man, and told him he was keen to work, but not at the weekend. His dad was very supportive and told his son to 'leave it with' him. Sam continued to toil away at the grocery store until the day his father took him aside and told him he was starting in the shipyards as a plater's boy on the Monday morning. His new employer was William Beardmore and Company, an active engineering and shipbuilding firm in Dalmuir which, at its peak, employed some 13,000 people.

In 1900, Beardmore had working shipyards in Govan and Dalmuir, situated on opposite banks of the River Clyde from one another. Notable warships produced by the firm included HMS *Conqueror* and HMS *Benbow*, as well as HMS *Argus*, the first aircraft carrier to have a full-length flight deck. The firm was soon involved in the manufacture of all sorts of arms and armaments. They were working hard to buck the trend of lost contracts and laying off men, and were still the major employer in the Dalmuir area.

A plater was a skilled job and, as the plater's boy, Sam would be responsible for helping to lay plates of steel which would form a ship's hull. These would be rolled in the various contours required to form the curvature of the hull. The plates would then have to be riveted or welded together. It would have been hard going for young Sam as plates were generally too heavy for one man to lift, and the conditions would also have been tough. In the winter it was a hardy and thankless task.

But every cloud has a silver lining, and in this case the silver lining for Sam came in the form of Dalmuir Albion, the Beardmore football team. Sam wasn't yet 16 but he was growing up fast and playing for the works' side toughened him up no end. Despite the unforgiving nature of his job, Sam enjoyed his time at Beardmore, mainly due to the half-hour he got at dinner time, when there would be at least three games of football taking place on the waste ground outside the yard. It was all hands on deck and players would come and go as breaks were staggered and they would be designated a team as and when they arrived to join in the action.

Sam served his time as a plater and no sooner had his apprenticeship ended than he was on the move, around two miles or so along Dumbarton Road. It was perhaps the equivalent of moving from Partick Thistle to Rangers, without a fee, of course. When Sam took up a job in the sheet metal department, in 1926, John Brown was still one of the most highly regarded, and internationally famous, shipbuilding companies in the world.

Once again, though, one of the main attractions for this football-mad teenager was the thriving sports scene they had going at Brown. In fact, in his first year with the firm, Sam was part of the Sheet Metal Department team that won the John Brown Shop League. A team-mate in that side was Alex Allan, who played for Queen's Park, but 'give the ball to Sam and he'll stick it in the rigging' was a familiar cry. For Sam, this period of his life was as carefree as it got, and he cherished every moment.

But he wasn't the only member of his family with a keen interest in the round ball. Older brother Richard was also a talented footballer, and plied his trade on the right wing, creating opportunities for numerous strikers throughout his ten-year career playing at Junior level.

At the beginning of the 1926/27 season, Richard signed for Old Kilpatrick, who played in the Scottish Junior League (perhaps the equivalent of non-league football in England) and were based at Lusset Park, which was just off busy Great Western Road. Dick, as he was known to all, had scored a couple of goals and made quite an impact by the time he managed to persuade the manager to give his kid brother, who hadn't long turned 18, a chance with the team.

One of the first games Sam played for Old Kilpatrick was a Dunbartonshire Junior Charity Cup tie at Lusset against Singer's, a Clydebank works' team. Sam scored to give his side the lead – a goal set up by his brother – but with ten minutes remaining, and the home side leading 2-0, the referee called a halt to the game as darkness had enveloped the ground. There were no floodlights, so Sam's first goal at Junior level was disappointingly struck from the records, although there would be plenty more like it at that level in the next three or four years.

For the moment, though, Sam was in and out of the team – more out – for the remainder of the campaign as the manager preferred the more experienced centre-forward, Kane, to the youthful exuberance of the young and raw English.

And Sam was a spectator when Old Kilpatrick reached the final of the Dumbartonshire Junior Cup at the end of the season. Richard lined up against Dumbarton Harp but was left disappointed on the Senior turf of Kilbowie as the Harp ran out 4-2 winners. Recalling his inauspicious start to Junior football, Sam told the *Daily Express* in 1963, 'My brother Dick and I played for Old Kilpatrick and we received one shilling a game, although we didn't even always get that. I recall on one occasion we were up against Paisley Juniors, at Lusset Park, and some of their players came straight to Old Kilpatrick from their work. After the game, it turned out a few of them didn't have enough to pay their fare home and so officials of our club took our shillings back to help ensure they got home.'

Sam was only with Old Kilpatrick for a single season, as was Dick. And while opportunities were thin on the ground for the younger of the English brothers, the experience gained in the time he played was invaluable. In the 1920s, the gap between Senior and Junior level wasn't nearly as big as it is today, and crowds at the leading games were often counted in five figures.

Old Kilpatrick were a provincial Junior side but still played at a decent level, although when the new season started it was a similar story as the elder of the brothers was once again in demand. Dick was wanted by a couple of clubs but Port Glasgow won the race for his signature. Mind you, Sam was never too far from his side and was a regular at Garvel Park as the season started in August 1927. On one occasion, the Port were short of someone to play up front and Sam was signed as an emergency trialist. He showed up well and was offered terms to sign on for the season, which would be an interesting one, as plans were under way by the Glasgow Junior Football League (GJL) to break away from the Scottish Junior Football Association (SJFA). The plans soon came to fruition – and the renegade Intermediate League was born.

The GJL was the strongest Junior league in Scotland, having provided 15 of the 26 Scottish Junior Cup winners since the turn of the century, but member clubs had grown increasingly dissatisfied with the behaviour of Senior clubs, on both sides of the border, as they would often approach a player without first contacting his club, and offer little in the way of compensation. The GJL had attempted to introduce a registration form which was designed to give clubs greater protection and compensation should they lose a player. It was unsuccessful, but this form would become the cornerstone of the new Intermediate movement.

A total of 62 clubs met at the tail end of the 1926/27 season, and while they had the sympathy of the SJFA, the members of the GJL felt the game's governing body had been weak in their negotiations with the Senior association and failed in their duty to look after the best interests of its member clubs. They decided it was time for radical change.

The SJFA refused to sanction the breakaway Intermediate League, and the reaction of the Scottish Football Association (SFA) was merely to prohibit the signing of any registered Intermediate player. The result was that in the summer of 1927, the powerful GJL dissolved itself at its AGM and its 20 member clubs were joined by a further 20 from other leagues to form the Scottish Intermediate Football Association (SIFA). Clubs in Ayrshire broke away from the Western Junior Football League and reformed as the Western Intermediate Football League at the same time with 16 of the 18 clubs supporting the dispute. From the beginning of the 1927/28 season, Intermediate clubs began to compete in separate competitions, including their own Scottish Intermediate Cup.

The dispute would last for four years, and in that period, Senior clubs were forbidden from signing players from the Intermediate Leagues. That meant stability for the clubs involved in the breakaway associations, and as a result the quality and standard of the league remained incredibly high. In an interview many years later, Sam would say, 'I still maintain the standard of football played by many of the Junior clubs was the highest ever reached in Scotland – better even than many of the continental teams who played over here in the 1960s.'

But we're getting ahead of ourselves. Sam had signed for Port Glasgow and while he didn't feature in the first few matches of the season, Dick played a pivotal role. Sam eventually made his debut under the well-known pseudonym of the time, 'Newman', against Maryhill in a league match at Garvel Park. Sam played his part in an impressive 3-0 win for his new side as both he and the Port adapted to life in the tough and competitive Intermediate set-up.

On Saturday, 17 September the Port journeyed across the water to Helensburgh and Sam announced his arrival by scoring three times in a 6-1 romp. His first hat-trick in the Juniors was followed by a couple of singles and then, four weeks later, a second treble as the Port entertained high-flying St Roch's. Sadly, Sam's side lost 4-3, but his individual stock was rising, and folk were starting to sit up and take notice of this dashing teenage centre-forward with the easily identifiable shock of flaxen hair.

He was playing well and contributing to the team on a weekly basis. He was learning all the time and also enjoying his football, especially playing alongside his brother, who was a real creative talent. At the end of January, Sam was in sparkling form at Johnstone Rovers, and helped make the winner in a thrilling encounter. The following Saturday, Port locals were looking forward to the visit of Ashfield – a top Glasgow team – and Sam was set to test himself against one of the meanest defences in the division. It was a cracking game, but unfortunately the gods intervened and a torrential downpour 15 minutes from the end led to the referee abandoning the game.

Seven days later, Sam scored to win Port a valuable point at Renfrew, but after drawing a blank in a 1-0 defeat at Camelon, he was dropped for a Scottish Intermediate Cup tie against Troon, although his replacement, Cook, was deemed a flop.

The younger English was reintroduced to the side for a cup tie against Shettleston, but was well marshalled by imposing centre-half Basil Leitch who, it is recorded, attached himself to English like a leech to skin. Still, he was deemed a success and played in the replay the following week in Glasgow. Port lost 1-0, but the next day, the committee released the following statement: 'Some of our players have been getting a lot of abuse from supporters in recent games, which has prompted us to warn those fans that abuse will not be tolerated at Garvel Park or anywhere else. Supporters who continue this futile barracking will be ejected from the ground and banned if caught.'

When Ashfield visited Garvel for the re-arranged league fixture, 5,000 spectators packed into the trim ground. However, there was a shock in store for the English brothers as only Dick was listed in the starting 11. The Port had signed a new centre-forward, McKeegan, and he scored both goals in a memorable 2-1 success.

Sam found himself surplus to requirements but still attended every match, looking on as the much more experienced McKeegan scored regularly until the end of the season, when in a shock recall, Sam found himself in the line-up for the final league match against Maryhill at Lochburn Park. The Port lost 3-1 and it was the last time Sam would turn out for the club as he was released a few days later.

To shed a young player after a single season, especially one who had shown excellent potential, seemed rather short-sighted, given he was still a teenager and had scored a couple of hat-tricks. He had also gained valuable experience against some of the top Junior sides in the game, and despite the goals drying up to an extent, he finished the season with nine, which was a decent return for a 19-year-old playing his first full season at this level. One would have thought the Port committee might have been able to look beyond a mid-season barren spell, and try to take advantage of both the player's youth and the obvious experience he had gained, but they were quick to let him go, which prompted one newspaperman to say, just a couple of months later, 'Oops, someone at Port Glasgow has blundered badly.'

Sam was philosophical about the parting of the ways, and recalled, 'After just the one season with Port Glasgow I received a free transfer. My apprenticeship as a sheet metal worker in John Brown's was about halfway finished, although I was more interested in going dancing every night.

'I had almost decided to abandon the game, and how much happier if I had. But Yoker Athletic officials came to the house one Sunday afternoon. My father took them through to the front room, and there he told them bluntly, "This boy will be no good to you. He's never home any night before midnight!"

'But his words didn't deter them and they offered me a £5 signing-on fee, and I thought I might as well take it. Three great years followed. Wages were good enough, £2 for an ordinary league game, sometimes three of them a week. Journeymen's wages then were less than £3. And because of the intense rivalry between Yoker and nearby Clydebank, Junior gates often soared to 10,000.'

A new chapter in the short life of Sam English was about to begin and, as far as the football was concerned, it would be the happiest period of his career. The dancing might have been forsaken, but this twinkle-toed youngster was all set to put both feet to far better use.

Three

SAM ENGLISH skipped down the stairs of the double-decker bus and alighted opposite an eight-foot high red brick wall. He was nervous as he walked the short distance from the bus stop to the place that was to be his new football home. He crossed Dumbarton Road, boots tucked tightly between his upper arm and ribcage, and followed the path round the wall to the entrance of the trim little ground.

'Welcome to Holm Park!'

After having put pen to paper and signed for Yoker Athletic, Sam was viewed as an important piece of the jigsaw. The Yoker committee were constructing a formidable side, one that would eventually see them become one of the main players in the Scottish Intermediate movement – and one of the top clubs in Scottish Junior football. But it wouldn't happen overnight.

Holm Park lay in the shadow of the River Clyde, and at the heart of the vast shipbuilding industry of which Sam was already a part. He was just shy of his 20th birthday, and very much learning his trade, both in industry and football, but the likes of Davie Stewart and Duncan Mills were already among the best half-backs in the game, and the hope was that these Yoker stalwarts could provide Sam with the ammunition to bang in the goals. They had clearly seen in Sam something that Port Glasgow hadn't and felt he was well worth taking a punt on, given the signing-on fee which had changed hands.

The Holm Park side would be looking for a good return on their investment and viewed Sam as the man to help them go head-to-head with fellow Glasgow sides Ashfield, Pollok and Bridgeton Waverley. These clubs were the real threat to a resurgent Yoker, and their head-to-head battles would go a long way to determining the destination of the 1928/29 season's honours.

With both shipbuilding and team-building taking centre stage in the Yoker area, the committee had gone about their business quietly and effectively. Those in charge were also aware that if there was no quick solution to the Intermediate dispute, then there would be a rare opportunity to build something meaningful at Holm Park, and they were ready to take full advantage of the situation.

The players were put through a rigorous pre-season training programme. Sam trained until he dropped, and by the time the new football season kicked off on Wednesday, 1 August 1928, he was raring to go. Of course, he had to be, as Yoker were scheduled to play an incredible 14 matches during the month of August alone – almost one game every two days.

There was a real buzz of expectancy when the fixtures were released; Clydebank away on the opening day. It didn't get any better for supporters of both sides – and the neutral. In fact, more than 4,000 filed into the original Kilbowie Park and they weren't to be disappointed. It was thrill-a-minute stuff as the teams shared eight goals. Sam scored on his debut and was still tingling with excitement when the game was over and the players made their way back to the dressing rooms. The spectators were also delighted as they had got their money's worth, an important consideration in these cash-strapped times.

And 48 hours later he was at Holm Park, scoring twice as Yoker edged Glasgow giants St Roch's 4-3. It was an early message of intent. The next day he was back on familiar turf, as Yoker headed to Garvel Park to take on Port Glasgow. Sam was playing on a pitch he knew only too well and helped Yoker rack up another two league points. There were some long faces on the Garvel terracing as they watched Sam lead the Yoker line with aplomb and an old head way beyond his years. Another goal was the icing on the cake.

The games were coming thick and fast, and that tough pre-season training kicked in, but the players were given an unexpected rest when Camelon refused to travel to Holm Park, suggesting the 7pm kick-off was far too early for their players to be able to get home from work and then travel from Falkirk to Glasgow. The game was postponed and the authorities no doubt agreed as they rescheduled it for a Saturday afternoon later on in the season. A lack of midweek action failed to dampen Sam's enthusiasm, nor break his stride, as the hungry young goal-getter scored a staggering 20 times in the month of August. Included in this total was a four-goal salvo in a 7-1 rout of Neilston Victoria at Holm Park.

Even so early in his fledgling Junior career he was showing signs of possessing all the necessary attributes to make him a success. Goals – the number one priority in any game – were coming thick and fast, but it was his ability to bring others into the game which made him the perfect link man, and, of course, he was developing a penchant for shooting with either foot. He was also thriving on the type of service he received from the creative influences around him and the early signs were positive. Give this lad an opportunity and he was likely to convert it.

And Yoker started September like an express train – although against Glasgow Perthshire they received a little help from the referee. Four minutes before the interval, Mills flashed a low shot across the face of the Shire goal. The ball struck the post and rebounded out, straight into the arms of the goalkeeper. He picked up the ball and kicked it upfield but to everyone's astonishment, the referee signalled for a goal. Yoker went on to win 6-1, and the only other surprising aspect of the game was that Sam failed to score – although he did make a couple.

He wasn't exactly short of goals when the month ended, with the blank against Perthshire his only scoreless game from the five he played, as Yoker – nicknamed the Whe Ho – progressed in three cup competitions. Sam simply couldn't stop scoring.

When Yoker and Clydebank resumed hostilities at the end of October, the 'Ground Full' signs were up at Holm Park long before kick-off. This was the one everyone wanted to see. When the teams emerged from the tunnel for this Glasgow Intermediate Cup clash, up went the roars. The crowd, split almost evenly, were treated to another cracker, and saw Yoker take the lead through English, who took up the perfect position to hook in the opener. The Bankies scored either side of the break to overturn the deficit but English nodded home to tie the scores. Clydebank scored twice to make it 4-2 before the Irishman showed his class by deftly chipping the ball over Mathieson's head to make it 4-3. Yoker were out of the competition but Sam had turned in another top performance with a stunning hat-trick.

The impressive displays and wins kept on coming and by Christmas, Yoker were among the front runners for the league title. They had also successfully negotiated a couple of rounds of the Scottish Intermediate Cup – the premier trophy in the Junior game – but then came the third round against Wishaw, which by the time it had been concluded would read more like the plot of a long-running soap opera. It all began four days after Christmas, on the morning of Saturday, 29 December, when more than 200 supporters from Yoker set off on a special train, arriving at Recreation Park in plenty of time for the 2.15pm kick-off. A little later, the players and officials left Holm Park on a specially commissioned coach. There had been a slight worry over the condition of the Wishaw ground, as there had been an overnight frost, but the game was given the go-ahead just after midday.

Approaching 2pm, the ground was starting to fill up nicely, and the home players were out warming up on the pitch – but there was still no sign of the visiting team. When the scheduled kick-off time had come and gone, and the crowd were becoming increasingly restless, referee Aitken of Coatbridge phoned the Scottish Intermediate secretary to discuss the situation. It was 3pm and they agreed to call off the match, especially with darkness descending. It was decided that even if the match was to start, the chances of it being played to a finish were minimal. Fifteen minutes after that call, the visitors arrived, only to be informed that the game was off. Apparently the bus had taken a wrong turning at Parkhead Cross, and while it was a largely disappointed crowd which filed out of Recreation Park, the tie was quickly re-arranged for the following Saturday.

But disappointment again reigned supreme as a heavy frost got the better of the surface and the match was cancelled. The teams did, however, manage to get the game played the following Saturday and supporters were treated to a pulsating cup tie. Sam was on target for Yoker but the game ended honours even at two apiece and so the replay was set for Holm Park the following Saturday; week four of this epic struggle.

The teams were still inseparable after a further 90 minutes, with the best chance falling to Yoker when English set up Mills, although his goal-bound effort was deflected for a corner. No extra time and penalties in those days, so at the end of the match, the captains tossed the coin for choice of venue for the second replay, and it fell on the side of Yoker.

Yet another gruelling 90 minutes – which this time produced four goals – failed to separate these two great sides and the fourth match, played at Wishaw, was finally won by the home team. Sam found the net in the 4-2 loss but was ultimately left disappointed as his team had put so much into the tie. It had taken six hours of red-hot cup-tie football to separate the teams, but it was Wishaw who progressed. In the final match, the Lanarkshire side had led 3-1 with five minutes remaining. English scored to give his side hope but Colvin completed his hat-trick with virtually the last kick of the ball. A tie initially scheduled for December 1928 had finished in February 1929.

It was a huge disappointment for Yoker but they still had so much to play for. And they proved they had the bit between the teeth by embarking on an unbeaten run which saw them progress in the Dunbartonshire and Renfrewshire Cup and the Scottish Consolation Cup as well as making good headway in the league.

As the season entered its final stretch, Pollok arrived at Holm Park for what was more or less a straight shoot-out for second place in the Scottish Intermediate League. Four lost games in the opening month of the season had left just too big a gap for the team to close and it looked as though the runners-up spot would be the best they could achieve. Sadly, though, the big crowd looked on in disappointment as Sam seemed to have left his shooting boots at home. He missed a gilt-edged opportunity to fire Yoker ahead just before the break, and missed the target completely from seven yards moments into the second half. It simply wasn't his day. Yoker had started the second half well but referee Wilson stopped the game shortly afterwards to dismiss the Yoker linesman for 'ungentlemanly conduct'. The visitors were well on top and scored twice without reply.

As the campaign edged towards its climax, Yoker tumbled out of both the Kirkwood Shield and Dunbartonshire and Renfrewshire Cup competitions at the semi-final stages. A season that had promised so much was now seemingly set to deliver little in the way of silverware, but there was still one trophy left to play for – the end-of-season Elder Cottage Cup. Just before the last-four clash against St Anthony's, the Yoker players had a meeting at training and vowed to give it their best shot. They were clearly disappointed at the manner in which their season had panned out and were keen to make the Ants pay. They did just that, sticking eight past the beleaguered Govan side with Sam scoring four times.

And the talented striker was at it again in the final against Clydebank with four more. Yoker were comprehensive 6-0 winners and it was the perfect way to end a long and arduous campaign for both Sam and his club. It also vindicated the Yoker officials for sticking to their principles and insisting on playing open, attractive football, with an emphasis on keeping the ball on the ground. It was now regarded as 'the Yoker way' and would eventually bring success to the club.

Following stop-start campaigns with Old Kilpatrick and Port Glasgow, Sam had just completed his first full season at Junior level, and boy how he proved he had the tools to do the job. He'd scored around 80 goals in competitive matches and marked himself down as one of the leading lights in the league – and he was still just 20 years old. To score such a terrific number of goals against some of the toughest defenders in Scottish football was a fine achievement, although perhaps the downside was that both the Yoker Athletic officials and supporters would be looking for more of the same from the blond-haired centre-forward the following season. But Sam was determined to deliver and there was no doubt he was capable. He was a vital cog in the Yoker machine, and his star would only gain in popularity in the coming years.

There was a feeling of optimism around as the Yoker committee held their annual meeting at Holm Park on the eve of the new season. The team had achieved good things during 1928/29, and it was felt that the squad – which contained the majority of the players from the previous season – were capable of taking the next step and matching the so-called 'bigger clubs' when the league kicked off at the beginning of August. One or two little additions had been made, but no major surgery had been required.

Clydebank once again opened the season for the Whe Ho and, depending on which match report you read, the crowd inside Holm Park for the Friday night encounter numbered anything between five and ten thousand. What isn't in doubt, though, was the quality of football played by the hosts. The Bankies were pulled all over the park from the first minute until the last and English contributed two goals in Yoker's 6-1 win, picking up exactly where he'd left off.

Sadly though the action on the park was marred by the behaviour of a large number of supporters off it, and attracted newspaper headlines such as 'ROWDYISM AT YOKER' the following day. Police were called to disperse an unruly section of the crowd at the end of the game, just as the players were leaving the field. A Yoker player, it was alleged, struck and knocked down one of his opponents. The visiting fans were seething and a large number invaded the park. They were followed on to the playing surface by supporters of the home side and a pitched battle ensued. When the police arrived they worked hard to restore order but it was 10pm before they were able to eject the battling supporters from the stadium.

The following day, Yoker were back in league action, again at home, with Kirkintilloch Rob Roy this time providing the opposition. The players showed little sign of tiredness, especially English, who scored four times to make it six goals in 24 hours.

Yoker won 7-2, but it was anything but a stroll in the park. For 20 minutes, the Rabs looked the real deal, and even had the audacity to take a two-goal lead. This riled the home side and a beautiful left-foot drive by English started the rout. The Irishman was outstanding, with Davie Stewart a close second.

Many supporters left the ground – this time in orderly fashion – thinking that if their favourites could reproduce this kind of form away from home, they would surely give the rest of the league something to think about.

The goals kept coming and, at the start of September, Yoker climbed a massive hurdle by defeating Bridgeton Waverley – one of the era's top sides – away from home in the Glasgow and District Cup. The match was played at Waverley's new Barrowfield Park, which was situated on the boundary of Bridgeton and Camlachie. It was a hostile place to visit but Yoker won a hard-fought match 2-1 and Sam scored both goals. Psychologically, it was an important win.

Seven days later, Sam was on target four times as Yoker crushed Camelon 8-0 in the *Evening News* Cup. A Sunday newspaper report stated, 'Yoker certainly conveyed the impression to the very casual onlooker that they will be hard to beat this season. They have five dashing forwards, including a masterful marksman in Sam English, three stalwart half-backs, and a resolute pair of backs.'

But pride normally comes before a fall and Athletic were unceremoniously dumped out of the Scottish Cup by Duntocher Hibs at Glenhead Park. The home side won 3-0 and Sam was hardly given a sniff of the ball. It was a tough one to take. In fact, in their next match, there may still have been a sense of frustration in the air as in the process of easily beating Perthshire 3-0, tempers became frayed and there was a stand-up fight in the middle of the park. Strangely, the referee refused to send both players off. But it didn't seem to put English – described as an agile leader – off his game and he scored twice, his second goal being of the very highest quality.

Next up was a visit to the south side of Glasgow, and a match against the shut-out kings of the Intermediate League, Pollok, who went into the game having failed to concede in their previous 14 outings. The record ended that day, as Yoker edged it 2-1, and even though Sam failed to score, he was the architect of both goals.

And then the match that introduced English as not only one of the top strikers in the Junior game – but *the* striker at that level. Saturday, 2 November and big guns Petershill were the visitors to Holm Park. They were tipped to leave with both points, but Yoker were in no mood to be usurped at their Clydeside fortress and by the end of an incredible fixture they had scored 15 times. Yes, 15, and Sam had scored seven of them. The visitors looked shell-shocked at the end of a torrid 90 minutes. Yoker had just used Petershill to convey a message to the others in the league – 'ignore us at your peril'.

Strange thing is, it was goalless after 20 minutes, which means Yoker averaged a goal roughly every four minutes. And the course of the game changed when a Yoker player was ordered off. The home side were reduced to ten men when Blair was sent to the pavilion, and their numerical disadvantage served only to galvanise the remaining ten. They were 6-1 up at the interval, with English firing a first-half hat-trick.

There was a shock in store for the Petershill manager at the break when his goalkeeper, McCloy, refused to come out for the second half – as, 'What was the point?' Inside-left Beith donned the keeper's jersey, and was forced to visit the back of the net nine times, with Mills grabbing a hat-trick and English scoring a further four goals, which would contribute to his greatest haul in a single game. Afterwards, the Yoker manager reminded his players that they had received just two points for the win – but inside he must secretly have been buzzing.

They carried that form into the next league match, at Port Glasgow seven days later, and were four up just five minutes into the second half, due to a far superior passing game, when the referee abandoned the match due to heavy rain. The result, therefore, was null and void and Yoker slipped to fourth in the table, five points behind leaders Clydebank but with a game in hand.

The following Saturday, Yoker were again leading a league match, this time against Benburb, when the referee was forced to abandon the game due to darkness with just ten minutes remaining. Yet another Sam English goal was struck from the records.

Significantly, at the next league meeting, Yoker were fined ten shillings for a series of late kick-offs.

Thankfully, the League Cup tie against Clydebank four days before Christmas kicked off bang on time, and English made light work of the treacherous Holm Park surface to carve out a couple of early chances – but found former Stenhousemuir goalkeeper Shortt in terrific form for the Bankies.

After the break, Yoker opened in grand style, and in the first minute Shortt saved brilliantly from English's clever and deceptive screw shot, but the centre-forward managed to set up Cunningham, who scored the opener. As a result, the majority of the 3,500 crowd tossed their caps in the air. Clydebank equalised but with time running out, English was 'grassed' when he seemed set to score, and the appeal for a penalty was ignored.

But Sam wasn't to be denied when Glasgow giants Ashfield were first-footers to Holm Park for a vital league match. Yoker, even though they won quite comfortably, were far from convincing, and by the end of a tough 90 minutes, one man proved the difference between one point and two: English.

Until Sam had scored a second, there was always the possibility of the visitors snatching an equaliser, for their defence at times seemed impenetrable. As early as the first minute, Stewart slipped English through and only a timely tackle by Rennie saved the situation.

Yoker missed a penalty, but the overdue goal arrived on the stroke of half-time. Boyd sent in a rocket drive, which Ashfield keeper Kyle saved, but couldn't hold, and before he could clear, the lightning-quick English bundled both ball and keeper into the net, which was, of course, perfectly legal.

Early in the second half, English smartly netted a cross from Boyd, and after several missed chances by the forwards, English darted through to register his hat-trick. His final goal of the afternoon was his 38th of the season. The razor sharp instinct he had honed in front of goal rarely let him down, and he remained a constant thorn in the side of most defences.

Sam later admitted, 'Mainly I scored goals – which after all is what football is mostly about. In three years with Yoker Athletic I averaged [almost] 100 goals a season. My shot was never big. It was just that I could place the ball where I wanted it, or near about. That was what I did best.

'Looking back now, it seems strange that, for all our efforts, Clydebank and Dalmuir never produced more outstanding players. Patsy Gallacher had a spell with Clydebank Juniors. Jimmy McGrory was farmed out to them. And I remember Duncan Mills, Yoker's outside-left – the man with the 100-ton shot. We called him "pussy", but never to his face. He had a straight left as strong as Jack Dempsey's and a harder shot than the great Hungarian player, Puskas.'

One week later, Sam was out of luck in a Scottish Intermediate Consolation Cup tie at home to Shettleston. The Irishman did everything except find the net, including rattling the bar from distance, but with Yoker leading 2-1, and around 20 minutes left to play, snow which had been falling lightly started to come down heavily and when one of the visiting players slid for almost 30 yards before crashing into the perimeter fence, the referee stopped the match. The lines had also become unnoticeable so play ground to a premature halt.

When the match was replayed, a fortnight later, the supporters in the big crowd were treated to an absolute thriller. They looked on open-mouthed as Shettleston roared into a 4-1 lead – with English grabbing Yoker's goal. However, Sam was the victim of some rough play and when he reacted to one particularly nasty challenge, he was sent off. English, a stockily built forward, was used to handling close attention from rugged centre-halves, but on this occasion he felt it was excessive and took matters into his own hands.

The home side looked down and out, three goals in arrears and their greatest hope of a goal or two back in the pavilion. But when the chips are down … back came Yoker to score five times without reply to win 6-4.

English scored in his next two outings but was suspended for a league match against St Anthony's, which Yoker eventually won after the sides had scored eight goals between them.

As the season moved towards the end of March, league points were vital, so the home match against St Roch's was a must-win for the Holm Park side. The game would provide spectators with a marked contrast in playing methods. Yoker moved very methodically, but at times a proneness to develop a close passing game on the heavy surface robbed their play of greater success. The 'Candy Rock', on the other hand, swung the ball about in telling fashion and were always dangerous in and around the Yoker goal.

But only five minutes had elapsed when Yoker grabbed the lead, and once again it illuminated English's prowess in the six-yard box. Rock goalkeeper Blackstock brilliantly saved a strong drive from Mills, but when Blair pushed an accurate centre between the Garngad backs, English took advantage of fractional hesitation to push the ball home. Mills then made the game safe for Yoker.

English's talents were soon recognised at representative level when he was chosen to play for a Renfrewshire and Dunbartonshire Select against a Scottish Intermediate League XI in aid of struggling Duntocher Hibs at Glenhead Park. Two team-mates from the Whe Ho joined him.

The games were coming thick and fast and next up was a colossal struggle against fellow title challengers Glasgow Perthshire at their Balmore Park home. The big crowd were treated to a rousing game which finished with the visitors securing two vital league points. The home team were made to look mediocre at times and Yoker, who had a player sent off after four minutes, were leading 1-0 with 12 minutes remaining when English made the points safe with a fine header.

Big wins over Pollok and Maryhill – with Sam scoring in both – had Yoker hovering around the top three alongside Parkhead and Ashfield. It was anyone's title, but before a double header against Benburb and Duntocher Hibs, Sam had another match to attend, and this one was personal. On Wednesday, 30 April Sam walked down the aisle with his sweetheart, Sarah Morrison. Both were 21 years old and the ceremony took place at Old Kilpatrick Parish Church. At the time, Sam was living in Dumbarton Road, Dalmuir, and was a sheet iron worker in the yards. Sarah, like many other young women in her area, was employed by Singer's sewing factory as a machinist. She lived at Kirkton Place, in

Old Kilpatrick, and her proud parents, James, an engineer, and Charlotte, cried tears of happiness as their daughter became Mrs English. Sarah's sister, Janet, was best maid, while David English, Sam's brother, who was six years older, performed his best man duties admirably.

Sam had a few days off to celebrate and then it was back to work, and to the football, where the Holm Park side gave themselves every chance of winning the league by sticking five past both Benburb and Duntocher Hibs, to set up the first of the title deciders against Parkhead.

But the night before the big match – which was to be played on the Wednesday at 2pm – Yoker were ordered to play a Glasgow Consolation Cup semi-final tie against Clydebank at Southcroft Park. A rumour circulated that Yoker were to play a scratch team against the Bankies to give themselves every chance against Parkhead. This was scotched as 'absurd' by Yoker officials, who stated that their usual team would be on show. And it was indeed as a big crowd watched the sides fight out an exciting 1-1 draw.

It's incredible to think that a team chasing the title was asked to play two important matches just 17 hours apart. The stakes couldn't have been higher. A win for Parkhead would see them crowned Western Division league champions, which showed the standard of opposition in all its glory. A home win would see Yoker set up a final title decider with Ashfield.

Yoker started well and were two goals up inside the first ten minutes – both scored by their talisman, English. But Parkhead were anything but cannon fodder. They fought back and ensured the big crowd got their money's worth. The remainder of the first half was a bitter struggle as both teams battled for supremacy. Yoker held the upper hand with their two-goal lead, although Parkhead were far from finished. Yoker started the second half the way had started the first, and English bagged his third. Duffy added a fourth and the contest was over. The final score stood at Yoker 5 Parkhead 1, and with one match remaining, a Yoker win would see them crowned league champions. Davie Stewart was hailed as the chief architect of Parkhead's downfall – although Yoker's dashing leader had scored three fantastic goals.

On Monday, 19 May Yoker travelled the short distance to Kilbowie Park, and disaster struck. Not the fact that the teams once again couldn't be separated, as they fought out a 2-2 draw, but with the title decider against Ashfield just a week away, English – who had led the line brilliantly – picked up a nasty-looking leg injury late in the second half.

The Whe Ho's trainer worked on the striker four nights of the seven between the games and on the day of the big match, Sam was passed fit to travel to Possilpark. It was generally felt that while the trainer had worked wonders on the damaged leg, there was no way English could've been 100 per cent fit. And their theory was put to the test as the Ashfield coach switched tactics mid-match and deployed two bulky defenders to follow him all over the pitch. If he'd nipped off for a leak, I'm sure the defenders would've followed him. The tactic was a success as the home side won 2-1.

Over-anxiety seemed to be Yoker's problem. As the game wore on, they appeared to lose confidence and failed to do themselves justice. Ashfield started the better team and took the lead, but from a long and high ball up the park, English brought it under control with supreme confidence and lobbed it over the keeper's head to tie the scores. It was a sublime goal, and Yoker were well on top at this point but the extra defender deployed on English was making it nigh-on impossible for him to find any space and Ashfield finished the job. It was disappointing for the Holm Park men and their followers.

But there was some consolation over the next few days as Yoker made it to the final of the Glasgow Consolation Cup by edging the all-conquering Clydebank 2-1 in a second replay at Southcroft Park. Time and time again, English was robbed at the point of shooting as Yoker looked to put their arch-rivals to the sword, but it was in the second half that the Whe Ho were seen at their best. A cross from the right was headed on by English to Duffy, whose header beat Shortt all ends up. It was level at 1-1 after 90 minutes but there was still time for big Duncan Mills to score the winner.

With the Junior football season again running on indefinitely, Yoker started their attempts to harness the *Glasgow Evening News* Charity Cup with a tricky trip to Springburn to face a Petershill side still smarting from their 15-1 mauling at Holm Park earlier in the season. It was a tousy tie with repeated fouling and abuse. The visitors were happy when the final whistle was blown, and a Sam English goal had taken them through to the next round – but their evening wasn't quite finished. As they attempted to leave the field, the Yoker players and committee were subjected to some 'rough handling', and the club made an official written complaint to the Scottish Intermediate Committee. The matter was discussed at a committee meeting and it was decided to send the complaint to Petershill for their views.

The games were coming thick and fast, and just 48 hours after their bruising encounter at Petershill, Yoker were back at Hawthorn Park for the Glasgow Intermediate Cup Final against east end hot-shots Bridgeton Waverley.

Scotland's former international half-back Jacky Robertson – by this time a reporter – was covering the match for the *Sunday Mail*, and he filed this report:

> Hawthorn Park is not a happy place for football on such a sunny, breezy afternoon. The ball was light, the strong sun irritating; but worst of all was the dust, which blew in clouds all over the place, at times obliterating the spectators' view

of the play. It was bad enough for the looker-on, but much worse for the players. Nevertheless, they put up a fair show.

The breeze had much to do with Waverley having the lead in the first half. Turned about, though, Yoker, with the wind behind them, soon took a grip of the game, and were well worth their eventual victory, which brought them the Glasgow Intermediate Consolation Cup. They were the better team as they knocked the ball about with confidence.

Waverley got their only goal on the half hour mark. A Sykes corner was fisted to the left by the goalkeeper. Whitney got possession on the bye-line, ricked the back, and lobbed the ball beautifully into goal, where Workman was placed nicely to breast it through.

Yoker equalised a minute after the interval. Blair took a free-kick from 20 yards and drove the ball directly past Skewis. Midway through, Duffy slipped a lovely pass through to English, who veered to the right and beat Culbert. With his view clear, he placed the ball neatly beyond the goalkeeper, Skewis, and the same player put the issue beyond doubt when he raced between the Waverley backs and tapped a deceptive ball past the keeper.

Neither team could be expected to do themselves full justice under the conditions, but both sides put on a good show. Stewart was Yoker's best working forward, and he kept making openings. English was useful for his goals, the first of which was cleverly taken. The final score of 3-1 to Yoker was a fair reflection of the play.

The victorious Yoker side was: Blackstock, Milne, Bourhill, Henderson, Blair, Kelly, Boyd, Stewart, English, Duffy and Mills. The referee was Mr W. Wilson from Maryhill. The gate totalled £145, representing a crowd of 10,000 at 6d admission.

With the Glasgow Intermediate Consolation Cup in the trophy cabinet, there was still lots to play for, despite being deep into the month of June. The Elder Cottage Cup, a competition for teams within a certain radius of the Govan area, was up for grabs, while Yoker were also in the hunt for the *Glasgow Evening News* Charity Cup.

After knocking Shawfield out of the Elder Cottage Cup, Yoker were paired with old foes Clydebank in the semi-finals. Both sides expected a tough match, although for the Bankies it was a good deal tougher as the ever-improving Yoker won 5-2.

Seven days later, Clydebank had a chance of revenge as the teams met in the second round of the Glasgow Charity Cup. Once again, Holm Park was chock full for the tie – and the recent form of both sides suggested a close-run thing. It was the NINTH encounter of the season between the old foes, but spectators looked on agog as they witnessed one of the most one-sided matches of the season.

Clydebank were unable to field their normal 11 and made six changes, while Yoker were minus two of their regulars. However, it was soon evident that the home men were out for goals, and English and Mills scored in quick succession after delightful outfield play. Continuing to keep their grip of the game, Blair volleyed home from a free kick, and English added number four.

Despite splendid work by Smith, Clydebank were making no impression on the Yoker defence, and after tea-time English, who was in lively form at centre, chalked up two more, with Mills and Ferguson completing an 8-0 rout. Once again, English was the name on the lips of most supporters as they filed out of the ground and on to the busy Dumbarton Road. His four goals had marked him down as the game's outstanding contributor. Charity was also the winner with £55 taken at the gate.

The following Monday, Yoker crashed out of the competition after a tough semi-final at Ashfield's Saracen Park, Maryhill running out 3-2 winners.

All that was left to play for was the Elder Cottage Cup, and the first leg against St Anthony's took place at Holm Park. English scored twice as Yoker beat the Ants 4-2, and while the Irishman may not have made it on to the scoresheet in the second leg at Moore Park, in Govan, he still played his part in another 4-2 success, thus giving Yoker the cup.

That was it for another season, and while it had been a tough 11-month campaign, at least Yoker had something tangible to show for their efforts. They had stepped it up a notch from the previous season, but to a man they knew that to get in among the major honours, they would have to do it all again in a month or two – but did they have it in the tank to do so? You bet they did, and for Mr English it would be the perfect swansong at Junior level.

Four

HOW TO eclipse seven goals in a single match, five hat-tricks and many doubles. That was the dilemma facing Sam English on the eve of the new season. But if the team could continue to improve at the rate of the past two seasons, then eminent success was surely on the horizon, and no one individual would be happier than Sam; the consummate team player.

As an individual, it was questionable as to whether he could offer more than the 80-plus goals he had contributed in each of the last two seasons. The fact that Sam suffered few 'dry' periods had turned him from prolific striker to hot property. But were Yoker, as a group, now capable of 'cashing in' on a striker who could guarantee so many goals, and shake off their 'bridesmaids' label?

When his third season in a Yoker jersey began he was still just 22 years old. He was ready to play on a bigger stage, but that remained out of his hands. Those playing in the renegade Intermediate League were still looked upon as outcasts; lepers, almost. The signing embargo imposed by both the SJFA and SFA remained in place. Even the impasse had reached an impasse and a breakthrough seemed as far away as ever.

The good folk of Yoker were fine with that. They were focussed on taking the club to the next stage and getting in among the top prizes – like the league and Scottish Cup. The Intermediate League still had the top teams and players, and Sam was learning weekly from playing against the best at his level. Put simply, he was getting better and better. But then a strange phenomenon occurred. Yoker's first four games saw them face Clydebank, Pollok, Rob Roy and Neilston. A tough start for the club, but they lost three of the four and Sam failed to score in any – and he was sent off against the Kirkintilloch side. The narrative changed. Had the Yoker bubble burst? Were the plaudits for Sam a little premature? Both questions would be answered rather quickly – and in emphatic style.

August was always the busiest month in the Junior calendar, and by winning six of their eight other fixtures that month (the other two were drawn), the Whe Ho proved it was an early season blip. And by scoring a dozen times in these games – including his first hat-trick of the season in a 5-0 win against St Anthony's – Sam proved he had lost none of his old sparkle in front of goal.

Yoker were quickly back in their stride, and their disgruntled supporters were smiling again. When they thrashed Arthurlie 8-0 in a league match, in which Sam was suspended, they proved they had goals in other areas of the team. They were on a fine winning run when they travelled through to Gasworks Park to face Larkhall Thistle, one of Scotland's oldest Junior teams, and were leading 2-1 midway through the second half when they started yet another promising move. As they switched the ball effortlessly from defence to midfield, the referee, Mr Wilson, from Maryhill, collapsed in a heap in the centre of the field. Medical aid was immediately procured, but the match official had slipped into unconsciousness. He was taken to hospital and the game was abandoned. Thankfully he recovered after further treatment.

Next up was Stewarton Athletic in the first round of the Scottish Intermediate Cup. This was the big one, and a match the players had been looking forward to for weeks. Word on the Holm Park terracing was that the squad they had was good enough to win the national trophy, but only time would tell. They made the perfect start against the Ayrshiremen. English was in stunning form and scored three times as Yoker romped to an 8-0 win.

Back-to-back league victories in Govan against Benburb and St Anthony's – with Sam scoring in both – was followed by the visit of West Lothian side Fauldhouse United to Holm Park for a first-round Glasgow Cup tie. A newspaper report stated, 'The visitors were completely outplayed, and for football craft I have yet to see a better display than that given by Yoker and, in my opinion, the team who beat the Holm Park side will win the cup.'

Yoker were on the front foot from the first whistle, and after a couple of missed chances, Keane placed a corner kick perfectly for English to head the opening goal. Henderson and Kelly had good opportunities to increase the lead but it was left to English to add a second two minutes from half-time with a great left-foot drive, and he completed the almost inevitable hat-trick in the second half as Yoker won 8-0.

The match report ended with these words: 'Yoker, as a whole, played a sound game, and possess the 100 per cent centre-forward in English.'

When the Yoker party jumped aboard the Renfrew Ferry for a 100 Guineas Cup tie at Western Park, English was marked out for 'special attention'. Still, the Whe Ho were far from a one-man team, and while Sam went home that night with some extra bruises, he still managed to score twice as Yoker chalked up their tenth successive win in all competitions with a 5-3 victory. Yoker were an excellent football side, but also tough-as-teak and certainly no pushovers for the bully boys. The perfect combination for the era they played in.

Saturday, 8 November was a watershed moment for Yoker – and English. Ashfield travelled to Holm Park for a Scottish Cup third-round tie. As one of the best in the business, Ashfield represented a difficult hurdle, and the home officials and players were wary of the threat they carried. It would be quite a game, and had Ashfield converted a gilt-edged opportunity in the opening minutes, the result could have been different. Instead, Parker shot high and wide of the Yoker goal – and that was the end of the Saracen Parkers.

With a quarter of an hour on the clock, English worked a nice opening for Stewart, and crafty Davie put the home side one up. Moments later a Mills piledriver was spilled by the Ashfield keeper and English pounced like a wildcat to tap home. It was 2-0 at half-time and Yoker were confident they could see out the tie.

The second half opened sensationally, with English scoring from a Mills cross two minutes in, and a minute later he got the fourth, and his own third, from a solo effort. Ashfield, by now a dispirited lot, all but threw in the towel. Yoker scored three more goals before English completed the scoring after a lovely team move involving eight players. After the game, former Scotland international Jacky Robertson called Yoker 'the finest combination in Junior football'. 'He wasn't normally wrong, and once again Yoker had scored eight.

In their next outing, Yoker stuck seven past Maryhill in a game which no doubt created a record that might never be equalled. They were five goals up inside 15 minutes – and each of the five forwards had grabbed one. A real novelty, or perhaps a record to be proud of.

There was no stopping this goalscoring powerhouse and two days after Christmas, Clydebank keeper Boland was credited with keeping the score in single figures. Of course, English scored a couple as Yoker won 4-0, but one wag suggested Boland was like a circus shot-stopper with eight arms, saving attempt after attempt windmill-style as the home side virtually camped in the Bankies' box.

Of course, Clydebank had their moments, but found it tough to break down Yoker's 'rock-like defence', which when allied to their stinging attack, made them a formidable outfit.

As the season moved into 1931, Pollok led the Western Division of the Scottish Intermediate League by five points from Yoker but having played two games more. The clubs had still to meet at Holm Park. Renfrew were just a point behind the Whe Ho but had played three games more, due to Yoker's continued involvement in all competitions.

The league games kept coming, with both St Roch's and Duntocher Hibs duly despatched, and when Bellshill Athletic turned up at Holm Park, for a Glasgow Cup fourth-round tie, it proved to be quite an afternoon. The game had only been going four minutes when Yoker took the lead. However, a ten-minute spell saw Yoker score again, and miss a penalty, before Bellshill scored twice before the break to draw level.

Keane edged Yoker ahead a few minutes into the second half, and when Yoker were awarded a penalty moments later, the ball was handed to English – as Mills had missed in the first half. English shot straight at the keeper, which prompted Bellshill left-back Leonard to say something to Sam. There was a mass brawl in the visitors' penalty box, and the upshot was a red card to Leonard. This prompted a pitch invasion by home supporters trying to get at the Bellshill player, but swift action by the police – as they surrounded Leonard – ensured he made it back to the pavilion in one piece.

Armstrong, of Bellshill, was sent off three minutes from the end, and although it proved difficult to get him off the field, the game was able to re-start after police moved in to drag the player back to the pavilion. Yoker grabbed another two goals late on to win the match 5-2 – their 20th win in a row and also their 28th game unbeaten.

February was the month that really set Yoker apart from the rest. And while it started inauspiciously with a 3-0 win over Benburb in the 100 Guineas Cup – in which Sam was again on target – the next match against Parkhead at Holm Park proved beyond all reasonable doubt that Yoker were at the very top of their game.

After the first ten minutes the result was never in doubt. Morrison, the Parkhead keeper, played a great game; in fact, their entire defence did well, but Yoker were irresistible. After Mills had missed two fine openings he scored Yoker's first goal, and within ten minutes English had added a couple.

It was more of the same after the interval, and English scored a further three times to take his individual haul to five. Not many teams scored eight against Parkhead, so it was clearly going to take something special to halt this fine Yoker side.

The following Saturday, Petershill had a go at Holm Park, but came up way short. English bagged another hat-trick, and while Peasie did well to restrict the home side to six – after shipping 15 at the same venue 12 months earlier – the simple truth is they were swatted aside by a ruthless outfit who took pity on no one. Many years later, Sam would insist that the Yoker side of 1930/31 was the equal to anything he witnessed in the remainder of his career, and while some folk may have scoffed at such a suggestion, perhaps he wasn't too far wide of the mark.

And the Irish-born forward completed an incredible personal milestone the following weekend in a home league match against Renfrew. Sam scored four times against the Frew, with his third being his 200th goal since joining Yoker two and a half seasons previous. It was an astonishing return, and the few left in the

Scottish game who hadn't heard of Sam English, had by this time surely joined his fan club.

In the month of February, Yoker had played four matches, won the lot, and scored 24 goals. Sam had scored 13 of them. As for the team, their colours hadn't been lowered since early August. Renfrew had played well, but when English scored that landmark third, Renfrew crumbled. As a result, Yoker had closed the gap at the top of the table, albeit slightly. Pollok were three points clear and Yoker had a game in hand. A well-beaten Renfrew remained third.

Perthshire were next to visit the lion's den, this time in a Scottish Cup fourth-round tie – and they almost left with a well-deserved victory. For a change, English didn't get on the scoresheet, but he made the first goal for Davie Stewart. Keane scored Yoker's second, and while Shire got one back late on, it was Yoker who went into the hat for the fifth-round draw. The big crowd had witnessed a dour struggle but were impressed by Perthshire, easily the best team seen at Holm Park that season.

By the time Yoker rolled up at Saracen Park to play Ashfield, on the first weekend of April, they were a point ahead of Pollok, but had played a game more. After 90 torrid minutes of full-thrust Junior football action, Yoker left Possilpark battered, bruised and with two points dropped. A 6-3 win for the hosts was about the right result, but Yoker had little time to feel sorry for themselves as they were due to play Pollok in a crucial league match at Holm Park on the Monday night.

The place was packed for the game of the season, almost 10,000 inside the ground, but how would Yoker fare after losing so heavily just 48 hours beforehand, and suffering their first loss in almost 30 matches?

For the first 80 minutes, one side was as good as the other – fast and clever in raiding, with the inside-forward play exceptionally smart, and the half-back standard high. Yoker were just a shade more alert in their movements, but Pollok made up for that by their studied methods.

For the final ten minutes, though, it was a different story. Yoker moved up a gear and took their opportunities. Up until then, a draw might have been fair, but after Yoker got the first, they found it easier to get a second four minutes later. English scored both. For his first, the ball was pushed through the centre. Hurst and Hopewell seemed to leave it to Williamson, but the goalkeeper hesitated and English touched the ball into the net out of his reach.

The second goal was top-drawer. Whether or not there was a little slackness on the part of the Pollok defence was immaterial, because English was alert and made a clever job of it. He ran into the inside-right channel, took the ball on to his left foot, and finished off by whipping the ball into the net from a difficult angle. It was the perfect piece of opportunism, and it settled the issue. That said, it was a hard, clean game – and a credit to both sides.

When the dust had settled on a great night's football, it was advantage Yoker, and the title race was now a straight shoot-out between Yoker and Pollok.

Saturday, 11 April was a significant day in terms of the championship. It was Scottish Cup Final day, with Motherwell and Celtic clashing at Hampden. Yoker had the day off, like most teams, but Pollok hosted Benburb, and it was the Govan side who left with both points courtesy of a 4-2 win. Yoker's championship destiny was now in their own hands.

The following Saturday they took a massive leap towards the title when they visited Maryhill's Lochburn Park and won 4-2, with English claiming his eighth hat-trick of the season. His first goal was a cracker. He picked up a long clearance from Bourhill, and neatly tricking the backs, shot well out of Blackwood's reach.

At the start of the second half, Yoker instantly bore down on the Maryhill goal, where Blackwood fumbled a cross from Mills, and left English an easy chance, which was promptly accepted. A faulty clearance by Russell then allowed English to score his third. The win put Yoker seven points clear of Pollok, who had three games in hand. Yoker had just two games left to play.

Forty-eight hours after beating Maryhill, Yoker were back in action, facing bogey side Perthshire, although once again English was on target – this time with a double – as the league leaders won 3-1.

The big games were coming thick and fast and after scoring the only goal of the game against Clydebank in the semi-final of the Glasgow Cup, Sam and his mates were up against the same side seven days later, this time in the *Evening News* Charity Cup. There was no stopping English as he single-handedly demolished the hapless Bankies with four goals, which prompted one journalist to write, 'English demonstrated that he has no superior in Intermediate football as a centre-forward!'

The day after the match, Clydebank revealed they were in dire straits. Financially, they were a mess and there was talk of the club's players being given free transfers, and Yoker getting Clydebank's ground – Clydeholm Park. It was claimed the club was around £8,000 in debt.

After thumping the Bankies, Yoker beat Arthurlie 4-1 in the Renfrewshire/Dumbartonshire Cup semi-final on the Friday night at Western Park, Renfrew, before drawing 0-0 with Renfrew in the final 72 hours later. But the big one was just a few days away. St Roch's v Yoker Athletic in the final league match of the season. It was simple: win, and win the league. The Whe Ho refused to contemplate anything less, and yet again they came up with the goods, winning 4-2 against a good side, and with English again on the scoresheet.

The title was Yoker's, and it was a deserved success. But if the players thought they might nip along to a pub on Dumbarton Road for a little celebration, they were forced to think again. The following day they had the replay of the Renfrew/Dumbarton Cup Final, and although English again scored, it proved a consolation as Renfrew lifted the trophy. Perhaps the players had indeed gone out to celebrate winning the league the previous evening.

Barrowfield Park, home of Bridgeton Waverley, was the neutral venue for the Scottish Cup semi-final against St Roch's, and after 90 minutes there was nothing to separate the teams. It was a similar story in the replay, which again ended in a 2-2 draw, this time at Petershill's Hawthorn Park. The teams required a third match to split them, and it was third time lucky for Yoker, who won by the odd goal in three.

In between the Scottish Cup semi-final ties, there was the not-so-insignificant matter of the Glasgow District Cup Final against Strathclyde to squeeze in, and once again Barrowfield Park was the choice of location. It was 6d admission all round, and Yoker had endured quite a journey to get to the final. In the first round they had been drawn against Larkhall Thistle away from home. However, that tie was abandoned when the referee collapsed and was rendered unconscious. Players from both sides helped carry the stricken official to an ambulance, where he was conveyed to hospital. When the tie was rescheduled, Yoker eased through 2-0, with English on target.

Fauldhouse United were next up, and were routed 8-0, with English scoring a fine hat-trick. Yoker marched on and Perthshire were next to fall, at the start of November. English got his customary goal in a 3-1 victory. In the quarter-finals,

Yoker thumped Bellshill Athletic 5-2 before seeing off arch-rivals Clydebank in the semi-finals by the only goal.

On the eve of the big game, Yoker manager Willie Malloy said, 'My injured players have made splendid progress so our first-pick team will take the field.'

The kick off was delayed 30 minutes to allow the large crowd of 15,000 into the ground, and they saw the cup lost and won when Strathclyde scored two goals in rapid succession midway through the first half. Banks gave Yoker keeper Hill no chance with the first, and the east end team were well on top at this stage. Two minutes later, Strathclyde doubled their advantage.

Yoker tried desperately hard to get back into the match and had the better of things at the start of the second half. When Yoker managed to break up the field it was their policy to give the ball to English, but their good intentions were frequently upset by the watchdog tactics of Cook.

English, however, did get his chance with a ball that came across from the right and was then sent up the middle. The Yoker marksman just moved on a couple of yards and Calderwood was beaten.

It was Yoker's turn now but Strathclyde were fighting hard to retain their lead.

A melee in front of goal culminated in English being fouled when the ball was away and referee Williamson pointed to the spot. Muir was entrusted with the kick, but Calderwood produced an exceptional save.

Undaunted, Yoker piled forward in search of the equaliser, but the Strathies' defence stood strong, and three minutes from the end a third goal sealed the issue. Yoker were not at their best and their forwards seemed pretty disorganised. English was always a menace to the opposition, but he was too well watched to carry the side to victory.

The big games were coming thick and fast – for Yoker at least – and next up was the Scottish Intermediate League play-off final at Springfield Park, the new home of Strathclyde Juniors.

Like the Glasgow Cup Final, it was an east v west struggle, but what gave the game its added sparkle was that the teams were champions of their respective divisions.

The teams may have been equal in spirit and talent but Bridgeton Waverley would be the fresher of the sides as they had been idle for a fortnight, while Yoker had played four games in that period, two of them on Monday and Wednesday of the same week.

Waverley, therefore, had a great chance to accomplish what hadn't been achieved before, and that was to take the blue ribbon of Intermediate football to the east of the city.

The *Daily Record* sent its top reporter – nom-de-plume, Waverley – to cover the match, and this is part of his report:

> I enjoyed this decider thoroughly and let me say right away that the Scottish Intermediate Championship has gone to the sectional leaders that best deserved it. On the day, Bridgeton Waverley, the winners, were a better side than Yoker, who were disappointing.
>
> By comparison with the stronger, better conditioned, combined and bolder Bridgeton band, who possessed also an ever-so-much better idea of position, the Holm Park fellows were something of a ram-stam lot. True, they gave Waverley a frightful gruelling for a bit in the second half. And hereabout they had no luck.
>
> Yes, the ball did not run kindly for them, and for English in particular. As to the ability of this well set, fair-haired man I must reserve my opinion. Had he thought and acted quickly enough once – in the same instant – this in the second half before Mills had made siccar for Waverley,

English would only have done what a centre-forward of his reputation should.

Unfortunately he 'enjoyed' a bad afternoon, but his associates tell me he will make up for this on Strathclyde's Springfield Park next Saturday. The same teams will do it all over again – this time in the Scottish Cup Final. But on Saturday's showing, my packet of fags, if I were having a modest bet, would be on the Waverley.

To return to English. He found himself up against a Waverley centre-half who had no illusions regarding Yoker's centre-forward. Waddell his name, he knew it was his duty to keep English off the ball, and keep him off it he did. One of English's few untaken opportunities came after Waverley's second goal. He also had an overhead kick – which seemed goal-bound – but was headed clear.

A whole host of English managers attended the match: including Percy Smith (Tottenham), Willie Orr (Leicester City), Jack Tinn (Portsmouth) who also had his chairman and two directors with him, Peter Hodge (Manchester City), John Cochrane (Sunderland) and Alec Macfarlane (Charlton Athletic).

Not a good 90 minutes for the Whe Ho, but they could still have their day. Sure, they were extremely disappointed that after what can only be described as an exceptional season, they weren't able to perform when the stakes were highest. But the big one – the Scottish Cup Final – was still to come, and manager Willie Malloy was intent on having his troupe ready to perform to the best of their abilities. The initial staging of the match had been postponed due to a heavy rainstorm, and although it might have seemed unfair to host the big game in the backyard of their rivals, Yoker remained undaunted.

Yoker had four days to prepare for one of the biggest games of their 45-year existence, because on the Monday before the final, they faced Shawfield at Southcroft Park in the 100 Guineas Cup. They were 2-0 up at half-time, with English on target, but lost two goals after the break, which meant yet another fixture in the already congested month of June.

But just like their supporters, who chartered three special trains, they travelled to Springfield Park full of hope and keen to exact revenge on Bridgeton Waverley. At the start of the campaign, this was the type of game they had been building towards and they were determined to add the national trophy to their league title. They were certainly good enough.

Naturally, Waverley were favourites following the league play-off, but when they won the coin toss for choice of ends, and elected to shoot against a strong end-to-end wind, it seemed a strange decision. Many of their supporters thought this could cost them the tie but, in fact, they played very well in the first half.

The big crowd were treated to a fast-moving game of football, but Yoker's movement and speed of thought proved just too much for their opponents. Mills, the Waverley centre-forward, was a trier, but Boyd, the Yoker centre-half, was ever on top of the Bridgeton boy. A grand half-back, he had an equally grand colleague operating on his left side – Danny Muir, a hit while at Dumbarton.

While the Holm Park backs gave little away, it was in the forward department that they excelled. For instance, Waddell's failure to repeat his stranglehold on English was a big factor. The Yoker centre-forward was more like the English we all knew and loved. He was aye ready; he was sharper; he was up for the scrap, and he was there on the half-hour when his side took the lead. English jousted with Waddell for the ball just inside the Waverley area, and came out on top. He laid it off beautifully to Stewart, who rammed home a shot that gave Lindsay no chance.

Yoker – all in white - were well on top at this point but knew that one goal would never be enough against a team with the never-say-die attitude of Waverley. Five minutes later, Keen, who had whipped in several good balls, let go a howitzer. The ball fizzed past Lindsay, hit the underside of the bar and came down just over the line. Referee Willie Wilson signalled 'goal' without hesitation, and Willie Malloy's men were two to the good.

The half-time whistle arrived with the Holm Park side 2-0 up, and by the time the teams emerged from the pavilion to begin the second half, guess what? Yes, the wind had died down, and gone was the advantage the Waverley lads had been relying on.

They did have the first opportunity after the break when Whitney shot from the edge of the 18-yard box, but Hill was equal to it and saved well. He then broke Waverley hearts with a string of top-class saves before Sam English sealed victory with a goal of the highest class. Eight minutes remained when he latched on to a long, raking through ball and found himself with only the keeper to beat. English showed great maturity as Lindsay came out to narrow his options. Using his right foot as a sand wedge, he beautifully lofted the ball up and over the keeper and into the back of the net. It was a top finish, and Lindsay hadn't a chance of saving.

Waverley had been outplayed and outmanoeuvred by a slick, skilful and confident Yoker, who had improved tenfold on seven days previous. They were worthy winners.

But much more than this individual success, Yoker's time had come. Three years of patient team-building and careful annual additions had paid off, and under the charge of Malloy, they had become the most feared combination in the Intermediate ranks. And Sam English had played his part.

Five

THE INTERMEDIATE dispute was over and the stampede began. Senior managers, now free to approach the Junior game's star players, legally, at least, were quickly out of the traps. It was Monday, 29 June and Yoker officials were keen to protect their star assets from the circling vultures. The 1930/31 season was drawing to a close, but Yoker were still battling on four fronts for silverware, and manager Malloy, quite frankly, could have done without the awful timing of this distraction. Of course, the big ones, the Scottish Cup and League (Western Division) were already sitting proudly in the Holm Park trophy cabinet, but Malloy was still hopeful of adding the 100 Guineas Cup, Kirkwood Shield, Elder Cottage Cup and Glasgow Charity Cup.

In the week leading up to the disbanding of the renegade Intermediate Association, on successive nights, the Whe Ho had dumped Shawfield out of the 100 Guineas and Charity cups. It was the first two fixtures of five in just seven days, and with a small pool of players at their disposal, Yoker simply couldn't maintain the necessary energy levels and on the Saturday afternoon, lost 2-1 to Irvine Meadow at Dunterlie Park, Arthurlie in the semi-finals of the 100 Guineas.

On the Monday evening, they travelled to Hawthorn Park, in Springburn, for a Kirkwood Shield last-four tie with Rob Roy. Again, they lost 2-1, but significantly this was the last time Sam English would pull on the blue shirt of Yoker. He was desperately disappointed that he couldn't go out on a winning note, but there was no doubt he had played a starring role in bringing the good times back to Holm Park.

The moment the game was over and the players had taken a shower, the 'guard' on the inside of the dressing room was filtering each individual as they attempted to leave. 'Okay, yip, on ye go. Hang on, nope,' and Johnny Blair (who would eventually snub Rangers to sign for Motherwell) was asked to sit back down on the wooden bench. Sam English, drying off his thick blond thatch, was given the same instruction. Once the remainder of their team-mates had left, Malloy held court. It was imperative he speak to his star players before they exit the dressing room and into the clutches of unscrupulous 'representatives' and managers from an assortment of clubs.

Sam was well aware that a great number of clubs were interested in signing him. Rangers, Hearts, Sunderland, Stoke City, Newcastle United etc., but what Mr Malloy was about to say took him completely by surprise. The great Arsenal manager, Herbert Chapman, was waiting to receive Sam at his Glasgow city centre hotel, and the 22-year-old Dalmuir lad was told in no uncertain terms that this move was the club's preferred choice. Yoker had helped bring Sam on to a high standard during his three years at Holm Park and this, potentially, was payback time.

If he moved to a Scottish club, under the terms of an agreement with the SFA, the most Yoker could hope to trouser was £75. Still a fair chunk of compensation for a Junior club, but if the north of London, and Highbury in particular, would prove to be Sam's final destination, the sky was the limit in terms of monetary remuneration as no such agreement was in place for cross-border transfers. It was decision time.

Looking back, Sam recalled the way it was in the run-up to the end of the Intermediate dispute, 'Because Junior clubs – then called Intermediates – were outside the control of the SFA, no Senior manager was permitted to approach us officially. Of course, they came just the same.

'Willie McCartney, of Hearts, was a frequent visitor around Yoker, always with a red rose in his lapel. Mr McCartney never made me an offer. But always he would say, "Here's a little something for you – and remember me when the time comes." Inevitably, I would be a few pounds richer.

'Jack Tinn, of Portsmouth, spats and all, held court in a Sauchiehall Street hotel. Leicester's Willie Orr interviewed me in Wyper's, in Renfield Street, the first pub I was ever in, while Paddy Travers, then of Aberdeen, was interested, as were Stoke City.

'And every week for two seasons, four pound notes would be delivered to me in an envelope at John Brown's from manager Bill Struth of Rangers.

'So, the Mr Bigs of football, with the cash, kept in touch with the rebel wayside Junior teams. When the authorities patched up their differences and the Intermediates were re-introduced back into the SFA fold, the Senior managers wanted to be ready to move in with their chequebooks. Their "tips" plus my shipyard wages had meant a lot of money coming into the house at a time when nearly all the others were unemployed.'

Sam was a reasonable man. He completely understood the club's position so agreed to meet Mr Chapman at the St Enoch Station Hotel, one of the grandest in the city, and he would be accompanied by Mr Malloy. When they eventually left Hawthorn

Park to head into town, the place was all but deserted. The nets were down, corner flags in, and most committee members had retired to the nearest pub. Sam and Mr Malloy climbed into a taxi and set off for the hotel. It was a 25-minute journey, give or take.

When they arrived at reception, they were shown straight to Mr Chapman's room. The legendary Arsenal boss was wearing a dressing gown, while a heavy strapping covered his left ankle. He explained how he'd just had an operation to fix a troublesome cartilage.

The men sat down to talk and listened to Mr Chapman's opening gambit with great interest. He looked Sam in the eye and said, 'If I'm being 100 per cent honest young man, I've never seen you play, but I see the interest your availability has caused and so you must have something special to offer. I would be a fool if I didn't join the queue.'

Sam was respectful in his reply and the three men sat for more than an hour chatting before the talented centre-forward told Mr Chapman he had promised to speak to a couple of other managers before coming to his final decision. The men stood up, shook hands and the Yoker duo left the hotel, and while no doubt Herbert Chapman still managed to sleep like a baby, the same probably couldn't be said for Sam. It would later transpire that Arsenal had offered £1,000 to Yoker for his signature, equivalent to around £65,000 today, and far more than the statutory £75 they would later collect.

Sam recalled, 'Mr Chapman told me I could do better for myself in London than anywhere else. Opportunities were unequalled there. I said Sadie and I weren't long married, and that I'd never been to England. Finally, over coffee, Mr Chapman virtually offered me a blank cheque to go to Highbury. Any offer Rangers made, he would better, he promised. It was after midnight before I left him and took a taxi to Ibrox.'

When the taxi pulled up outside Ibrox, a solitary light shone inside the stadium as manager Bill Struth awaited the arrival of the young Northern Irishman. As he got out on Edmiston Drive, Sam took one look up at the imposing red brick façade and gasped for breath. It was an awe-inspiring sight. He couldn't even begin to imagine that one day he might be walking through the front door as a Ranger.

He dusted himself down and the two gentlemen walked towards the entrance. Before them stood grand columns and the famous marble staircase – and the man who would eventually go down in history as the most successful manager of the world's most successful football club. Mr Struth offered his hand first to Mr Malloy, and then young Sam. He welcomed both to Ibrox before leading the way up to his office on the first floor. The office was at the top of the staircase and as they edged closer to it, Sam was struck by the beauty and elegance of the Ibrox interior. Mr Struth opened the door and showed both gentlemen inside. It was a magnificent office, with the boss's traditional bowler hat hanging on a coat stand in the far left-hand corner, just to the right of his desk. The manager motioned for both to sit down, before taking his place behind the large, leather-covered desk.

Despite his obvious talent and record-breaking exploits of the previous three years, Sam was a bag of nerves. He was a confident lad on the pitch, but at this moment he sat staring down at the floor as Mr Struth began to speak. The short meeting passed in a blur for the player and all he remembered of the evening was signing his name on a piece of paper. Mr Struth was delighted; Mr Malloy perhaps not so, but while Rangers were one of just three Scottish league clubs to adhere to the £75 maximum compensation agreement, struck between the Scottish FA and the Intermediate clubs, they did offer to take a team to Holm Park for a pre-season friendly with Yoker. There's no doubt it was a bitter pill for Mr

Malloy and his club to swallow, but ultimately he wanted the best for his players, and he was delighted that Sam had got his big move to Ibrox. God knows it was deserved.

So, Sam English was no longer a Yoker player. He had signed for Rangers, and Mr Struth would say later, 'When I bought Sam English from Yoker it seemed that everybody wanted him. All I did was to send a message saying that I would see him at Ibrox. He turned up and I signed him – and I don't believe he was even sure of the terms.'

Sam added, 'I signed papers and we shook hands. Mr Struth himself drove me home with £600 worth of crisp new banknotes in my pocket. I was a Ranger.'

All thoughts of Herbert Chapman and the bright lights of London had long since faded. Sam was sitting in Mr Struth's comfortable car, and on his way home with a wad of cash that would considerably ease the pressure on his mother as she worked hard to make ends meet. Sam would be plying his trade much closer to home, and it wouldn't be too long before he came to terms with the fact that his working life would no longer consist of the short journey from his Dalmuir home to the John Brown shipyard for an 8am start on cold winter mornings. No more toiling in a dingy yard as a sheet metal worker with a limited dinner break and even shorter tea breaks. No, his working day would now begin two hours later and consist mainly of a few laps of the Ibrox running track, before working on ball drills and other tactical manoeuvres with the training staff at Rangers. Life was about to change dramatically for Sam English.

But Yoker still had a few games left to play and Sam's replacement, a young lad called Finnan, took over centre-forward duties and scored a couple of goals on his debut in a 6-0 thrashing of Pollok. It was a Glasgow Charity Cup semi-final tie at Lochburn Park, in Maryhill, and Sam attended the game to support his friends and former team-mates, and he reserved a special cheer as the new lad hit the ground running. His jersey was in capable hands; the Yoker production line was already in full swing, with a series of young replacements rolling off the conveyor belt.

But Sam had one more day out with his Yoker mates to enjoy. They were off on a bus run down the coast to Helensburgh, where a government minister presented the victorious Whe Ho players with their Scottish Intermediate Cup winners medals. Afterwards, the players and committee enjoyed a fish tea in a swanky waterfront hotel before walking off the extra pounds with a stroll along the pier. It was the perfect way to say cheerio to some great friends and colleagues.

One of the first things Sam did as a signed Rangers player was to enjoy three weeks off. The Scottish League season had finished long before the Junior campaign and most of the players were already at their holiday destination of choice. Sam handed in his notice at the shipyard and promptly received the congratulations and good wishes of all those he worked alongside.

He managed to grab a break with his wife of just over a year, Sarah, and their baby daughter, Charlotte, before getting down to the business of preparing for the new season. And that meant coming to terms with his new workplace – especially on day one. Later, he would recall the one thing that stood out that day more than most. He said, 'I reported nervously to Ibrox on my first day and the thing that struck me immediately was the league championship flag fluttering in the mild breeze above the stadium. Boy, was that a statement. At our one and only meeting, Mr Struth had also said to me that he believed I was good enough to go straight into the first team – the first ex-Junior to do so. There was pressure, but a basic wage of £12 a week was a nice comfort.'

English was a level-headed 22-year-old and journeyed on the bus from his home in Dalmuir for his first day at his new club.

He was met at reception by Davie Meiklejohn, arguably Rangers' greatest ever player and captain of the famous Ibrox club, master of the cross-field pass and an expert tactician.

Sam recalled, 'They were a happy family at Ibrox then, with Mr Struth very much the father figure. He was an autocratic man. He was the Boss. His word was law – except on the field. There, captain Davie Meiklejohn ruled completely. Older players told me that if the Boss ever tried to switch the team during a game Davie would have left the field, and I believe he would.

'Davie introduced me – just a youngster of 22 – in a friendly and direct way to the occupants of this star-studded dressing room. Alan Morton, who was starting his 12th season as a Ranger, grinned and said softly, "Don't be looking for me out there. You find the open space and I'll find you." Alan could have placed the ball in your hip pocket. It was formidable playing with him on the left wing and another veteran, Sandy Archibald on the right. Sandy cannoned the ball across. Do more than touch it, and your head would have finished up in the net with the ball! Meanwhile, Alan's lobs sailed over and hung in the air. Defenders would jump too early and be on their way down again before an Alan Morton cross started to drop.'

Always keen to impress, Sam turned up rather early for training on one occasion – and made sure he was never early again. He recalled, 'I was determined not to be late, and one day I reported 15 minutes early for ten o'clock training. None of the other boys showed their face until ten o'clock on the dot. Mr Struth was just going out for his daily sprint and invited me – I suppose "invited" is the wrong word – to join him.

'Running shoulder to shoulder he told me of every slip I had made in the previous match. How I could improve. How I should play the centre-forward role in the next match – if selected. All this at the top of his voice during six lung-tearing laps of the field. I was never too early for training again!'

Sam was joining the Scottish League champions, with Rangers having won the title the season previous by two points from Celtic. Motherwell, a strong, emerging force, were just a couple of points shy of Celtic in third place.

Rangers were always well equipped for the next challenge, with a fantastic array of talent at Ibrox, and Sam was only too happy to recall some of the lads he played alongside. He said, 'Dougie Gray was the finest right-back in Scotland for his size, and an amazingly agile substitute goalkeeper. There has never been anybody like him for shepherding a winger along the touchline, robbing him, and starting an attack with a cunning ball, placed wide of the goal.

'"Al Capone" played in that team – otherwise known as left-back Bob McAulay. Once he had gone to Canada for the harvesting and stayed over to play football in America. In front of him was the precise George Brown. He was a school teacher who worked his way up to headmaster, and who would become a director of the club with Alan Morton.

'Tommy Hamilton or Jerry Dawson kept goal. Tommy was a big bunch of good nature but utter master of his domain inside the 18-yard box. On a clear day his bellowed "It's ma ba" must have been heard all the way to his home town of Renfrew. He owned a billiards hall in Dalmuir.

'Football was now my profession. I had always played football for money. For I know what it means to be short of money, and I know what it meant for my mother to be short of it. But it was my main source of earning now and I wanted to make the most of it.

'But apart from the fact that it seemed rich enough, I was innocent of Senior football. I had been to only four matches, and seen John Thomson in action once. That was the 1930/31 cup final when Allan Craig disastrously headed the ball past his own Motherwell goalkeeper to give Celtic a replay – and the cup.

'Whether I had wanted to go Senior or not, Mr Struth had asked me to come and see him at Ibrox after Yoker's last game of the season, and his invitation was as good as a summons.'

And Sam was mighty pleased he had taken up Mr Struth on his 'offer', as his life was about to change, initially for the better. Pre-season training was in full swing and Ibrox was a hive of activity. Supporters were milling around outside the main entrance on Edmiston Drive, hoping to catch a glimpse of the players and they themselves always made time for the men who ultimately paid their wages. They were a happy lot at Ibrox, and they were ready for the challenge the new season would bring.

Six

PRE-SEASON TRAINING, in its rawest of forms, was over. The players were fit, raring to go and counting down the days until the start of the new season. There was growing speculation in the media that manager Bill Struth might spring a surprise on the huge Rangers following by announcing the rookie Irishman Sam English in his starting 11 to face Dundee at Ibrox on the opening day of the season.

In the club's official trial game, the former Yoker man had showed up well, especially in dealing with high balls from the wing and in his distributive play. He was said to be first class, and earned the plaudits and acceptance of those who made up the 20,000 crowd.

But Sam was taking nothing for granted and on the day of the match, waited nervously for the team lines to be pinned up in the dressing room. He wouldn't be disappointed. As he worked his way through the 11, there, ninth name down, was that of Sam English. He was in. After impressing in the trial game, he had been given the nod ahead of both Jimmy Fleming and Jimmy Smith, which perhaps highlighted a shift in thinking by Struth.

Unlike most centres of that era, English believed in working with his inside men, and if Dr Jamie Marshall and Bob McPhail bought into the young centre-forward's philosophy, it was quite conceivable that both Smith and Fleming would find it difficult to get back into the first team.

One thing was certain, though – English would prove a grand draw, as he possessed all the necessary attributes of the ideal centre. There was a sense of anticipation ahead of his debut.

With the advent of the sectional League Cup still some 15 years away, it was straight into the league campaign. Points were up for grabs, and it was imperative Rangers make a good start, as an emerging Motherwell side, under the expert guidance of John 'Sailor' Hunter, were starting to make waves in the Scottish game.

But Rangers had an expert of their own, and under Bill Struth had won the Scottish Division One title for the previous five seasons. Of course, arch-rivals Celtic would be there or thereabouts, but it was the Fir Park men Struth was keeping a watchful eye on, and his assessment of the opposition was seldom wrong. Win the title again, and Rangers would equal Celtic's record of six successive championships.

Just over 30,000 fans were at Ibrox to witness this bright new beginning, and while the overall standard of play was mediocre, the keenness shown by both sets of players was at times exhilarating and made for a good spectacle on opening day.

Of course, everybody had more than one eye on the two fresh-faced centre-forwards, lint-locked English in particular, but also Dundee's Craigie. As for English, he was plied with the ball from all directions, and though at first perhaps being disposed of parting with it too quickly, he caused the Dundee defence a lot of anxiety by his quickness in darting this way and that. He went for everything, high and low – clearly a player who would require a lot of watching. It took the new boy little time to get up to speed with this new standard of football and he was soon stamping his authority on the game, although when he came within sight of goal, his shooting was a little off, certainly in the first half.

Rangers had the first real opportunity in the game, but McPhail's snap-shot was cleared with consummate ease. English then took up good positions inside the box on two separate occasions, but both times he was out of luck.

Ten minutes before the break, the home side edged in front. A swinging pass from Brown to Archibald was returned to English. The centre-forward shot hard against Marsh, who failed to hold the ball, and it rebounded out to Marshall, who made no mistake. Just before half-time, English doubled Rangers' advantage when he powered home a header, taking advantage of some hesitation in the Dundee defence to ghost away from his marker and find the target.

It was a special moment and the debutant celebrated the goal with great excitement, running straight to a section of the crowd who had travelled from Yoker to see their former favourite make history. He drank in the applause of the home crowd before slowly making his way back to the centre circle for the resumption of the game. It was such a special moment for this extremely likeable young footballer.

After the break it was all Rangers, and it was a case of how many. Clever play on the part of Archibald led to a third for the Light Blues. In a seemingly simple manner he drew and tricked the defence, and then sent over a well-placed cross to the unmarked Nicholson, who met the ball on the drop and drove it past Marsh.

Shortly after this, Dundee enjoyed a brief flurry of possession, and nicked a consolation, but with time running out, Nicholson – deputising for Alan Morton – went on a mazy run down the left and sent over a delightful cross for Sam to head home his second of the afternoon, and Rangers' fourth. But while it may have been an excellent day for English, it wasn't so good for his opposite number, Craigie, who enjoyed nothing like the same support. Besides, Meiklejohn was always on his case, although the Dundonian had the best of it when he scored his goal, taking both the Ibrox captain and Hamilton by surprise.

It had been English's day. It was a fantastic afternoon for the ex-Yoker Athletic man, and to get two goals on his debut – just a few weeks after stepping up from the Junior ranks – was a great achievement. And it begged the question – was Sam the type of player who was blessed with supreme talent, and able to step up to whatever level he found himself playing at; comfortable in the company of the top players? Or was the gulf between Senior and Junior football not as big in the 1930s as it is today? Perhaps the true answer lay somewhere in between, although there was little doubt that Rangers had made a smart acquisition. No wonder Herbert Chapman had joined the queue.

It was the perfect start for Struth as he negotiated the defence of Rangers' title and a warning shot to those who fancied seeing the flag flying above their stadium at the start of the following season. It was business as usual for the champions and, for Sam English, he headed home to Dalmuir – aboard a corporation bus – to bask in the personal glory of being a Rangers player, and one who had scored two goals in his first match.

The following day, Sam awoke to find himself headline news in the Sunday morning papers. He had to give himself a shake to ensure it hadn't all been part of some far-fetched dream. However, along with the adulation, he was also feeling a lot of pain in one of his legs. He had taken a hefty kick during the game, but the euphoria of making his mark in such a triumphant manner had acted as the greatest form of pain relief and he hadn't noticed the injury. When he reported to Ibrox on Monday morning, it was straight on to trainer Arthur Dixon's treatment table and while the prognosis was far from serious, it was still bad enough to keep him out of Rangers' next game, at home to Airdrie just 48 hours later.

Jimmy Smith proved an able deputy although the Light Blues limped over the finishing line by the odd goal in three. The two points were vital but the Ibrox hierarchy were just a little concerned at the failure of their players to finish off a struggling Airdrie side, especially when they'd enjoyed the lion's share of play.

Sam's leg injury was proving tough to shake off and he was forced to sit out the clash of the titans at Fir Park on the Saturday afternoon. It was important to lay down a marker so early in the season but Rangers lost 4-2 to title rivals Motherwell. Struth, though, refused to hit the panic button, preferring instead to retain a sense of perspective.

Ten days after his first outing in Rangers colours, Sam was back in the starting line-up for the home match against Morton. There were no more than 15,000 present at the midweek encounter, but those in attendance witnessed the birth of a star. In an incredible 90 minutes, young Sam scored five times as Rangers romped to a 7-3 win. Those who entered through the 'shilling' gate were treated to just shy of a goal a penny, but while the final scoreline meant plaudits for the forwards, it did little for the reputation of the Ibrox defence.

The 13th minute brought the opening goal and it was certainly unlucky for the Greenock men. Sam took a delightful pass from Bob McPhail and powered straight through the centre of the visitors' defence before calmly slotting home with his left foot. McPhail scored a second, and Rangers were in control until a highly controversial moment in the 25th minute. Morton's McCartney shot at goal and the ball was collected by Jerry Dawson, but as the Rangers keeper decided what to do with possession, Black followed through and bundled man and ball into the net, and the goal was allowed to stand.

Rangers' advantage was halved, but five minutes from the interval, English took advantage of a misunderstanding between Bulloch and Hunter to ghost in and score a third, and before half time the same player accepted a pass from Marshall to fire home Rangers' fourth.

But his finest goal arrived ten minutes after the break. The ball was centred by Nicholson, and English, running on to it with precision timing, showed exactly what coolness and deftness of touch could achieve. After a sublime first touch he used the side of his foot to place the ball into the net. His fifth goal was also calmly taken. This lad looked as if he was here to stay, and when supporters were filing out of the stadium into surrounding streets, the talk was of little else apart from English.

Following the disappointing performances against Airdrie and Motherwell, a return to sparkling form for the team had coincided with the return of English, and while it may have been unfair to place so much responsibility on such young shoulders, while English appeared to be revelling in it, Struth saw no reason to upset the applecart.

Rangers were back in action at Ibrox just four days later – five of their first six league fixtures were played at home – and this time St Mirren were the visitors. Rangers were ruthless. Sure, they won 4-0, but a more realistic tally would have been double figures. Bob McPhail was imperious in attack and coordinated the movement between the half-backs and forwards superbly. English, playing only his third Senior match, looked every inch the veteran. He exuded confidence and swagger and showed little respect to the Saints defence by bullying and harrying them all afternoon.

Rangers took the lead on seven minutes through English, who took advantage of a mistimed header by Ancell to nip in and hoover up the opportunity with glee. Brown, Meiklejohn and Nicholson merely confirmed their superiority, and in a sporting contest, the only unfortunate incident was an injury to English, who was charged down by Hay, the St Mirren right-back, after getting a shot in at goal. He finished the game limping, but was fit enough to take his place in the Rangers side for their next outing, at Ibrox against the minnows of Leith Athletic.

The Edinburgh side weren't expected to leave with much, and just 6,000 supporters bothered to turn up. Perhaps the fans weren't the only ones to feel apathetic about a visit from Leith, as it seemed the majority of Rangers players had struggled to motivate themselves for the game and the first half was played at a tempo far slower than Rangers' normal Ibrox exertions. Word of this young phenomenon had obviously reached the east end of the capital as the Leith management had decided to go with two defenders permanently on English. As the Rangers inside and outside men looked for English at every turn, he wasn't just well marshalled, but positively crowded out. Still, English ploughed a lonely furrow up top and never once did he give the air of someone who felt brow-beaten. His lack of height belied his strength and work rate, and his bravery knew no bounds. Jimmy Fleming – finding extra space – scored in either half, while McPhail and English also countered after the break to put a touch of gloss on the final result.

Next up for Rangers was a trip to the seaside; Somerset Park in Ayr to be more precise, and it turned out a comfortable enough afternoon, even though they were a bit below par. McPhail missed a penalty in the first minute but Rangers didn't let that affect them too much and ran out 3-1 winners. One match report included the following paragraph, 'Now for English, whom I was seeing for the first time. I liked him, and believe he will get a lot of goals for Rangers. The lad has plenty of pluck, a good turn of speed, which will improve with proper training such as he will get at Ibrox, he can shoot, and has fairly good control. He took his goals cleverly, the first from 15 yards after being put through by McPhail, and the second from an awkward angle, although he was clearly offside.'

The games were coming thick and fast and next up was a midweek trip to Brockville to face a plucky Falkirk 11. And once again English was the man for all occasions when he put Rangers in front after ten minutes. All five members of the forward line were in super form and it was said that 'their movement and combination was a joy to behold'.

When McPhail scored on the half-hour the points looked safe, but soon after Falkirk took command and Stevenson saw Dawson save his penalty. However, a second penalty was awarded and this time Hamill scored from the spot. There was a real danger now that Falkirk would grab a share of the points, but in Bob McAulay they found a giant of a man barring their route to goal.

When Rangers were awarded the third penalty of the evening, Thomson dived full length to stop English's well-taken kick. It mattered little, though, as Rangers held on for a well-deserved victory.

Rangers had played eight league games in just 25 days, and their ninth – a first encounter of the season against Celtic – was a matter of days away. English had played in six of these league games and scored a dozen goals. He was the form striker in the country, edging out even the great Jimmy McGrory and Motherwell talisman Willie MacFadyen at that point. He had made rapid strides in a short space of time, and defenders were still coming to terms with his robust, but controlled, style.

In a later newspaper interview, Sam would say, 'My first three weeks at Ibrox passed happily. The boss insisted we were always well dressed. He even had us all wearing bowler hats. But on the field we were encouraged to play a natural game. I had felt almost disappointed by his briefing for the first game against Dundee. "Just play as you did with Yoker," he said. The advice was good because after only a few minutes I found my feet. This was no faster than the Intermediate game. With half-time approaching, a beautifully judged cross dropped close in to the far post – and landed on my head. I had scored my first goal. It was as easy as that.

'From the terracing came a hearty roar of "Whe Ho", which was the old battle cry at Yoker and Clydebank. Later, I was told that a crowd of 10,000 had followed me from my old stomping ground to Ibrox for the game, which was astonishing.

'I put another one past Dundee goalkeeper Wilson Marsh in our total of four goals. Whe Ho. Even the boss seemed pleased! And captain Davie Meiklejohn was excited. "If that's your first game – you'll do," he said briefly. He decided that in future I would be called Blondie. I had a dressing-room nickname. I was in.

'My haystack thatch of fair hair made me prominent on the field. More outstanding than my 5ft 8in – or my ability – called for. And far more easy to pick out than I wanted after the accident.

'Through August, we did rather better than even the boss insisted. Mr Struth's rule was, "Remember that two points from every home game and one from every away trip are enough to win any league."

'By the end of the month we topped the table. Celtic trailed us in third place. I seemed to be fitting in – two goals against Dundee, five against Morton, two against St Mirren, two from Ayr and one against Falkirk. It was all going even better than I could ever have imagined.'

And now, looming large, was the match that all of Scotland always looked forward to; the Old Firm, Rangers v Celtic, and, as usual, there was much more at stake than just two league points.

Seven

'I can control my destiny, but not my fate. Destiny means there are opportunities to turn right or left, but fate is a one-way street.' Paulo Coelho

THREE DAYS before the first Old Firm game of the season, Sam had starred for Rangers against Falkirk at Brockville. It was just his sixth appearance in the colours of the Ibrox club, but after scoring in the midweek 2-1 win, he had taken a kick to the ankle. It was a painful one, and even though he carried on after treatment, manager Bill Struth had decided to leave him out of the home match against great rivals Celtic.

It was the second time in just six games that he had been singled out for rough attention, and it was a theme which would continue throughout his career. In deciding to replace him with Jimmy Smith for the Old Firm encounter, perhaps Struth was trying to 'manage' his precocious young talent as best he could.

On the morning of the match, the *Glasgow Herald* printed the team line-ups. Smith was listed at centre-forward. There was no place for Sam, which would have disappointed thousands of

Rangers supporters reading their paper, and no one would be more disappointed than the player himself. Barring a last-minute injury to someone listed, those line-ups were taken as gospel. But this was one of those days.

When Smith reported for duty at Ibrox, he was quite clearly suffering from a heavy cold, or even flu. As a precaution to ensure no other players became infected, he was immediately sent home. Struth then asked his trainer to scour the corridors of Ibrox to find English and tell him to prepare for action – and a painful ankle wasn't about to keep this hungry youngster from missing out on the biggest game of his life. Sam was in.

And then the nerves started.

English explained, 'During that last midweek match at Brockville I picked up an ankle knock. There were stories in the newspapers that Jimmy Smith would be in the middle for the Saturday game. Despite my injury, I hoped not. I had been looking forward to my first meeting with Celtic.'

But despite being in a strong position to win the first Old Firm match of the season, English recalled nerves being present in every corner of the Ibrox changing room. He said, 'Personally, I had never been so nervous, but before the match, even veterans Davie Meiklejohn and Bob McPhail showed signs of strain, and there was certainly none of the usual dressing-room joshing. Dougie Gray looked jumpy as a cat. Dougie was on edge before every game. He had to hit turf and kick his first ball before he settled, but that day was as tense as I'd seen him.

'Only Sandy Archibald, who wasn't playing, managed a joke. He told wee Alan Morton, "If you behave yourself, son, we'll mebbe let you have a game with the big yins today." On the quick, thin burst of laughter the quip raised, I went out for a look at the crowd. From the lip of the tunnel it looked like a vast tidal wave moving down the terracing. Already there were about

60,000 in the bowl, filling out the empty spaces with slow, massive impatience.

'I hurried back to my place in the dressing room. We always stripped in team order. Goalkeeper Jerry Dawson had the first position. The rest sat round the room through to Alan Morton. I hung my coat on the peg between Bob McPhail and Dr Jamie Marshall. Getting ready, I tried to keep a hold of myself, draining my thoughts of everything except the simple business of getting ready. I hadn't long turned 23 and this was my first big game. Rangers against Celtic at Ibrox. League champions versus the cup holders.

'From the dressing room the crowd was a distant, growing murmur. "Well, you know what this means to you," Mr Struth said briefly as we filed out. Under the marble stairway. Across the indoor running track. Through the tunnel. Then the roar as we came out, blinking a little, into the sunshine. I had never seen so many people. Eighty thousand towered above us under a thick halo of cigarette smoke.'

And then the referee, William Holborn, emerged from the tunnel. This was it; the latest instalment in the finest club match on earth. It was just a few moments from starting but also light years from anything Sam had experienced while playing for Yoker. Sure, there had been crowds of 10,000 crammed into Holm Park, but this was another level, not just from anything else in Scottish football, but the world over.

Mr Holborn put the whistle to his mouth, and with a single burst of wind, the pea shot round the inside of the vessel and the game began.

Before the match, Celtic were being touted by some as favourites for the title, with one journalist saying, 'Celtic, after a lapse of several years, during which the Parkhead team passed through a transitory period, have found a league championship 11.'

Only a few games of the 38-week season had elapsed, but there were two hurdles over which Celtic would have to scramble before they would be able to fulfil that prophecy; namely Rangers and Motherwell, who had arguably the most dynamic team in their history.

Some suggested the size of the Ibrox attendance for this Old Firm game – in the region of 80,000 – was down to the resurgence of Celtic, but there was little evidence to support this. The Old Firm was always well patronised. The spectators were clearly looking for thrills; for first-class football, and for a battle of craft and cleverness. On all accounts, they would come away both disappointed and disgruntled, as though being cheated out of something. And no wonder. Of thrills there were none, of scientific football there was a complete absence, of craft and cleverness hardly a hint, but there were never any guarantees when the Old Firm met.

What they did see, though, according to a *Sunday Mail* reporter was 'stuff that was a blot on the fair name of sport'. The reporter added, 'Early in the game the old Celtic–Rangers weakness of "footbody" instead of football was evident. It didn't creep into the proceedings: it completely enveloped them from the outset, and not a minute passed without the referee's whistle blowing for some sort of infringement or other. Trainers and assistant trainers were the busiest men on show.'

The first half was something of a non-event, with very little football played and the stop-start nature of this clash of the giants infuriating. It was hoped, at least by the large crowd, that the second 45 minutes would be far more entertaining.

Five minutes after the re-start, Celtic were pressing high in an attempt to get an opener. The ball was in Rangers' quarter of the field when Marshall managed to steal possession. He transferred at right angles to Meiklejohn, who slipped it forward to Fleming, standing on the touchline a few yards on the Celtic side of the halfway line. McGonagle came tearing across, but Fleming dodged him and sent the ball low up the centre to be chased by English. The middle of the Celtic defence had a gaping hole and, with McStay in a hopeless position to catch him, Thomson decided to leave his goal in an effort to halt English. Just inside his penalty area, the keeper, with that bravery which was one of his greatest attributes, dived for the ball. Slightly beforehand, English made to shoot, and Thomson seemed to get the slightest of touches on the ball which sent it spinning past the outside of the goal. But in following through, the goalkeeper's head made contact with the inside of English's leg. He lay motionless on the turf. Almost immediately, a stretcher was called for.

The Rangers supporters behind the goal, believing Thomson to be play-acting, started cat-calling and jeering for him to get up. But John Thomson wasn't play-acting, and he wasn't getting up. On noticing the seriousness of the situation, Davie Meiklejohn left the field and made for the fans, urging them to calm down. They listened to their captain and respected his appeal. A deathly hush enveloped the ground.

After five or so minutes' attention on the field Thomson was eased on to a stretcher and ferried to the pavilion, where he was examined by Dr William Kivlichan, who diagnosed a depressed fracture of the skull and ordered the player's immediate removal to the infirmary.

An ambulance was summoned and Thomson was taken to the Victoria Infirmary. While awaiting its arrival, there was a knock at the door of the Ibrox medical room. It was a young girl with tears in her eyes: Miss Finlay, the young goalkeeper's fiancée. She asked permission to see John, which was granted, and one can only imagine the scene as she looked down at his unconscious form. At the moment the accident had taken place, it's said there was a high-pitched shriek from the Main Stand. Quickly realising it was the partner of the Celtic goalkeeper, Mrs Dallas, the secretary of Bill Struth, escorted the young woman down to her office for a cup of tea, before taking her along to the medical room.

In the meantime, realising how critical was the condition of Thomson, Dr Kivlichan made arrangements for the parents of the young man to be informed, and Mr and Mrs Thomson on receipt of the message at once left their Fife village of Cardenden by motor car. They arrived in Glasgow some time before the death of their son, who passed away at 9.25pm, but the doctor's quick thinking had at least allowed Mr and Mrs Thomson to spend precious moments with John.

Prior to that, in a last attempt to save his life, an operation was performed. During this anxious time several Celtic directors were present at the infirmary, along with Celtic manager Willie Maley, who was given permission to see the lad as he lay in a screened-off part of the ward.

On coming out of the ward Mr Maley stated that only a miracle could save young John.

Between the time of his being taken to the infirmary and his death, phones were ringing off the hook at all Glasgow newspapers, which was a favoured way in those days for the public to get the latest news. It was particularly busy this Saturday night as John was such a popular lad.

Outside the infirmary, and in the vicinity of the Bank Restaurant, the social rendezvous of the Celtic players and officials, large numbers of supporters gathered to await word. The mood was sombre, and the tragedy talked of only in whispers.

A quiet, clean-living young man, Thomson had endeared himself to all true lovers of the game, and there wasn't a more popular footballer in Scotland.

Normal protocol in the event of such a tragedy was for a post-mortem to be held on the body, and a report sent to Mr J.D. Strathern, the procurator fiscal. There would also be held, of course, a fatal accident inquiry before a sheriff and jury.

The game itself now seemed immaterial. As has already been indicated, it wasn't the most watchable of Old Firm games, as for the most part it was devoid of much skill and the moments worth talking about could be numbered on a single hand. There was no denying the collective level of skill on the field but for one reason or another it wasn't evident during a rough and tumble 90 minutes.

The match petered out into a 0-0 draw. Defences ruled throughout, but they did so in a manner that was not always pretty to watch. The forwards were simply not allowed, at any cost, to get away with the ball, and elbowing, shoving, heel-tapping and all the other unfair manoeuvres were only too evident. It started off with McAulay, in the first minute, deliberately drawing the legs away from Bert Thomson, and it finished with McGonagle doing the same with Fleming in the last.

In the first half, play was even. There was plenty of effort, hard kicking and unintelligent distribution of the ball. This latter fault was chiefly among the forwards, who simply couldn't get going. Celtic seemed intent to slap the ball up the middle, but McGrory was too well policed to get any decent possession. He always had Jimmy Simpson breathing down his neck, while George Brown, so far as McGrory was concerned, had a very nasty habit of being in the centre of the field when the ball was there. When he did get hold of the leather, McGrory on several occasions was slow to gather, or well out in his calculations when trying to distribute it.

Bob McPhail was the strong man in the Rangers attack. With physical strength, allied to a measure of skill, he went all out to make openings. He tried Alan Morton with ground passes, but quickly found the wee fellow couldn't get away with them, and varied his stuff with raking balls up the centre to English. The ex-Yoker man, like his prototype, had a 'policeman' at his shoulder in the shape of McStay, but he scored over McGrory in that he often found space to shove the ball out to Jimmy Fleming. The outside-right responded only indifferently. He tried to be too dainty and his returns were often just a yard short.

Play for the most part was in the region of midfield, and one can understand how safe the respective goals were, how untroubled the respective keepers, when 24 minutes had elapsed before a corner kick was given. It was Celtic's, but it served no purpose and Brown nipped in to clear.

Just after half an hour's play, Fleming was given a golden opportunity, but he messed it up. McPhail, twisting and swerving, had the defence guessing. He shoved the ball forward slightly to the right. Celtic, to a man, stopped, and claimed offside against English. The referee waved his hands to carry on. Fleming dashed in but with only Thomson to beat he toed the ball too hard and had the embarrassment of seeing it whistle past the post.

And then we had one of the game's few thrilling passages. In a slick passing move, Rangers edged ever closer towards the Celtic goal, but despite many attempts to play a final through ball, they found the route to goal blocked by the impressive Chic Geatons, who eventually cleared for Bert Thomson to race away and change the focus of attack.

With Celtic minus their goalkeeper five minutes after the restart, and Geatons taking his place, Rangers were favourites to win the game. Celtic, after the loss, made a spirited foray, but it petered out, and Rangers tried their utmost to press home the advantage. The Parkhead defence stood up to everything, and for minutes on end only McGrory stood out from the rest of his side, the others trying to block the road to the net.

If it was poor stuff in the first half, it was poorer in the second. Rangers' left wing had more or less faded out, and their right never looked like breaking down the barrier raised in front of them. Time dragged on drearily, with Rangers always threatening to do something, but never doing it.

Indeed, in the last few minutes they came very close to meeting with their second defeat of the season. Scarff was the man responsible. For the first time in the game he started one of his solo runs and weaved his way in and out towards Jerry Dawson. He finished up three or four yards from the right-hand post, and was raising his boot to finish affairs when a foot shot out, and he was dispossessed. A fraction of a second made all the difference.

If there was one man out there on the Ibrox turf who deserved credit for his performance, it was the referee. He handled the game efficiently and with the minimum of fuss, especially in a game which must have been very difficult for him.

Sam's view of the game differs little from the match report. He remembers the game lacking in any real quality, and added, 'It was poor fare, full of stoppages for free kicks and so many throw-ins even the reporters high in the press box stopped counting. Both teams marked closely, following instructions, taking no chances. Each side was like a boxer sizing the other up. There would be a rush to one end, a rush to the other. But no real action.

'All through the first half I don't remember having a single shot at goal. Most of the time I was out on the wings trying to take centre-half Jimmy McStay for a walk. But Jimmy was having none of it. He had the rare knack of never seeming to be more than six or seven yards away, yet always lying handy to guard the middle of the field and the way to goal.

'After 35 minutes Bob McPhail carried the ball upfield. He dummied me. The Celtic backs appealed for offside. McPhail switched out to Fleming instead, but Jimmy shot over. Tempers frayed and I remember McPhail clashing with Peter Wilson; Bob McAulay jousting with Bertie Thomson.

'I had one chance – a high cross well out, near the 18-yard line. I jumped for it but John Thomson – just over an inch taller than me – coolly lifted the ball off my head. "Hard lines, young fellow," he said. These were the first and only words we ever shared.

'Half-time came as a relief. I had an orange and a cup of tea in the dressing room as usual. As usual, too, manager Struth paced to and fro in the middle of the room. There was not much talking and no special instructions. It was still anybody's game.

'Five minutes after the re-start Jimmy Fleming had the ball, making ground right out on the wing. His cross came over low towards me just outside the 18-yard line. Both Celtic backs are lying wide. Billy Cook is left of me and behind. I can see McGonagle to my right. He is maybe six yards away. I don't know. Anyhow, he's too far away for it to matter. There is only the keeper to beat. The ball comes to me from the side. I can see John Thomson moving out of his goal. He hesitates about the six-yard line to balance himself. He's got the goalmouth completely blocked. There is no bounce in the ball. I can't lift it over his head. But if he comes out further I have a chance to go round him. I can run forward faster than he can run back.

'He does come out. I have a view of two feet to a yard of the goal. By now I have pulled the ball round in line with my body, using my right foot. I kick it, again with my right, cutting across the front of the ball to try to swerve it in.

'John is on me in a rugby tackle. His head thumps into the inside of my left knee. I feel nothing. Later examination finds no mark on that knee, but a small scratch on the right one where he must have clutched at me, going down.

'I fall over him. The ball trickles over the byline, barely moving.

'I bend over John [to see how he is]. Billy Cook pulls me back. "It wasn't your fault," he says.

'Cheering swells out from the terracing of Rangers supporters behind the goal. Davie Meiklejohn runs forward, waving it down. A sudden heavy silence fills Ibrox.

'Jimmy McStay and Jimmy Fleming are standing beside the unconscious Thomson, waving for a stretcher. It was only when I saw Chic Geatons taking the goalkeeper's orange jersey that I realised how serious John Thomson's condition might be.

'Somehow the game finished. No goals were scored. I don't remember. I kept looking all the time towards the tunnel, waiting for him to come back, but at the end 21 players trooped off.'

As 80,000 supporters filed quietly out of the stadium, the players made their way back to their respective dressing rooms. Barely a word was spoken. It was there that Sam was given an update on John Thomson's condition.

He recalled, 'They told me John Thomson had a fractured skull and had been taken to hospital. His brother was with him. I had a bath and got into my street clothes. There was a hush in the dressing room. Mr Struth came over, "Go home and don't worry. We'll take care of everything."

'I didn't see William Maley, the Celtic manager, or any of the Celtic players. The teams didn't mix much then.

'"You'll be all right Blondie," Davie Meiklejohn said as he left.

'George Brown asked if I should like to get away for a weekend's sailing around Arran on his motor cruiser. But I just wanted to get home and big Tommy Hamilton drove me to Dalmuir in his car. Later that evening I felt suddenly restless. Tommy's billiards hall was next door. I went there. We were standing talking under the green smoky lights when a local man we both knew came in. "Johnny Thomson is dead," he said. It would be about 10.45pm.

'We didn't believe him. "It's true," he said. "There are special papers out."

'Tommy locked his office and the glass case where he kept sweets and lemonade. We ran out across the canal bridge for the nearest phone at the end of Nairn Street, where Tommy phoned the infirmary. I squeezed into the box beside him. I could hear from what Tommy was saying that the news was true. But still I could not believe it.

'Then along the darkening street I could hear the newsboys running and shouting "John Thomson dead".'

John Thomson had died more than an hour before the phone call Tommy Hamilton made, and roughly five and a half hours after the accident – at 9.25pm of a depressed fracture of the skull. His mother and father, called urgently from Fife, were with him when he passed away.

Sam said, 'My wife Sadie and I took our little daughter Charlotte from her bed and went to my mother's house; it seemed the place to be. Automatically, my mother made tea. And through the long reaches of that night my father sat with me by the fire, talking. He talked as I had never heard him before, deliberately and endlessly. I forget about what. About everything and anything, I suppose, except the accident. At last the morning came.

'Mr Struth arrived early with a police inspector from Glasgow. The inspector asked a few questions about what had happened, told me there would be an inquiry, but that it would be only a formality.

'I had to get out. I went to Helensburgh and walked to Garelochhead and back again. It was little comfort. Everywhere there seemed to be news bills with Johnny Thomson's name on them.

'I thought, "Why me?" I asked that question every day of my life since the accident. And, of course, there can never be any answer to it. Football was just a game to me, and nothing more. It happened I had some skill for it and could earn money playing. I have never intended anyone any harm. I was never a rough player. I had never played against Johnny Thomson before. I had not met him, had never even spoken to him.

'Of the Celtic team I knew only Billy Cook, a mate from the old Port Glasgow days. Jimmy McStay, the Parkhead captain, who was to play opposite me on the day of the accident was a canny, close-marking centre-half, scrupulously fair. He had a leisurely, unworried air about him. Once I asked him how he could remain so relaxed. "I like to enjoy my football," he explained. But I doubt if either team enjoyed the Old Firm encounters in those days – or even now. They were dour defensive affairs. And always it was the mood of the crowd which dominated the match.'

In the half dozen games Sam had played for Rangers before the tragic Old Firm encounter, he had gained a reputation for being a livewire centre-forward whom a defender couldn't take their eyes off for a solitary moment, lest he would be in about the six-yard box feeding on loose balls. He had never been held up as the type of player who adopted a win-at-all-costs attitude, which was borne out by a newspaper report, which included the following paragraph: 'While many players must be held culpable for causing injury to their opponents, English must be completely absolved from any blame whatsoever from the terrible hurt that came the way of John Thomson. Here was an accident in every sense of that much-abused word.'

Behind the goal that afternoon, cameramen clicked away, hoping to get one decent photograph for the next day's papers. One such snapper, crouched behind the byline when John Thomson moved from his goal line to intercept the ball, was Jack Gibson, himself the same age as the young goalkeeper. He was a 'staffer' at the *Daily Express*, and was the man responsible for capturing the almost grotesque image which would be produced as evidence at the fatal accident inquiry.

Mr Gibson recalled, 'It was a typical Rangers–Celtic match. Most of the action was played out in the midfield. I had made only one exposure before this picture in the 50th minute.

'John Thomson made to move forward, stopped, then moved forward again. I clearly remember seeing daylight between Thomson's body and the ground, and the ball coming through under him. I took my picture.

'I was not surprised when he didn't rise, for I thought he must be winded. When they turned him over I saw his face was twisted. Only then did I realise his injuries might be more serious.'

John Thomson died that evening, and a part of Sam English died too.

Sam, left, with two of his brothers, outside the home where they grew up in Crevolea

Young Sam's view from his front door in Crevolea

The house in Crevolea where Sam was born

Looking up to the house in
Crevolea where Sam was born

Glenruther Terrace, Dalmuir: Home for the English family on
their arrival from Ireland

Sam English was a pupil at Dalmuir School

Sam, front, centre, and his team-mates won the
John Brown's Shop League in 1926

The all-conquering Yoker Athletic team of the early 1930s

A portrait of Sam in his Yoker days

One of the many medals Sam won during his time at Yoker Athletic

The two managers who battled for Sam's signature when he was leaving Yoker. Bill Struth, of Rangers, left, and Arsenal's Herbert Chapman

Sam heads for goal during his Rangers debut at Ibrox against Dundee in 1931

Hearts goalkeeper Jack Harkness saves from Sam English

Sam, left, appeals for a corner against Third Lanark

John Thomson dives at the feet of Sam English. Later that night, the goalkeeper lost his fight for life (courtesy of SMG)

Sam and his wife pictured with John Thomson's father at the unveiling of a memorial statue in Fife

Sam takes a moment off from his 9 to 5 for a quick chat

A smiling Sam in his training jumper

Sam English in his Rangers attire – cartoon style!

Sam, extreme right, holds court at a Rangers' players dance in the Grosvenor Hotel, Glasgow

Sam claims for a corner kick

Sam, left, scores against Hamilton Accies in the Scottish Cup semi-finals

Sam, right, was a keen golfer

Scottish Cup winner 1932. Pictured, from left, Bob McPhail, Sam, Davie Meiklejohn and Jimmy Fleming

Sam, extreme left, scores against Kilmarnock in the Scottish Cup Final

Rangers' victorious squad pictured with the 1932 Scottish Cup

Sam, partly hidden by another player, in action against Arbroath in a Scottish Cup tie at Ibrox in 1933

Signing for Liverpool, Sam shakes hands with new team-mate Ernie Blenkinsop. Also pictured are Berry Nieuwenhuys, right, and Tom Cooper

The Liverpool Echo *hails the arrival of English*

Sam scores his first goal for Liverpool

Eight

THE FAMILY of John Thomson wasted no time in issuing a statement absolving Sam English of any blame in their son's death. Within 48 hours of the accident, Mr and Mrs Thomson announced through the press that they viewed the incident as purely accidental. The family also wanted to express their gratitude for the uniform sympathy that had been extended to them from people all over the country. It was a kind gesture and, hopefully, provided some relief for Sam and his family.

It was also fitting that the announcement came on the day that a memorial service was held at Trinity Church, in Glasgow, to remember the brave young goalkeeper. Thousands were in attendance, and several women who fainted were taken to hospital. Reinforcements of police arrived and restored order. Sam English sat with his head buried in his handkerchief throughout the service, and tears were shed by the footballer.

Sam recalled, 'Along with other Rangers and Celtic players I attended a memorial service at Trinity Congregational Church in Glasgow on the Tuesday after the accident. Our captain Davie Meiklejohn read one of the lessons, but Celtic skipper Jimmy

McStay was unable to break through the crowd outside the church to take part in the service.

'The crowd is all I remember. Three thousand packed the street; jostling, pushing. Policemen seemed everywhere. Women in shawls. As I passed through them, one said, "But he's only a boy." Somehow she seemed disappointed.

'One newspaper report said I looked "visibly moved". From the first organ note of "Nearer My God to Thee" I wept. Team-mate Jimmy Simpson sat throughout the service with his arm round my shoulders. And next day was the funeral.

'A soccer-sized crowd attended the burial of John Thomson in the tiny Fife village of Cardenden. Three trains carried them from Glasgow; there were three lorries filled with flowers. Miner friends of the Thomsons gave up a day's pay to be there. Some unemployed men walked the 55 miles from Glasgow, camping out for the night in the hills above Auchterderran.

'And all morning the coffin lay in the front room of the Thomson house under a canopy of rambling roses. By early afternoon, 30,000 crammed the narrow half-mile village street to the cemetery.

'Jimmy McGrory and other Celtic players shared the burden of the coffin with John Thomson's brothers.

'I walked alone.

'Inside the cemetery Alan Morton pushed his way to my side. The crowd broke in through the gate, trampled over graves, massed round the chief mourners. Silently, a cordon of police formed thickly round Alan and me. I never saw John Thomson's grave that day ... and on the next there was a match at Ibrox.'

The *Daily Record* reported, 'Unparalleled scenes were witnessed in the Fife mining village when John Thomson was laid to rest in the quiet little cemetery that adjoins Dundonald Road. Hundreds of miners, grimy and toil-stained from their work in the nearby colliery, rubbed shoulders with scrupulously dressed men from many of the big cities.

'Thousands of Glasgow boys who had seen John play in many a well-fought contest gathered in little silent groups before the service. Women, too, who had travelled scores of miles waited patiently for the cortege to pass, while many of them wiped tears from their eyes as they discussed his death.

'Never at any time was the passing of a footballer so widely mourned, nor so deeply. Men experiencing hard times, and unable to afford the train or bus fare, had walked miles to pay their last respects. One man had walked from Kilmarnock, and reached the village barely two hours before the service. He was almost exhausted, but took his place in the crowds at the roadside and waited as patiently as the others.

'In three special trains, five thousand people from Glasgow had poured into the village. The residents were out man, woman and child.

'The coffin lay in a simple little room on the right hand side of the entrance. All furniture had been removed, and the coffin in the centre was the only thing in the room. On it lay several wreaths and a little bunch of white heather. And one of John's international caps. His sister had placed it there. "It was what he desired most in life, and I see no reason why he should not have it now," she said.

'By two in the afternoon the route to the cemetery was lined with thousands of people. They clambered up the banks at the roadsides, they climbed to the tops of walls, even on to the roofs of buildings.

'On the arrival of the special trains the passengers formed fours and marched to Balgreggie Park. The streets echoed to the tramp of marching men for more than an hour. There were many floral tributes, with a beautiful one in white roses and chrysanthemums from the Rangers Supporters' Club in Bridgeton. The supporters of Rangers and Celtic in Raglan Street, Maryhill, had clubbed together to present another little token of the respect in which John was held by fans of both clubs.

'As the clock approached 3pm the crowd fell silent. There was scarcely movement among them, and the silence had an air of tense expectancy. The coffin was brought to the front door of the house and a simple service was conducted by Mr Duncan Adamson, an elder of the Church of Christ. One hundred yards along the road two bands waited to accompany John to his final resting place. Many of the bandsmen had been to school with him.

'Seated at the window of an upper room sat a lady looking down on the mass of people and straining her ears to catch every word that was uttered over the oak coffin. "His mother," someone whispered, and there were many sympathetic glances towards the window where she sat, supported by her son William. She was silent and immobile while the words of the service floated up and away in the wind. Since her son's death, she had been unwell.

'At last, the flower-covered coffin was raised on the shoulders of his club mates, who carried it to the grave, a quarter of a mile away. Men and women drew back to make way for John's passing.

'Men doffed their hats and caps and women bowed their heads. Only the sound of an occasional sob punctured the quiet as they carried him to the corner of the street. The pipe band struck up a slow and plaintive air, and to the stately tread of the pipers John Thomson was carried from the home of those who had loved him so well.

'And through it all, the silent figure at the window sat still, while the sound of the piper grew fainter and fainter, and she strained her eyes to catch the last sight of the coffin containing her famous son.

'The procession was nearly a mile long.

'Towards the end of the service the Rangers players arrived and stood quietly by until the finish. Some carried flowers. It had been a fitting send-off for the young man they called The Prince of Goalkeepers.'

Just seven days after the accident, as Sam was at Firhill Stadium, preparing for a league match against Partick Thistle, a telegram was delivered to the front door of the ground. It was addressed to 'Sam English, Rangers Football Club, c/o Partick Thistle, Firhill Stadium' and it was accepted and taken to the Rangers dressing room, where manager Bill Struth was addressing his players. The changing room prior to a game was normally out of bounds for anyone outwith the playing side of the club, but on this occasion Mr Struth made an exception and invited the messenger inside.

When it was handed to Sam, and he opened it up, a tear immediately slid down his cheek. On realising the contents, Struth ushered him outside and English handed the note to his manager. It said, simply, 'TO SAM ENGLISH – GOOD LUCK FROM JOHN THOMSON'S MOTHER'.

Sam was deeply touched by the thoughtfulness of Mrs Thomson. Nothing else would come close to comforting him more than that one line on the telegram.

Celtic's official programme, for the match against Queen's Park on the same day, naturally included a lengthy tribute to their young goalkeeper, but included the words, 'We are sure that all who were present at Ibrox will agree in exonerating English completely from blame ... and we are certain that he will welcome a statement such as this.'

On Wednesday, 16 September, Sam came face to face with Mrs Thomson at her home in Cardenden. He was accompanied by Bill Struth and Davie Meiklejohn, after the trio had motored through to Fife at the invitation of John's parents, who wanted a calm and consoling talk with Sam. In their neat cottage home, the little party gathered for an hour or two, and what transpired was comforting to all.

Mr and Mrs Thomson gave the young Rangers centre further assurance of their deep sympathy for him, trusted he would not allow himself to worry over the sad event at Ibrox, and wished him a long and successful career. He was deeply moved by the affectionate kindness not only of John's parents, but of the other members of the family. On parting, all expressed the hope that they would meet again soon.

As for Rangers and Celtic, they met for the first time since the accident around a fortnight later. On this occasion the match was played on a Monday evening at Celtic Park and up for grabs was a place in the final of the Glasgow Cup.

For the first time in many a year, a truce had been called on the fanatical partisanship normally reserved for these occasions. As a mark of respect to the late goalkeeper, no club or party colours were displayed in any form whatsoever. However, the only thing which disturbed the peace was the outbursts of booing or cheering and counter-cheering whenever certain incidents took place.

It was unfortunate that even these demonstrations should have been in evidence, but considering the strained atmosphere in which the game was played, and watched by nearly 60,000, they were practically unavoidable.

For some time after the game began, the players conducted themselves in a fine, sportsmanlike way, and the football was fast and delightful to watch. And this pattern continued almost until half-time, when tempers became a bit mixed. Tensions were raised, and after the first bad challenge of the game, others soon followed. Some were jaw-dropping in their ferocity and might well have been best avoided, although perhaps that was too much to ask of the players within such a highly-charged atmosphere. Some of the tackles had a nasty look about them, and on such occasions large sections of the crowd were very noisy and persistent in their vocal expressions of disapproval.

It was particularly unfortunate that the first injury to a player in the game involved Sam English. Early in the second half, McDonald swung in a cross, which Celtic keeper Falconer was in the act of catching, when English jumped to intercept with his head. But instead of getting the ball, the Rangers centre's head made contact with Falconer's jaw and the home keeper fell to the ground.

A great hush descended over the stadium, and a little bit of pushing and shoving, and finger-pointing, ensued, but when Falconer got to his feet the scene quickly calmed down. The injury to Falconer also caused a section of the Celtic support to make English a target for their ire, but the mood changed when, from the resulting free kick, Celtic ran up the park and scored, with Alec Thomson on target.

Shortly after the goal, it was the turn of the Rangers supporters to vent their anger towards certain Celtic players when English was twice hacked to the ground and had to be helped from the field to receive treatment. He had clearly been singled out for extra-special attention by the very players who only a couple of weeks earlier had declared him innocent in the John Thomson accident.

Eventually, Rangers skipper Meiklejohn stopped the game to speak earnestly to the referee, who walked from the centre of the field to the pavilion entrance and talked with an official. The game was then restarted. It is understood that Meiklejohn's complaint had something to do with the booing of English by sections of the crowd. About this time, too, a squad of police went among the spectators behind one of the goals; but otherwise there was no sign of disturbance.

Moments later, Rangers equalised. Nicholson played a lovely ball towards English, who was aggressively bundled off his feet by

McGonagle. It was a clear but foolish penalty, for the ball might never have reached English, but referee Mungo Hutton had no hesitation in pointing to the spot, and Jamie Marshall remained the coolest man on the park to shoot past Falconer.

Then the Rangers left-winger swooped down on the Celtic defence. The ball was sent through to English, who jumped high with the intention of heading out to Nicholson. Coming down he came into contact with Billy Cook, his old Port Glasgow team mate, and was injured. He was again forced off to receive attention.

Six minutes into the second half, the struggling English and Fleming swapped places, and moments later, Rangers squandered the best chance of the game. English passed to Marshall, who squared for Nicholson five yards out, but he made a complete hash of the chance and a great opportunity was lost. The injury to English had certainly upset Rangers' rhythm.

After the match, which most people found extremely interesting and often very thrilling, the crowd left the ground in orderly fashion.

Of the match, Sam recalled, 'I played only once at Parkhead, a few weeks after John Thomson's death. There was an incident on the field. A bottle was thrown and one of my team-mates pretended he was about to throw it back. The crowd in one corner surged forward, threatening to break in. "Get into the middle," Davie Meiklejohn shouted to me, but I stood where I was. If they really wanted me, I wasn't going to run.

'The incident passed. It was brief and isolated. For at first I enjoyed only sympathy and understanding from players and officials, and even from that cruellest of all animals – the football crowd. The oppression grew gradually.'

Two days before Rangers were due to host Queen's Park in a league match, English was forced to relive the John Thomson incident all over again at the Fatal Accident Inquiry into the goalkeeper's death. The inquiry took place in Glasgow on Thursday, 15 October 1931, and a verdict of death by accident was returned. The inquiry, held before a sheriff and jury, looked into every aspect of the death of the Celtic goalkeeper. People well known in the football world were present, and the witnesses cited included Bill Struth, Willie Maley, manager of Celtic, Sam English, and the press photographer who took a picture of the two players at the time of the accident.

Altogether around a dozen witnesses were summoned by the Crown, but a number of these, including English, were not called to give evidence. Both clubs were represented by legal teams, headed up by Colonel Shaughnessy (for Celtic), and William McAndrew, who appeared on behalf of Rangers and English.

Mr Maley showed signs of emotion when giving his evidence. He was asked by John MacKay, the fiscal, to describe what had happened when, shortly after the second half began, the ball was sent towards the Celtic goal, and English chased it down.

Mr Maley said, 'I was in the stand, a good distance from the actual occurrence, and I cannot really say what happened. I saw the clash when the two men came together and I noticed that Thomson did not get up. I remarked to a friend, "something serious must have happened", but that is the extent of my knowledge of the occurrence. My impression was that Thomson attempted to save when English was shooting.'

Mr Maley said he knew that Thomson, seriously injured, was taken off the field and died in the Victoria Infirmary.

Mr MacKay asked, 'In your opinion it was an accident?'

Mr Maley replied, 'I hope it was an accident, but I cannot form an opinion of what happened.'

In the eyes of many, the first six words of that sentence condemned English. It was such a foolish thing for Maley to say, because it meant nothing. Many years later folk still wondered why he felt the need to say it at all. If the parents of John Thomson had been gracious enough to absolve Sam of any blame, then what right did Maley have to put doubt in people's minds?

Next up at the inquiry was the referee, William Holborn, who told of how he saw the ball being played forward towards the Celtic goal. The Rangers centre-forward made after the ball and was in the act of shooting when Thomson ran from the goal and dived at English's feet. Both men fell. Mr Holborn saw that Thomson was badly injured and had him removed. He ordered the resumption of the game by a goal kick.

The fiscal asked Mr Holborn, 'The whole thing was an accident?' to which Mr Holborn replied, simply, 'Yes.'

Dr Fulton Kivlichan, casualty surgeon at the Central Police Station, who had been present at the match, said he examined Thomson in the pavilion. He diagnosed the injury as a depressed fracture of the skull and had Thomson taken to the Victoria Infirmary. He did not consider that there was any blame attached to anyone.

Sheriff Wilton asked Dr Kivlichan if he considered the injury to be a fatal one, to which the doctor replied, 'At the time I thought the goalkeeper was going to die.'

Dr Kivlichan said he conveyed this view to the officials of both clubs.

Asked if it was not usual to stop the game in such circumstances, Dr Kivlichan replied that it was just his view that Thomson was going to die.

The next witness was Dr William Gillespie, house surgeon of the Victoria Infirmary, who said that Thomson was in his care from the time he came into the Infirmary.

Thomson was suffering from a depressed fracture of the skull, and a last effort was made to save his life. An operation was performed but, unfortunately, it did not have the results they hoped for.

The dead goalkeeper's brother, James Ferguson Thomson, who was an eye witness, also gave evidence. He stated that he was present in the Victoria Infirmary where his brother died at 9.25pm on the day in question.

The formal verdict of the jury was, 'That the deceased, while acting in his employment as a professional football player with the Celtic Football Club, and acting as goalkeeper in the football match with Rangers at Ibrox Park, Glasgow, on September 5, and in the course of the match, sustained an injury to his head by accidentally coming into contact with the body of Sam English, playing centre-forward for Rangers, and in an attempt to save a goal by diving towards Sam English when in the act of kicking the ball, he sustained a fracture of the skull from which he died in the Victoria Infirmary from injuries so sustained.'

Addressing the jury, the sheriff said that this had been a very distressing occurrence on the football field. 'You are no doubt satisfied,' he said to the members, 'that it was an accident.'

The *Daily Record* reported the findings of the Fatal Accident Inquiry extensively in its paper the following morning, but afterwards insisted it would not be entering into any further discussions on the subject. A report read, 'We have received a large number of letters relating to the evidence heard at the inquiry into the death of John Thomson, but think it is better that no issue should be raised which would involve any recrudescence of feeling on the matter. Our readers will hopefully understand that this is in the public interest and for the good of the game.'

Jimmy Kerr was the Rangers trainer at the time of the accident, and was the first person to attend to the stricken goalkeeper. Many years later, while being interviewed by a national newspaper, he said, 'Sam English shot for goal, the ball glanced off John

Thomson's right side and passed near to the right post. I measured the distance he ran out to his left. It was 47 feet. As your man on the spot has said, he moved out one step, hesitated, then made his effort.

'I remember Mr Maley coming on to the field, asking if it was serious. I told him it was very serious, and it would be a fight for John's life. Mr Maley tried to speak, but his heart was too full. The game finished with no scoring. I don't think any of the players on either side had the heart to play on. I wonder what would have happened if the game had been abandoned.'

Celtic stalwart Chic Geatons played in goal for the remainder of the game. The talented left-half – later to become a Glasgow publican – remembered that day and night vividly, describing it as 'a cloud settling over the city as we learned that Jock had died'.

He recalled, 'Sam English was just becoming one of the best centre-forwards of his time. He was not a rough player, relying on strength. He was a cultured footballer. I know that if anyone could have avoided that impact it would have been a player like Sam.

'I took over in goal afterwards – as I had done two or three times that season when Jock had taken knocks. After the game, the Celtic team went, as usual, to the Bank Restaurant in Queen Street for a meal. The crowds outside were exceptional – all waiting for word of Jock. Round about nine o'clock we heard he had died.

'It was a shock to us all. But I can assure Sam that from that moment the sympathy of every Celtic player was with him. We knew how he would be feeling. His play suffered as a result. Later he went to play in English football, which I always considered a mistake. They hounded him down there. He came back and played in Scottish football again later but was not the same; his heart wasn't in it.

'Sam English was a gentleman footballer, as well as a great one. But he was very young when this happened and never seemed to be able to forget it. But I can assure Sam that neither I nor any player on the field that day blamed him for what happened. It could happen to anyone in football.'

As Geatons alluded to, the long-term psychological effect of the accident on Sam would be enormous. To be directly involved in the death of a fellow sportsman would have been incredibly tough, but ten times harder as it was played out so publicly, although in time, that very public would become less and less forgiving. Sam was in no doubt that the catalyst for much of the resentment towards him was down to the irresponsible comment made by Willie Maley at the FAI.

He recalled, 'Looking back, I seemed to detect a whiff of [the resentment] even at the inquiry into the accident. I still cannot imagine why Mr Maley would say what he did that day. It was then my father warned me I would never be allowed to forget. He advised me to go to America where I had two brothers and a sister; to cut myself off entirely.

'Even then, at 23, I realised that might be the wise course. But I played on for seven long years.

'Why? Because I believe a man must do what he can do. And football was my job.

'I felt on top of the world at Ibrox. And no man with a young family growing up wanted to go back into the shipyards of the 1930s unless he had to. To choose football was possibly not sensible. To have done anything else would have seemed to me like running away.'

Referee William Holborn was so affected by the tragic events that he penned a poignant letter to Mr and Mrs Thomson. It was one of many thousands received by the family.

Mr Holburn wrote, 'Dear Mr and Mrs Thomson, I am grieved to know that the accident on Saturday ended so tragically for your home, and that you have been bereaved of a loving son.

'John's death will cast a gloom over the entire field of sport, and football circles especially will mourn the loss of a comrade. As a referee of the Scottish Football Association I am brought into close touch with players of the various clubs and I have an opportunity, therefore, of studying the character of the men. In John I always found one of high purpose, whom it was always a pleasure to meet, and who not only played the game on the football field, but whose every action was that of a gentleman.

'By his death I have lost a dear friend, but I will cherish my associations with him as happy memories. Words fail me to express adequately my sorrow for you and your family in your great grief, but I would ask you to accept my heartfelt sympathy in this hour of sorrow. That the great, all-wise Providence will be your comfort in the sincere wish of – Yours very sincerely, William G. Holborn.'

It had often been said of John Thomson that he did not need to learn the art of goalkeeping, as it came to him as naturally as swimming to a duck. With Celtic he almost immediately sprang to prominence: the hallmark of class was upon him. He had been with Celtic five years when tragedy struck, and was known not only as a great goalkeeper, but also as a young man with unlimited bravery. In February 1930, while in the act of making a save against Airdrie at Celtic Park, he had been seriously injured, suffering a broken jaw, several fractured ribs, a damaged collarbone and two lost teeth. The incident threatened to end his career, but the youngster's indomitable spirit helped him through tough times and he won the first of his four caps for Scotland just three months later.

Friend and foe admired Thomson on the field. He was a sportsman and a gentleman. And off the field he was the same. His tragic death, at the age of 22, was the third in the history of Scottish football. On Christmas Day 1909, at Firhill, James Main, the Hibernian right-back, was kicked in the stomach – an accident, as the Partick Thistle player had slipped on ice while tackling him – and suffered a ruptured bowel. He died in Edinburgh Royal Infirmary four days later.

In November 1921, Rangers hosted Dumbarton in a league match. Joshua Wilkinson kept goal for the Sons, who were struggling at the time, and the former Ranger was outstanding, playing a huge part in helping his side secure a 1-1 draw. Wilkinson had taken a couple of knocks during the game, and afterwards complained of feeling unwell. Peritonitis was diagnosed by a local doctor and he had an operation in hospital the following day. He remembered speaking to Bill Struth, who visited him after his operation on the Sunday, but sadly died on the Monday morning. The cause of the rupture remained unsolved but it was another sad loss for the football community.

Nine

THE DAY after John Thomson's funeral, there was a match to be played. Sam didn't think for a moment he would be involved in the Glasgow Cup tie against Third Lanark at Ibrox, but manager Bill Struth had other ideas.

On the morning of the game, Sam was at home in Dalmuir, having breakfast, when his mum asked him what he had planned for the day.

He recalled, 'When I told my mother we had a game at Ibrox, she said, "Surely they'll not ask you to turn out today." At that point I didn't have the answer. All I knew was I would have to report to Ibrox as normal. I got the bus from Clydebank with our goalkeeper, Tommy Hamilton, and he talked the entire journey, as cheerfully as he could, about my old carefree days playing for Dalmuir School. It certainly helped the time go by.'

Sam and Tommy got off the bus in Paisley Road West and cut along Broomloan Road to Ibrox. When they entered through the main door, the commissionaire welcomed both inside. They went straight to the dressing room, where the team was already pinned up on the wall.

Sam said, 'I remember the dull shock of getting to the stadium to find that Mr Struth had listed me to play. Our team that day was: Dawson, Gray, McAulay, Meiklejohn, Simpson, Brown, Main, Marshall, English, McPhail and Morton. At first I thought of refusing, of defying the absolute authority of manager Bill Struth, but he came immediately to me and said, "Keep your eye on the ball and remember you are playing football." He said it gruffly, but kindly enough.

'Reluctantly I ran out of the tunnel with the rest of the team. The crowd hushed. They seemed uncertain whether to cheer or not. There was a heavy air of suspense, but to tell you the truth, as soon as my feet hit the turf I felt a moment of relief.'

Like the dressing room, the playing surface was also sacred to the players, and where most of them felt at ease. And while Sam had felt trepidation at facing such a big crowd just 24 hours after John Thomson's funeral, it was the sight of a boyhood friend that gave him the courage to play the game.

Sam recalled, 'The best Clydebank-built player I knew was Neil Dewar, my favourite centre-forward. We went to school together. My teacher, Miss Mitchell, used to say all my brains were in my feet. But Neillie was dedicated. For school team away games he would turn up at the station with his green strip on under his coat and wearing his boots. We nicknamed him "silver sleeves" because he never seemed to have a handkerchief, or sometimes Cleeks because of his hen toes. He was a big, lanky, fragile boy, but he was my friend.

'For years we lost touch, until Tommy Hamilton had mentioned his name while we were travelling to the game that day on the bus. Tommy had tried to cheer me up by saying that the Dewar listed at centre-forward for Third Lanark was actually Cleeks himself. And when I ran on to the field sure enough it was – the very same long, hen-toed Neil, a brilliant ball player.

After the strain and ache of the memorial service and funeral it tore a laugh from my throat.

'I ran out to him in the centre circle. We shook hands. We said just the usual things about how long it had been since we met. But the relief of having an old friend on the field helped me through that first game.'

After leaving Third Lanark, Dewar would go on to play for Manchester United and Sheffield Wednesday, and scored four goals in three international appearances for Scotland, which included a hat-trick in France.

Perhaps it was a good thing that Sam hadn't been given too much time to think about the extent of the tragedy due to the close proximity of the Third Lanark game. Such a traumatic episode must have taken its toll, either consciously or subconsciously, on the young man, but in those days there was little time given over to psychological trauma.

The Third Lanark game was played just four days after the match against Celtic, and it would later transpire that Struth had intended for Jimmy Smith to fill the centre-forward role but once again Smith was unavailable due to injury so English played instead. Sam was fine about it and scored a beauty of a goal, due to a bit of quick thinking and coolness. It was a glorious strike after some intricate passing with Alan Morton. Jamie Marshall scored a couple, and Bob McPhail got the other in a 4-1 victory. English was outstanding, with his clever positioning a feature of the game.

That same week, Sam's brother Richard had been invited over to Northern Ireland to train with Coleraine. Richard, a Cambuslang Rangers player at the time, reported that the trial had gone very well and that he had been offered a deal to sign with the Bannsiders, but he turned it down and headed back to Scotland. He was very close to Sam and wanted to be there to help his young brother through a most traumatic period.

Next up for Rangers was a short hop across the city to face Partick Thistle, where a crowd of 30,000 packed Firhill and looked on as English picked up from where he had left off against the Hi-Hi. His movement was outstanding, and he would find openings where it seemed none existed. With just three minutes on the clock, Sam set up Bob McPhail for the opener, and midway through the first half his powerful shot deflected off Calderwood and flew past the helpless Jackson in the Jags' goal. English then engineered an opening and fired for goal; Jackson saved, but the effort elicited hearty appreciation from all present.

English and McPhail teamed up to great effect, with the former showing great perseverance and pluck. He was certainly well endowed with both qualities, and kept the Jags' defence on tenterhooks throughout, and they too did well to keep him out on many occasions.

The third and final goal involved a smart passing movement between English, Marshall and Nicholson, before Fleming scored. Another two points in the bag.

Rangers were back in action a couple of days later against Aberdeen at Ibrox and once again young English was the chief architect of the visitors' downfall. He failed to score, but led the line like a seasoned pro and in a rip-roaring first half, Rangers scored four times. They were far too strong and Aberdeen simply couldn't cope with English. He was a disturbing factor for the Dons' defence, as they never knew where he would pop up next.

English impressed the watching media even more than in some of the games in which he had scored. His feinting and anticipation were extremely clever, but this drew unwanted attention, and he was injured following a quite awful first-half challenge. One of his greatest qualities, though, was the ability to absorb physical attention and get on with the game without reacting. It was the same when he was with Yoker.

The win over Aberdeen was Rangers' ninth in 11 matches, and afterwards, due to the international break, the players had 11 days off until facing Hearts at Tynecastle. That was the cue to get the golf clubs out and head down the coast to Turnberry. Fourteen happy players left on the Friday, with a couple of others – including school teacher George Brown – joining up on the Saturday night after the international match.

It was Sam's first trip to Turnberry with the players (an Ibrox tradition in those days), and – like his Ibrox colleagues – the former Yoker centre-forward was properly equipped with the necessary 'bag o' clubs'. The next few days would be spent among colleagues and friends, playing golf and breathing in the beautiful coastal air.

Following the Glasgow Cup semi-final draw with Celtic, at the end of September, just 8,000 turned up for Rangers' next game, a 6-1 rout of Cowdenbeath at Ibrox. English was back among the scorers, and his brace included a fine glancing header before the break. There were also doubles for skipper Davie Meiklejohn and Jamie Marshall.

The Glasgow Cup semi-final replay, at Ibrox, was next up and it was a thrilling encounter. With just 30 seconds remaining, Rangers led 2-1 and looked bound for the final – but Celtic grabbed a dramatic equaliser. Thankfully it was a clean and competitive contest, and the 40,000 crowd behaved impeccably. English had two good chances in the first half but goalkeeper John Falconer was his equal. With half an hour played, English raced on to a through ball from Brown and stuck it past Falconer. It was a beautiful finish, but referee Hutton ruled it offside, although many doubted the accuracy of his call. Throughout the game, English appeared isolated up front, but he never once gave up and showed some wonderful touches.

The teams were back in action the following day for the second replay but English was ruled out with a knock. His replacement was the ever-dependable Jimmy Smith, who scored the only goal of the game to send Rangers into the final.

When the final against Queen's Park was played Sam was fit and ready to go, but Smith was given the nod at centre-forward. However, Struth still found a spot for English, and he started the game at outside-right. Sam was on top of his game and scored in a convincing 3-0 win. Meiklejohn had a hand in Sam's goal, which he took with all the composure of a veteran. 'Blondie' was the sole creator of the third, which was credited as an own goal, and although he looked ill at ease out on the wing at times, he was still able to create a number of opportunities for his team-mates. It was a stroll in the park for Rangers in front of 50,000, and the day after the game the players donated their bonus payments – amounting to almost £4 – to the John Thomson Memorial Fund.

Queen's exacted revenge seven days later when they turned up at Ibrox, executing the perfect smash-and-grab tactics to leave with both points. English again started on the right wing, but the crowd were quick to show their displeasure, and there was ironic cheering when Struth ordered him to swap places with Smith. However, the visiting defence stood firm and held out for the win. The result would have devastating consequences for Rangers' title hopes.

A week further on, Rangers were again in trouble early on when they fell behind to Hamilton Accies at Douglas Park. But just five minutes before the break, English snapped up a ball headed out by Bulloch and like a flash drove it into the corner of the net. Rangers went on to win the match.

When Dundee United arrived at Ibrox for a league fixture at the end of October, Rangers were without five of their top players. McAulay, Meiklejohn, Brown, McPhail and Morton were on international duty for Scotland against Wales in Cardiff, but rather than ask for a postponement, Struth forged ahead with the fixture. The afternoon proved a double success, with Rangers strolling to a 5-0 win and Scotland emerging victorious in Wales.

However, it was a foggy day at Ibrox, and some supporters complained of seeing little of the action. On the field, though, English had a big say in the victory, and not only did he record a hat-trick, but he led the line with commendable confidence, dash and cunning. McIntosh was beaten after 17 minutes when English, taking the ball on the drop as it came over from Archibald's free-kick, smashed it behind the helpless goalkeeper. After the break, English latched on to a great through ball and as McIntosh came out to intercept him, he cunningly bent it round the keeper. His next, eight minutes from the end, showed a real touch of class. Nicholson's overhead kick was palmed out and English was on to it in a flash, guiding the ball into the top corner of the net.

A match report stated, 'English took his three goals splendidly, but his worth didn't stop there. What I liked most about him was the way he flicked the ball right or left, and ran on to take the return.'

Just moments after the match finished, a new Ranger was introduced to his team-mates by Struth. George Coubrough, a native of Cathcart, in Glasgow, had been playing his football in America. He left the good ship *Transylvania* at Greenock, and was picked up and driven to Ibrox by a club official. He had been achieving great things in the States, but saw the move to Ibrox as a major step up in his career. A fellow passenger aboard the *Transylvania* told Coubrough, 'You are a jolly lucky chap; you are coming home to join the greatest football organisation in the world, and your future is assured. Be guided by Mr Struth, and all will be well.' Coubrough had been likened to Alan Morton in style and stature.

On the evening of Monday, 23 November the club held their annual dance at Glasgow's Grosvenor Hotel, and a good time was had by all. It was a black tie affair and most of the players and their wives were in attendance. Sam was seen to hold the attention of the Rangers party for several moments while he told one of his well-known funny stories.

When Rangers travelled through to the capital a few days later – to take on Leith Athletic at Marine Gardens – Sam proved his worth to the club by almost single-handedly destroying the home side.

In the first half, the Edinburgh minnows had battled gamely and restricted Rangers to a single-goal advantage, but if the home fans thought their favourites might just pull off a shock result in the second, they were sadly mistaken.

Enter English. With five second-half minutes gone, Rangers were three up and the game was as good as over. McAulay sent a hefty clearance upfield and English beat the Leith backs to it before turning the ball into the net well out of Todd's reach. A minute or two later he did it again, this time from a cross by McPhail. With the goal he had scored in the first half, it completed a fine hat-trick for the Ibrox centre.

It also knocked the stuffing out of Leith. Rangers, with the points securely tucked away, treated supporters to an exhibition of classy football, making the Athletic look third rate, and the final score of 5-2 looking more favourable to the hosts than the Light Blues.

Following his hat-trick, and all-round top performance, there were many calls from the press to the Irish FA selectors. 'Don't forget Sam English when you're naming your side to face Wales in the home internationals. He possesses the necessary birth qualification,' wrote one reporter.

It was certainly a good weekend for Sam, who was a contributor to Glasgow's Art Union fund. He was thrilled when his numbers came up at their annual draw at the beginning of December and he was rewarded with a £30 painting. When his name was announced, it evoked a loud cheer from those in attendance. The Art Union existed primarily to encourage and foster the love of art, but at the same time helped many young artists in their hour of need.

When Falkirk took on Rangers at Ibrox a couple of weeks before Christmas, English painted his own pretty picture, and the Light Blues had another two important points in the bag. Early on, Sam spotted a gap in the Bairns' defence and punished it mercilessly. On three other occasions in the first half, Hamill thwarted English when he was about to pull the trigger, or the Irishman could easily have had four goals before the break.

As it was, Rangers finished with four, three of them from English, and after the game, one reporter had this to say: 'The Ibrox centre was cool and sprightly, and was willing and able to dash ahead alone, yet he did not let the attack get out of gear by his individualism. His three goals stamped him as a menacing, alert leader.'

The final goal was the pick of the bunch. English ran half the length of the field and hoodwinked the entire Falkirk defence before adding the finishing touches with style.

A couple of days after yet another hat-trick, Sam was invited to take part in a star-studded benefit match for the legendary Celtic forward Patsy Gallacher. The match was due to take place at the start of 1932, and as well as Sam, Davie Meiklejohn and Alan Morton had also been invited. Gallacher, born in Ireland, lived just along the road from Sam in Clydebank.

When Rangers slipped up at Dens Park, losing 4-2 to a Scot Symon-inspired Dundee, Motherwell increased their lead at the top of the table to five points, albeit with a game more played. When the clubs met at Ibrox on Boxing Day, more than 50,000 were present. It was a must-win game for Rangers, and that was evident by the way they started the match. At the end of the 90 minutes, Rangers had edged Motherwell 1-0, but the message they sent out was far more powerful. By bossing virtually the entire match they had warned the Fir Park men they wouldn't be giving up their title without a fight.

One of the major contributors to the success was Jimmy Simpson. The big defender was outstanding and held the prolific Motherwell striker Willie MacFadyen in the palm of his hand, thus preventing the forward from claiming his 40th goal of the season.

The other major factor in the success was rookie striker Sam English. One newspaper reporter suggested that 'Sammy always settles' would be a good wee slogan for the Rangers. 'Against Motherwell,' he added, 'Sammy, who never wasted a ball, was the one finisher afield, although often fighting a lone battle.'

Up to Boxing Day, English had scored 28 goals, and the report continued, 'Until McPhail and Marshall, with their close play, remember that they have a centre-forward, only then will the Rangers attack function as they ought to.'

Another stern test awaited Struth's men on New Year's Day. The cross-city trip to Celtic Park would prove one of their toughest matches of the season, although goals by Archibald and Marshall would see them come away with the two points.

It was a cracking game, with both teams serving up a festival of fast, accurate, passing moves which the 55,000 crowd lapped up. The winning goal was sublime, and a product of the quick-thinking English, who received the ball and feinted to go straight through the middle on his own, but as Cook and McGonagle were drawn towards him, he tapped it to Marshall, who ran in and smashed it into the net. James 'Joe' Kennaway had no chance.

An after-match report said, 'English was always on his toes. I saw more of him than most people when he was an Intermediate:

he is better now than ever. The skidding ball did not trouble him at all. He was an artist. He got the chance he wanted in the first half when McPhail and Marshall were playing close up with him. When these two fell back afterwards, the effect was seen at once.'

After just half a season in the Seniors, English had taken to the higher level like a fish to water. He was turning in consistent performances week on week and putting many an established star to shame. Three days after winning at Parkhead, Rangers hosted Partick Thistle, and while English didn't get among the scorers, he was credited with 'running the show'. When Rangers were awarded a penalty kick, the crowd screamed for Sam to take it, but he smiled and handed the ball to Marshall, who despatched the kick with his usual aplomb.

Sam was carving out a reputation as a first-class player, but elevated that status in January 1932 when he scored hat-tricks in three successive games. It was a tremendous feat, irrespective of the opposition. Brechin City were first to fall in an early round of the Scottish Cup, and after missing a couple of decent chances in the first half, he scored three times after the break. Rangers scored four in either half and the Angus men got a couple of late consolations.

The following Saturday, Ayr United arrived at Ibrox on league business – and were promptly blown away. English's first two goals were the work of the 'always there forward'. He twice showed a razor sharp instinct in the box to pounce on defensive errors. However, his third goal would have impressed even the world's most famous contortionist. Supporters leaving Ibrox after the 6-1 win were still trying to work out just how Sam managed to get his body into such a position to enable him to score despite being surrounded by six Ayr United defenders. It was a feat of acrobatic genius that had supporters in the Main Stand on their feet applauding.

Rangers were back in Scottish Cup action on the last Saturday of the month with a trip to Stark's Park, Kirkcaldy. Raith Rovers had been playing well but were no match for rampant Rangers, and the 5-0 scoreline flattered the home side a little.

More than 18,000 – the biggest crowd at Stark's for many years – saw English score a beautiful second goal – with his eyes closed. The Irishman snapped at an Archibald cross and with the sun shining strongly in his eyes, it was a wonder he managed to stick the ball in the top corner.

Five minutes into the second half, English scored the most spectacular goal of the day. Picking up a forward pass from Fleming, he sidestepped Bell and went on to whack the ball past Wallace, who showed hesitancy, but in reality had little chance of stopping this thunderbolt. Shortly after, Sam completed his hat-trick by flashing into the net a beautiful cross from Marshall, who'd travelled fully 50 yards with the ball before leaving it for the centre to apply the finishing touch. English, besides leading the line with skill, showed masterly opportunism.

And on the Rangers bandwagon rolled into February, although supporters may have been a tad disappointed to see English manage just a single goal in a 4-2 win over Hearts at Ibrox. Mind you, a polished performance acted as the perfect curtain-raiser for the following week's big Scottish Cup tie between the same teams at Tynecastle. That said, Hearts weren't in Glasgow merely to make up the numbers, and it wasn't until English showed a dashing piece of individualism that Rangers could make the points safe.

Hearts relied far too much on their offside trap working to full effect, because with a speed merchant like English in opposition, there would be little chance of recovery if their high line failed. This led to a couple of peppery incidents. English, with his usual quickness, was dashing through with a pass down the middle when he was called up for offside. He looked 'on' by at least a yard. The referee's decision went down badly with the home crowd, but two minutes later, it was the visiting fans' turn to be furious. This time English seemed offside, but was allowed to carry on. He looked round to see if play had been stopped, then raced ahead and scored with a well-judged shot, despite Harkness leaving his line to narrow the angle. The two linesmen supported the referee's decision.

There was more controversial stuff to come, like when English was racing clear of the Hearts offside trap, and looking every inch a scorer, when Johnston clipped his heels from behind. The punishment? A free kick to Rangers, which was wholly inadequate. But the Ibrox side secured the points when English produced his master stroke. He went out to the right to take a pass from Marshall, again beat Johnston, cut in to give Fleming the pass and he had only to flick the ball into the net.

Hearts' back line did well to curtail English's exploits, but they never fully came to terms with the danger of offside tactics against such a quick mover. The Rangers centre watched for the pass, and travelled so fast that he was yards ahead of the backs by the time the ball had reached him and still onside. He was an absolute master of springing the offside trap and, it was said, often left his own shadow trailing in his wake. Yes, he was that quick!

Seven days later the teams met in Edinburgh, and this time a place in the last eight of the Scottish Cups was up for grabs. There was just short of 54,000 in the ground when the teams kicked off, a record for Tynecastle and, in fact, any Scottish game outside of Glasgow. The 7/6d seats had sold like hot cakes and virtually every inch of terracing was claimed.

Rangers' fans filled 16 special trains and a contingent of about 200 Gers supporters made the journey from Glasgow to Edinburgh on foot, despite being told that the capacity of the ground was limited and not everyone would get in. These calls were not entirely unjustified as an hour before kick-off, the stand was full. Half an hour later the terracing was crowded to such an extent that many fans called for medical assistance due to crushing.

And just before the teams emerged, when it looked as if even a sardine packer would have struggled to get many more in, the gates at those parts of the ground where the congestion was greatest were closed; a decision taken for safety reasons.

When the game started, the calls on the ambulance men ceased for a time, but during a tense moment of play one of the crush barriers at the Gorgie Road (Rangers) end gave way, and there was an ugly sway of a dense mass of humanity. Around 30 people required attention and two Rangers fans were taken to Edinburgh Royal Infirmary.

As the game began in earnest, an interesting individual battle soon developed, that of John Johnston and English. The Hearts centre-half, an Ayrshire school teacher in his day job, against one of the fastest-developing footballers in Great Britain – but would the pupil tame the master?

There weren't very many minutes on the clock when English went chasing a long through ball by Marshall and he was chopped down, not by Johnston but his team-mate Bob King. The referee, Willie Bell, had no option but to award the free kick, and it brought about the goal which, as it turned out, would be the only one of the game.

Archibald took the kick and centred for Fleming, who turned the ball across the face of the goal. It caught out Hearts keeper Harkness and Marshall was on hand to tap it into the net.

After the goal, it was an evenly balanced, thrilling match, with Hearts giving as good as they got, but their forward excursions, of which there were many, were always repelled by a resolute Rangers side hell-bent on defending what they had rather than increasing their advantage. Meiklejohn and Brown were too busy lending a hand to the rearguard to influence the front line. For the most part each contented himself by sending through an odd one to speedy Sam, who was more or less up front on his own. Still, English's rare forays took the pressure off Rangers' overworked defence for vital minutes at a time.

Bob King didn't have a good day. Near the end he was ordered off. English and the Hearts back tangled once again and the referee sent him to the pavilion. Johnston, on the other hand, fared a little better. He never gave in against English, who was after every ball like a flash. Johnston's job was to mark easily the most dangerous, fastest and most dashing forward afield, and to a certain extent he succeeded.

It was back to league business the following week as Rangers entertained Glasgow rivals Third Lanark. The league title was still a target, and Sam's double in a 6-1 victory kept the dream alive. A tap-in was followed by a bullet header and Sam had kept his impressive scoring run intact.

And the following Saturday, the dynamic young striker added another four to his growing tally when Rangers visited Hampden to play an in-form Queen's Park. The experts predicted a close game, and it would've been had all 11 Rangers players not at once become a destructive engine with all its components working at high pressure and in perfect rhythm. Even the icy wind, which blew from goal to goal, failed to cut through the Queen's defence as lethally as the Rangers attack. It was 1-1 at half-time, and by the time the final whistle had sounded, even the home fans applauded Rangers off the park. Perhaps the hosts were fortunate the score remained at six. But good fortune was with them. Alan Morton added a 'seventh' – the best of the match – but it was called offside, which was debatable at best.

McPhail scored the first goal, but the second half belonged to English. He raced clear of the home defence soon after the restart to smash home the first of his four. After that, he was unstoppable, and could have had a fifth but unselfishly passed to Marshall with the goal gaping.

The following morning, English was the subject of many column inches, with one newspaper saying, 'English, I should say, never played a better game. He worked the ball at high pressure, drew Gillespie this way and that, threw Kerr and Walker into two minds, and generally played as perhaps no centre has played since R.S. McColl on the same expanse of grass.'

With his four goals at Hampden, Sam took his haul for the season to 38, and he was far from finished.

The big games were coming thick and fast, and after polishing off Hearts in front of 54,000 at Tynecastle, league champions Motherwell were up next – in the Scottish Cup quarter-finals – at Ibrox. Everyone wanted to see this game, and when the teams took to the field, there were around 90,000 inside the ground.

It was a cracking encounter, befitting of the top two in the Scottish game, and while English failed to get his name on the scoresheet, Rangers won 2-0 and were worthy of their place in the last four. Sam was on top form and looked to have given Rangers an early lead but his nemesis, McClory, stopped the drive low to his right.

Alan Morton was also in stunning form, but far too often hung on to the ball when others were in a better position, like the time McPhail and English were waiting with an open goal at their mercy, but the winger overplayed.

English, sharp as a needle and ever up for the fight, was a constant source of trouble to the Motherwell defence, and was the catalyst for the win. He worked his socks off and after the game said, 'So long as a ball is in play, it is always worth going for.'

Two days later, the Rangers players were in action again – but this time on the golf course at Troon. And the relaxed atmosphere on the Lochgreen course suggested excursions to the Ayrshire coast were extremely beneficial for the players. The weather was glorious and three- and four-ball partnerships were the order of the day, while some of the players who didn't really have an interest in playing contented themselves by walking round the links with their mates, enjoying the fine weather and the occasional wisecrack. Trainer Kerr engaged in a tussle with Bob McAulay, and discovered that the Wishaw man had a fine sense of direction with the wee ball. Considering he had just taken up the game, Sam English was soon showing he was equally at home playing with a large or smaller ball.

Dundee United were next up, and Bill Struth reckoned the trip to Tannadice could be a potential banana skin. And after watching an exciting first 45 minutes, nothing in his mind had changed. Sure, his Rangers side had dominated, but the United goalkeeper, Chic McIntosh, had pulled off three world-class saves. Arguably his finest arrived after half an hour when English outmanoeuvred three defenders and ran in to shoot at point-blank range from a couple of yards, but McIntosh stood tall and as if by a miracle, caught the ball and cleared brilliantly.

English did score just before the break following a clever lob from Meiklejohn, but not even McIntosh's heroics could prevent Rangers running out 5-0 winners as they piled on four goals in eight astonishing second-half minutes. During this spell they could easily have had four more. Few defences could have coped with a period of such concentrated aggression. English started the rout eight minutes into the second half, and then looked on as McIntosh somehow saved his goal-bound shot from six yards. Two from Fleming and an Archibald goal completed the scoring. On this occasion, the main architect of United's downfall was McPhail, whose passing was on the money and ruthlessly exploited even the smallest of gaps in the home defence.

When the draw for the Scottish Cup semi-finals was made, Rangers came out of the hat with Hamilton, while Kilmarnock drew Airdrie. It was a tough draw for the Light Blues, but it was put on the back burner as Rangers prepared to host Killie in a league match. The national trophy was all the mid-table Rugby Park side had left to play for, while Rangers were still realistically chasing the title. However, when Rangers and Killie went toe-to-toe at Ibrox one could've been forgiven for thinking the Ayrshiremen were still involved in the championship race, as they battled, scrapped and kicked their way through a tough 90 minutes. In fact, at one point the referee stopped the game to lecture Joe Nibloe for one too many kicks on English.

Twice Sam had the ball in the net in the first half, and twice the goal was ruled out. And then when he was clean through on goal, he took a blow to the side from Nibloe, and required medical attention. Moments later, Meiklejohn was crudely halted when carving a path through the Killie defence, and from the free kick, Rangers opened the scoring. Dougie Gray took the free kick and Bob McPhail chested the ball down before blasting it into the net. It was no more than Rangers deserved.

Moments after the goal, play was halted for the referee to speak to Nibloe.

The best goal of the afternoon came on the hour mark. Meiklejohn, out on the left, sent the ball over to McPhail, who fed Morton. The talented winger skipped past Leslie and centred for English, close in, who beat Bell with the cutest of finishes.

Rangers played some fine football after this, but Kilmarnock never gave in, although the game was over three minutes from the end. English was racing through when Nibloe again brought him down, and Marshall scored directly from the free kick.

The physical treatment meted out to English was nothing short of disgraceful, and he received little protection from the referee. Still, he got a goal, and realistically was unlucky not to have grabbed what would have been his ninth hat-trick of the season.

The following weekend, Rangers faced Hamilton Accies in the Scottish Cup semi-final at Parkhead – and Sam English faced his old Yoker buddy Dave Hill. It wouldn't be a pleasurable afternoon for Hill, that's for sure, as English was one of the form players in the country. And with the likes of Meiklejohn, Brown, Marshall and McPhail supplying the ammo, Accies were in for a torrid afternoon.

As it transpired, Rangers cruised into the final. After the game, someone remarked that if Hamilton had scored their two goals earlier in the contest it would have made a big difference. The truth is, that if Rangers hadn't had their five-goal lead, Accies wouldn't have scored.

Rangers were outstanding; a veritable machine, although for the first 20 minutes there was little between the teams, as far as industry was concerned. As usual, though, English was hopping around, and he caught the ball coming off the crossbar and let fly. Wright saved it, but the goalkeeper appeared to be well behind the line at the time. Rangers claimed a goal, but they were to be disappointed.

They wouldn't be denied for long, though, and when Meiklejohn lobbed a free kick into the goal area from 30 yards out, Marshall headed home. Two minutes later English followed suit by getting his head to a cross and doubling Rangers' advantage. It was a long way back for Accies.

As half-time approached, English got Rangers' third, although the credit went to Brown as he waltzed through the Accies defence before shooting for goal. The upright saved Hamilton but eagle-eyed English was on hand to fire home the rebound. Archibald and Marshall completed the scoring.

Scotland were due to meet England at Wembley a fortnight later and there was talk of calling Sam up for the international team. There was a problem, though, as English, despite living in Scotland since he was a little over 18 months old, had no Scottish heritage, and despite spending very little time in his native Ireland, they were the only country he could play for. One journalist lamented the fact that Scotland would go to Wembley without Sam. He added, 'If Sam English were not Irish, the thing to do would be to play seven Rangers up front for Scotland against England. Saturday's attack backed by Meiklejohn and Brown. But sadly Sam isn't eligible.'

Rangers received a massive blow to their title hopes when they lost to Third Lanark at Cathkin Park by the odd goal in seven just 48 hours after defeating Accies in the cup. Not since 1904 had a non-Old Firm side won the league – and that was the Hi-Hi. Now though, it looked increasingly likely.

The Ibrox club had started brightly, with English having a penalty claim turned down after being fouled inside the box, but it was the visitors who scored twice against the run of play to lead 2-0. Moments after their second goal, Morton scampered down the wing and pushed it inward, and English, with the prettiest judgement, sent it into the corner of the net.

After the interval, both English and McPhail, from just a few yards out, each failed to convert. These were costly misses, for a few minutes later Rangers were 3-1 down, although Marshall, and then English, scored to draw level. But just when they were getting on top and looking likely to win the game, Bob McPhail picked up an injury and was forced off. Thirds scored late on to clinch the points.

Rangers took their frustration out on Cowdenbeath at Central Park the following weekend by firing home seven goals, the sixth of which was scored by English – his 44th league goal in just 32 games. It was a phenomenal record and marked him down as one of Rangers' great forwards.

And so to the Scottish Cup Final at Hampden Park, in which Kilmarnock would provide the opposition. One man was guaranteed a start, and that was lightning-quick Sam English, who provided Rangers with their greatest goal threat since the days of Robert Cumming Hamilton. And tasked with 'looking after' Sam was Tom Smith, a powerful young centre-back with a great future ahead of him.

The crowd was 111,982 and it looked like there was barely a space to be found anywhere in the ground. In the opening moments Archibald flashed the ball across goal and English just failed to make contact. Morton then centred but Bell got there a fraction of a second quicker than the Irishman.

It was all Rangers, and when English tricked Nibloe he looked certain to score but Smith tackled strongly. Bell then made two great saves from English, before McPhail scored from an English pass, but the goal was ruled offside.

Rangers finally took the lead when English raced through on goal. Bell came out and saved at his feet but McPhail was on hand to knock it home. Bud Maxwell scored for Killie to take the tie to a replay.

Part of the reason for Rangers' failure to win the cup first time round was that both Jamie Marshall and George Brown were a little off colour, and English found that killer through ball in short supply. Still, English, sharp as a needle, was always on his toes waiting for an opportunity to arise, but found in Tom Smith a young man who gave him little rope.

All roads led to Hampden for the Wednesday night replay. A procession of special trains from Glasgow Central to Mount Florida were scheduled to carry thousands of fans to the national stadium but a derailment just outside Central threw travel plans for many into chaos. Staff worked tirelessly to fix the problem, but just when the rush was at its height bookings had to be suspended for 20 minutes. The result was that trams and buses were called upon to deal with an unusually heavy volume of traffic, and taxi drivers found people almost fighting for the use of their cars.

There was a bad jam with the two lines of traffic converging at Eglinton Toll, and a good number of men, fearing they would be late for kick-off, left the trams and buses and walked the rest of the way. Fortunately, the railway services were restored almost to normal, and the great bulk of the crowd, which was over 104,000, got to the stadium on time.

Many latecomers found a diversion in the car park. Policemen were seen running in and out of the cars trying to catch a boy who had broken a windscreen with a stone. After an alarming chase, the officers caught hold of the boy and he was tossed into the back of a police wagon.

If there was one difference between both ties, it was that Rangers were fully on song in the replay. They won with a bit to spare, and in doing so had to again put up with some brutish tactics by their opponents.

The real turning point came in the second half when Rangers, within a couple of minutes, scored their second and third goals. There was no way back for Killie after that.

Rangers went ahead in the 11th minute when, in an attempt to clear an overhead kick by Sam English, Bell put the ball out to his right. Fleming was on to it in a flash and smashed it into the net. Advantage Rangers. Shortly after this, English was hurt in a collision with an opponent and was led from the field with blood streaming from his nose, but soon returned to the action.

Rangers were making the running when the interval arrived, and they opened the second half in the same breezy style. But a halt had to be called when English and Leslie collided, and the

Ibrox centre had once again to go to the touchline for treatment. McPhail was then injured, but he too returned.

English was always in the thick of the action and when he controlled a centre by Archibald, he looked odds on to score but a last-gasp challenge by Leslie saved the day. Rangers were firmly on top and the pressure finally told on the Killie defence after 69 minutes when the second goal arrived. Leslie conceded a corner to Fleming, and when the ball was cleared it travelled to Archibald, who centred beautifully. English, clearly with purpose, avoided the ball, as he was covered by Smith. It was a wise move, for McPhail met it with his right foot and shot into the left-hand corner of the net.

Two minutes later, it was three and victory was sealed. Marshall shaped to take a free kick, but left it for Meiklejohn, and approaching as if going for a shot, placed it instead over the heads of the Killie defenders. Bell came out, but before he could reach the ball, English got to it with his head, and cleverly steered it into the net over the outstretched goalkeeper. English and Smith had enjoyed a ding-dong battle but Sam had his goal.

In the Queen's Park boardroom after the match, the cup was handed over to the Rangers chairman, ex-Bailie Buchanan, by Robert Campbell, the SFA chairman. It was Rangers' seventh Scottish Cup victory.

After the game, Willie Maley, the Celtic secretary-manager, popped into the Rangers dressing room and heartily congratulated the Ibrox players, shaking hands and speaking to each player individually.

But there was no time for proper celebrations as Rangers were soon back in league action – and there appeared to be a cup hangover lingering over the players. They were held to a 1-1 draw by Clyde at Shawfield, before losing 3-0 at Broomfield to Airdrie. A narrow victory over Hamilton and a 4-2 win at Kilmarnock ended what turned out to be an inglorious campaign. As an aside,

English was missing for the victory at Rugby Park, but once again the Ayrshire side seemed to have a problem with Rangers. The match report stated, 'Once or twice fists were raised, heads were used when the ball was not the object. The referee, Peter Craigmyle had by no means an enviable job. Tempers cooled by the interval, and the second half was tame by comparison.'

There was still the end-of-season Glasgow Charity Cup to play for and Rangers set up a final date with Third Lanark after beating Queen's Park 3-1 at Ibrox in front of 14,000. English created a couple of goals for Marshall, and the striker completed his hat-trick from the penalty spot.

The day before the final at Hampden Park, Rangers supporters were boosted by the news that English, and captain, Davie Meiklejohn, had agreed to re-sign for another season.

Mind you, the final was a dreadfully one-sided affair. Rangers won 6-1, but one reporter suggested a more realistic score might have been 26-1. Rangers took the lead after four minutes, and what a beautiful goal it was. English broke away on the right, back-heeled the ball to Archibald, who lost no time in crossing for McPhail, who smacked it with terrific power past the helpless Redford.

Rangers scored a second on 15 minutes. Archibald sent over a high ball which the ever-ready English headed for goal, and Redford allowed the leather to squirm out of his hands and over the line. The tie was over when English headed home his second of the game. McPhail ended up with a hat-trick although, if truth be told, most of the Rangers side had given up the ghost with almost half an hour to play. Well, everyone apart from English. It's said he was as 'keen as mustard' right up to the end.

Rangers might have lost the league to Motherwell, but they won the treble of Scottish Cup, Glasgow Cup and Glasgow Charity Cup, which was a decent season's work.

On the Monday night after the Charity Cup tie, Sam was back in action – although this time with a flag in his hand. Rangers goalkeeper Tom Hamilton agreed to referee a charity match at Yoker's Holm Park, and Sam offered to run the line. Proceeds were earmarked for Donald McNicol, who had met with an accident while playing for Victoria against Beardmore's shipyard team.

It was the end of a rather satisfactory debut season in Rangers colours for English, although in any other campaign, 44 league goals would surely have brought a championship medal. Motherwell, though, just happened to be a bit special that season.

It had seemed an eternity since early September, but the accident involving John Thomson was never far from his mind. In fact, it would haunt him not only for the remainder of his football career, but the rest of his life.

Ten

ON THE eve of the 1932/33 season, the Great Depression had taken hold in Scotland and footballers – especially those at the bigger clubs – were reminded of just how fortunate they were as the numbers visiting unemployment exchanges across the country reached record levels. As work halted on RMS *Queen Mary* at the John Brown shipyard, due to poor economic conditions, it affected members of Sam's family and many of his friends. It was only when Cunard, the liner's owners, applied to the government for a loan to be able to complete the vessel, that some workers were re-hired. On his way into Ibrox each day, Sam would pass the Clydebank Labour Exchange and see the queues snaking out on to the main road and round the block. It was a sorry sight.

At the start of July 1932, just as his team-mates had reported back for pre-season training, Sam travelled up to Fife for the unveiling of a memorial to John Thomson at Cardenden Cemetery. He had been invited by the late goalkeeper's family and was accompanied by his wife, Sarah, and Bill Struth.

The poignant event attracted a crowd of around 8,000 to the small village, and while it was a showery day, the rain stayed off during the memorial service. As the congregation both inside and outside the cemetery listened intently to a variety of eulogiums, many a moist eye was seen as the tragic death of the brilliant Celt was recalled.

Dr Angus Walker, from Leith, explained that when he was in residence in Cardenden, he was the Thomson family physician and, of course, he was well acquainted with young John as a boy. He told of an incident which showed that the spirit which young John later showed on the football field was already there in his early days. One day, Dr Walker was attending Mrs Thomson, and caused his patient to express symptoms of pain. This was too much for a nine-year-old John, who shouted out: 'Don't hurt ma mither,' and immediately took up a fighting stance. On the beautiful South Country granite memorial were inscribed the words, 'They never die who live in the hearts of those they leave behind.'

After the service, Sam and his wife spoke with members of the Thomson family before motoring down the road to Glasgow in Struth's car.

The following day he was present at training, and had just signed his new contract (in those days players signed only on a season-by-season basis) and was thrilled to learn he had been chosen as part of the Rangers five-a-side team for Clyde's annual gala day. The other members were Davie Meiklejohn, Tully Craig, James Kennedy and Jimmy Smith. They were given a bye in the first round and drawn against either Queen's Park or Celtic in the semi-finals.

More than 10,000 were present as Rangers beat Celtic 2-1 in their last-four clash, with Smith and English on target. In the final, against Partick Thistle, two goals from Sam were enough to give Rangers the trophy after extra time. The Rangers players were rewarded with handsome clocks, while the defeated Partick players, who had led 1-0, picked up wrist watches.

The following Saturday was Rangers Sports Day, the blue ribbon of pre-season, and Sam was again part of the Gers' fives team – and once again he was the star turn. The only change in personnel saw George Brown in for Kennedy. In the first round, a Jimmy Smith goal saw off Partick Thistle, and in the semi-final, a goalless tie against St Mirren was decided on 'points', awarded for getting the ball through a bigger set of goals, which were positioned behind the small goals. In the final, against Third Lanark, Rangers won 2-0, and Sam showed his trademark alertness by snatching both goals.

But while one English sibling was carrying off all before him, another wasn't having it so good. Richard had again travelled back to his native Ireland for a trial with Coleraine, who played a few miles north of his birthplace. Sadly, Sam's older brother – on a two-game try-out – was injured in the first match against Cliftonville and was unable to take his place in the side for the match against Ballymena. Richard, now with Yoker Athletic, looked likely to be out for at least a month.

Prior to the beginning of the league campaign, Sam was made to play second fiddle to a mate of his, Tim Williamson, the former Third Lanark and Stoke City centre-half. The pair were keen golfers and enjoyed a round on the Clydebank municipal course. While Sam showed up well during the game, Tim made the course look like a putting green. Out in 33, he came home in one stroke more, with his round of 67 the best ever recorded on the course. For once, Sam was happy for someone else to take centre stage and at the end of the round he gave his friend a thoroughly deserved handshake.

For Rangers, though, the league campaign started with a whimper rather than a bang when they travelled to Paisley on the opening day and lost 2-0 to St Mirren. It was a performance most unbecoming of the Light Blues, and 23,000 watched Sam stand accused of 'foozling' a great opportunity. The match report stated, 'In the first half, an Alan Morton cross should have produced the equaliser but English "foozled" his kick.' How dare he?

But there was no foozling of any sort in Rangers' next game, at home to Ayr United, when English bagged a couple of goals in a comfortable win. Mind you, it was a game in which others foozled. Bad shooting was the order of the day and the chief sinners were Jimmy Smith and Alan Morton and, as stated in one newspaper, Bob McPhail, who was a 'minor delinquent'. English's first goal was something of a trademark strike.

He had become known for shooting early, and this usually caught goalkeepers and defenders off guard. One of the centre-forward's great qualities was his alertness and ability to think on his feet. It often allowed him to steal a couple of yards on a dithering defender. Another of his qualities was his deftness of touch, which had improved significantly since his move to Rangers, and he displayed it fully when grabbing his second against the Honest Men. A George Brown through ball split the defence and Sam was on to it in a flash, took a touch and duly lofted it over goalkeeper Hepburn's head and into the net.

It now seemed that Rangers had a forward line who played for one another, with Jamie Marshall, Bob McPhail, Jimmy Smith, Alan Morton and Sam combining so well together that the neutral onlooker could have been forgiven for thinking that the 'Famous Five' had been playing together for many years.

One look at the goals record of English in 1931/32 might have led to an incorrect assumption that he was a selfish player, but had detailed records been kept by statisticians in the 1930s, Sam's would have shown a similar number of assists. He was a team player who could score regularly, and as such was worth his weight in gold.

That said, manager Struth proved he had options at the beginning of September 1932, when East Stirling visited Ibrox and English was left out. Smith scored a hat-trick against his old team and Sandy Archibald and Jimmy Fleming deputised for Sam and Alan Morton.

But Sam was back in his usual position for the next game, a trip to Parkhead to face Celtic. A crowd of 60,000 – the majority roaring on the home side – contributed to the dressing-room butterflies and it was a nervy opening five or ten minutes for both sides. But once the teams had settled into the game they produced a hard-fought match and, if not exactly blessed with pretty football, it was always interesting. It was a game of two halves with Celtic on top in the first 45, and Rangers dominating the second.

One of the main attractions was the battle between Rangers' central defender Jimmy Simpson and Celtic's old master, Jimmy McGrory. The pair scrapped for every loose ball and, even though McGrory fired Celtic into an early lead, the Ranger turned in a glorious display – although Simpson was never so glad to see his goalkeeper, Tommy Hamilton, pull off a world-class save from a McGrory piledriver moments after the Celt had found the net.

Rangers were fortunate to trail by just one at the break, and the home fans sensed a goals avalanche in the second period. What they got, though, was the reverse. Rangers were far from their passive first-half selves and not only had English found his shooting boots, but he was the outstanding man afield. He linked the midfield and forwards to near perfection, and the Celts had no answer to his prompting and industry. Allied to the three half-backs who were considerably more assertive than they had previously been, the game was flipped on its head.

English provided McPhail with the equaliser and it was the Rangers supporters who streamed out of the ground after the final whistle wondering how they hadn't won the game, especially as Celtic keeper Joe Kennaway had pulled off one of the greatest saves the reporter had ever seen, when he somehow clawed away a goal-bound header by Fleming. It was 'worth a guinea a box', one newspaper reported, and it saved Celtic from certain defeat.

It was a surprise, therefore, when English failed to make the starting 11 in the next two league games – against Partick Thistle and Cowdenbeath – both of which Rangers won fairly comfortably. Perhaps Struth was ahead of his time in utilising a squad rotation system, but the bottom line was Rangers were top of the league at the end of September, a point ahead of champions Motherwell, who had a game in hand. Hamilton Accies and Aberdeen were joint third.

Just a couple of months into the new season and already it looked like a two-horse race, with Celtic lagging behind somewhat. It was all about Rangers and Motherwell, and when the sides met on the first of October, the game was played out in front of a packed Ibrox, and supporters were far from short-changed. Sam was back in the centre-forward jersey, and played his part in what was described as 'a cracking game and a delightful mixture of carpet football and that smashing, forceful football where every man is on his toes and every man is expected to think and act almost simultaneously'. The reporter added, 'It was the best game I had seen in a long time.'

Motherwell were on top in the first half, and played Rangers perfectly, completely neutralising any threat the home side may have posed while also effecting their own highly offensive game plan, which brought the afternoon's opening goal.

Occasionally English darted upfield or Smith ambled up an avenue on the left touchline, but ultimately it came to nothing. But just like the match at Celtic Park, come the interval, and then the resumption of hostilities, Rangers reminded us of the guy who took off his coat to have a real go. They tore in with wonderful spirit, and by sheer strength had equalised within nine minutes.

Smith's run up the left, and cross into the middle, led to the eager McPhail driving home an equaliser. Rangers then beat a constant path to the visiting goal.

English, named man of the match, played in McPhail to grab a second on the hour, and it looked as though the home men would go on and claim the points, and extend their lead at the top of the table, but Ferrier, the Motherwell captain, equalised on 68 minutes, and it was good enough to gain his side a point. The experiment of playing Smith at outside-left was an interesting one, and was seen as a way for Struth to accommodate both he and English. Smith was predominantly a centre-forward, as was English, but both were adaptable, and they changed positions several times.

Seven days later, the match against Dundee at Dens Park was described by one newspaper as 'psychologically vital' to Rangers. It was said that Dens was their bogey ground, not only because defeat there the previous season had put paid to their title hopes, but also because of previous results there. But a sound 3-0 win, in which English played a big part, combining with Meiklejohn and McPhail in the opening minute to allow Smith to open the scoring, laid that hoodoo to rest. Rangers were well on top throughout, although when the teams came out for the second half, both were sporting changed kits. It was a strange sight, with Rangers having swapped their traditional light blue jerseys for dark blue with white shorts, and Dundee changing white jerseys for red.

Midway through October, Rangers and Partick Thistle contested the Glasgow Cup Final, and a single goal by Marshall saw the cup head back to Ibrox. English played well, and his five goals in the previous ties against Queen's Park and Third Lanark had largely been responsible for taking the Ibrox men to the final. During the game, Rangers came up against a most stubborn Thistle defence, with McAllister as watchful of English as he had been of Jimmy McGrory in previous games.

Following a single-goal defeat at Tynecastle, which set Rangers back in their title tussle with Motherwell, a tough game loomed at Ibrox against Kilmarnock. The heavy going made it difficult for players to perform to their usual standards, but the game was won and lost in the Killie penalty area. Once again English proved the vital link, and after he had brought out a fine save from Killie custodian, Milliken, Rangers took the lead when Archibald, with one of his low, hard drives, shot into the far corner of the net.

Marshall scored a grand second, and the players celebrated their success with a trip to a Glasgow city centre restaurant. They were enjoying an early evening meal when a newspaper vendor came into the restaurant selling the following day's paper. 'English set for Newcastle United in record transfer fee' was his cry, as he moved among the diners selling his wares. Little did he know that the man of the moment was sat in the corner of the restaurant with his team-mates, enjoying a bite to eat.

Of course, one of the Rangers party bought a newspaper, and there it was in black and white. 'What is behind the report that Newcastle United want the Rangers centre-forward Sam English? Is a record transfer fee really brewing?' The topic of conversation was set for the remainder of the evening, and Sam could do little more than shrug his shoulders. After all, he would have been one of the last to know if he was being transferred!

Throughout the month of November, Rangers played like true champions. On Bonfire Day, they made the short trip to Shawfield and thumped Clyde 5-0. The interchanging between the half-backs and forwards, the exploitation of the cross pass, and the solidity in defence made them a formidable outfit. All five forwards excelled, with McPhail the schemer. His artistry and driving power time and again cut a way through the host defence. Marshall notched three lovely goals, while the non-stop English was unfortunate not to score more than one, and it arrived 14 minutes after the restart. McDonald picked up a loose ball and pushed it through to Brown, who transferred it to English. He carried on, and whacked the ball into the back of the net. Just 60 seconds later, an English header looked goal-bound until the Clyde keeper Stevenson fell on the ball as it was tearing past him.

Seven days later, Rangers put six past Morton at Ibrox – after the Cappielow men had taken the lead – but when Meiklejohn equalised, the Morton roof fell in. English was again among the goals.

On 19 November, St Johnstone visited Glasgow, and for the first 30 minutes no one in the press box could see a thing. Fog was the issue. It hovered above the playing surface like a thick woolly blanket and it was only when one of the reporters went down to the touchline to ask one of the players – in this case Sam English, who had switched to the right wing – who had scored the first two goals that they could identify the scorers. They had known of the goals due to the muffled cheering from the terraces but thankfully Sam was able to identify the culprits. The match finished 3-0 to the Light Blues, and the Rangers juggernaut rolled on. Once more, Meiklejohn showed himself superior to his contemporaries with a masterly display in the middle of the park.

And so to the final game of the month – a trip to Brockville to take on Falkirk. Always a potential banana-skin venue, although on this occasion Rangers made light work of their hosts. At times the conditions looked more of a threat to the visitors than Falkirk, and the game was played against a driving wind, amounting almost to half a gale. It swept across the field, bringing in its trail a lashing rain that blinded the players and soaked them to the skin. To give one an idea of how bad it was, the Rangers keeper had to make a dramatic save after McPhail had played a cross-field pass to Marshall in the middle of the park.

And the elements contributed to the opening goal. Falkirk keeper Thomson badly misjudged the flight of a McPhail cross and the incoming English arrived just in time to guide the ball into the net.

Hamilton then saved a Falkirk penalty when Morgan was tripped in the box. The moment Hamill's kick was saved, there was a rush towards the referee by the Falkirk players. They wanted the kick taken again, but we will never know why as the press had been banned from interviewing players during this period.

After the break, Falkirk enjoyed a period of superiority and the Rangers attack consisted of one man, English. But when the ball did reach him, he was guaranteed to have support, as his team-mates broke forward at pace to offer their assistance. This tactic bore fruit on the hour mark when away went English. He held the ball up and laid it off to Meiklejohn, 25 yards from goal. Big Davie drove with his right foot, and his wind-assisted shot exploded high into the Falkirk net.

Rangers' forward line was below par. It seldom produced football of a combined nature, but after all, it depended more on the smash-and-grab stuff, with English carrying the brick to break the window.

The start of December brought more of the same, and English was on target twice in a 3-1 win over Aberdeen – Rangers' sixth successive league win. The Irishman was denied a hat-trick when he was deemed to have been offside before firing home. Rangers lost McPhail to injury when he got mud in his eye and was forced off.

As the month wore on, there was a slight downturn in performances and results, and successive draws against Queen's Park and Hamilton Accies brought an impressive run to a shuddering halt. The scoreless match at Hampden was followed by an eight-goal thriller at Ibrox as Accies more than held their own. The Light Blues were three up at half-time and cruising, but in an incredible second half, Hamilton scored four times in succession and it took a late Rangers equaliser to salvage a point.

However, the Gers got back to winning ways on Christmas Eve when St Mirren visited a half-full Ibrox. McPhail and Marshall had Rangers 2-1 up at the break, but the hosts were really up against it in the second half and it wasn't until English scored with a clever shot on the turn that the pressure eased. Three minutes later, a determined Sam thundered his way through the middle before releasing an accurate pass for Marshall to crash the ball into the net and make the points safe.

The New Year brought yet another change in the Rangers front line, with Bobby Main introduced in place of Marshall for the visit of Airdrie. The change was hailed by supporters as Main dazzled on the right, combining well with English, who filled the inside-right position.

The new front line played some remarkable football – close, sharp, low passing, quick movement, and there was an end product too as Rangers scored five. At times, it amounted almost to exhibition stuff. Main was a smart addition, and Struth's apparent strength in depth augured well for the second part of the season.

Saturday, 21 January was reserved for a special challenge match in which two contrasting styles of football met on the south side of Glasgow. The Austrian tourists of Rapid Vienna were in town and just over 50,000 witnessed an epic struggle which ended three goals apiece.

On a bitterly cold afternoon, it was a case of role reversal as the Austrians played a style of football once known as the 'beautiful game' in Scotland. Some younger supporters might not quite have got the irony of the Austrians refusing to play the 'aeroplane pass', instead determined to keep the ball on the ground and win the game through strategic passing rather than 'howfing' it in the air and chasing it down. Okay, so perhaps Rangers' style wasn't quite as Spartan as that, but there was a tendency for the Austrians to show up an absence of variety in Rangers' method of attack.

A draw, however, was a fair result, as Rangers did the bulk of the attacking, although at one point in the game it looked like the home men were in for a drubbing. Rapid led 3-1 at the interval, but a revival after the switching of positions by Smith and English saved the day.

Rapid opened the scoring on eight minutes, but 15 minutes later McPhail got his head to a well-taken corner by English. The changing of Smith and English a few minutes after the interval paid off almost instantly, as Smith reduced the leeway with a spot kick when Brown was pushed from behind. The equaliser arrived when English played in Smith to slot the ball beyond Raftl.

It didn't go unnoticed that the switching of English to a more creative role had been the catalyst for Rangers' revival. Here was a young man who had shown he had several strings to his bow, and that his value to the club had increased with his ability to move seamlessly into different parts of the forward line.

And it might even have been a hot topic at the social gathering in the St Enoch Hotel after the game, in which representatives of both clubs, along with many city dignitaries, enjoyed a pleasurable gathering. Everything was geniality, and ex-Bailie Duncan Graham, presiding, didn't hide his sentimentality. It was the first time, he said, that he had taken the chair under such auspices, and emphasised that Rangers would always aspire to make sport a refreshing recreation.

Sir John T. Cargill spoke in a similar strain, and said he was proud to be an honorary patron of the Rangers. More than politicians, statesmen, and diplomats, sport pervaded a better atmosphere among nations.

The chairman presented a silver Loving Cup to the Austrians as a memento of their visit, and the replies in German, ably translated by Mr Cummings of Paisley firm J&P Coats, revealed that several Austrian representatives believed they had just produced one of their proudest displays on a football field. The club president added, 'English football has not near the appeal of Scottish, and Austria and its surrounding countries would ring with the peal of the Rapid club's achievement against Scotland's premier club.' It was the first visit of an Austrian club to Scotland, and it's fair to say they departed with nothing but good memories.

Rangers warmed up for a huge league game at Motherwell by hosting the amateurs of Queen's Park in the Scottish Cup. Things didn't quite go according to plan and the hosts stuttered to a 1-1 draw. In fact, it was only an early goal by English – a brilliant piece of opportunism – that spared blushes.

The following weekend's Fir Park encounter was certainly more exciting. A goalkeeper sent off, two penalty goals, numerous injuries, and football of the he-man type, were the main features of a torrid 90 minutes. If the season's first meeting of the teams would be remembered as a classic football encounter, then this latest instalment would be recalled for other reasons. For the 26,000 crowd, there was no shortage of excitement.

Perhaps this was the game that would decide the destination of the championship, and if that was the case then Motherwell lost possession of their honour due to a couple of seconds of madness on the part of their keeper. Midway through the first half, with the match tied at 1-1, Rangers attacked the Motherwell goal. After scrambling around to grab the ball, McClory got possession and punted clear. He was about ten yards from his goal. As he ran back he passed English. Something happened. English fell to the ground and lay motionless while thousands of supporters howled themselves hoarse. The ball, by this time, was in the Rangers half, as was the referee. The shouting of the crowd, allied to his being made the object of emphatic protestation by members of the Light Blues' team, caused him to turn round.

Whatever was said by the Rangers men is up for discussion, but the whistler ran over to a linesman, had a hasty consultation with him, crossed to his other flag-waver, talked to him, and then dashed to the circle of players surrounding English, who, by this time, was on his feet receiving attention from the trainer, Arthur Dixon.

There was no hesitation on the referee's part. He approached McClory and pointed to the pavilion. More cheers from the Ibrox faithful interacted with jeers from the away fans. McClory pulled off his jersey, threw it to the ground, and walked off. On his way he had to pass the referee, and he made one last appeal, but the referee was adamant. McClory resumed his long walk.

Rangers were awarded a penalty kick as a result of the alleged indiscretion. Their supporters cheered the decision, while Motherwell fans cheered their dismissed man. However, McClory knew exactly what his dismissal meant to his team, and his face mirrored plainly the misery of his mind.

Rangers were already without Dougie Gray, who'd suffered an injury and been forced to leave the field, so the numbers were level. When all the fuss had died down, Jimmy Smith coolly despatched the spot kick. Advantage Rangers, and when English and Main set up Fleming for the all-important third goal, the points – and a title advantage – were with Rangers.

The game was significant for another reason. At the bottom of the match report, the journalist suggested that following the clash between English and McClory, much of the spark went out of the Rangers forward. It was as though the episode reminded him all too clearly of his clash with John Thomson – and one wonders if Bill Struth noticed much the same. The following Saturday, Rangers travelled to Rugby Park to face Kilmarnock in a Scottish Cup tie and meekly lost 1-0. It was suggested that a major factor in the defeat was Davie Meiklejohn's failure to last the pace. Indeed, he was a great deal slower than he once was and therefore his recovery time had increased. But the match report also stated, 'English, by his display, only confirmed what I thought of him last Saturday. He has gone back a bit, and is not as able as he was last season or at the beginning of this.'

Sam was left out of the side to face Dundee at Ibrox, and looked on from the stand as Rangers took the lead four times only to be pegged back each time. Thankfully, two late goals saw them win 6-4.

But English was back in the starting line-up at the beginning of March as Rangers travelled across the city to play Third Lanark, and scored from a fine header to seal a 3-1 victory. Rangers moved six points clear of second-placed Motherwell, although the Fir Park side had a game in hand.

Sam was again missing as Rangers fought out a thrilling 4-4 draw with Hearts at Ibrox, but was back in the inside-right berth for the league trip to Kilmarnock. Rangers were terrific, although English was said to be the least satisfying member of the front line despite scoring the second – when he reacted quickest after McPhail hit the bar – in a fantastic 6-2 success. As a result, Rangers pushed past the 100 league goals mark for the season.

The second part of the season continued to be a yo-yo existence for Sam as he missed Rangers' fruitful trip to Perth, being replaced by Tully Craig, who was, at that point, being used as more of a utility player. It was a strange move by Struth, although the 2-0 win guaranteed that Rangers maintained their healthy lead at the top of the table.

There were signs that English was perhaps becoming a little frustrated at being in and out of the squad, and moved from pillar to post to suit others. He recalled, 'Only once had I ventured upstairs to Bill Struth's office – when he started putting me out on the wing. He looked up surprised as I tiptoed to his desk. I told him all about how, since my schooldays, I had tried every forward position and centre-forward suited me best. Patiently, he heard me out, and then deliberately he put down his pen. "You will play where I put you – if selected," he declared. And that was that!'

The following midweek, the SFA hosted a disciplinary meeting in which Motherwell goalkeeper Alan McClory was the star turn. The meeting took place behind closed doors, but a report in the following morning's paper stated, 'There is something very mysterious about the case of Alan McClory, and I am not the only person to think that. The referee's report said he was informed by the linesman – he didn't see the incident himself – that McClory had "deliberately kicked English", and that he accordingly ordered him off. That sounds quite clear and decisive, but what do I read in the minutes of the Referee Committee's meeting? This, "Censured – A. McClory (Motherwell) for interfering with an opponent. Reported by J. Hudson."

'Just what "interfering with an opponent" means, I do not understand. It does not appear to be a heinous offence. Yet it called for a censure by the Referee Committee. But, according to the referee's report, McClory was not ordered off for interfering with an opponent, he was ordered off for kicking. If he didn't kick English he ought not to have been sent off, and the linesmen, who reported that kicking took place, were wrong. What have the committee done in regard to these officials? No steps have been taken to deal with them, so far as I am aware.'

English was again missing when Falkirk rolled up at Ibrox at the start of April, and again when Struth took his men north to meet Aberdeen. Inevitably, after the draw at Pittodrie, press men were asking questions of his exclusion.

And seven days later, with the Light Blues on the verge of clinching their 19th title at home to Queen's Park, Struth was asked if there was any truth in the rumour that Liverpool wanted to sign English. 'No comment' was the official line from Ibrox, but that didn't prevent this story from appearing the following day: 'I hear that Liverpool are moving to get Sam English, Rangers' snappy centre-forward. I believe manager George Patterson has made a personal call at Ibrox regarding Sam, and did not leave altogether disappointed. Don't be surprised if you hear more about this in the near future.'

But no amount of press speculation could take the gloss off what was to be a tremendous afternoon for players and supporters as a solitary goal was enough to see Rangers reclaim the title from Motherwell. The Light Blues were certainly the better team, while perhaps not playing like champions, but the all-important goal arrived midway through the first half. English shot for goal and the ball hit Smith's left-hand post. After rebounding across goal, McPhail dashed in to smash the leather into the rigging while the goalkeeper lay helpless on the turf, the result of his dive to save English's initial effort.

English had played well enough. He was clever in the second half at taking up position, and his heading of the ball was good. But one was left wondering what his future role at the club would be as his appearances had been severely restricted, while Smith's overall game time had gone way up. Sam was clearly still a fantastic player and a potent goal threat, but perhaps Struth felt he had lost his cutting edge.

He missed out on a Glasgow Charity Cup semi-final win over Partick Thistle, with Willie Nicholson this time given the nod, and also Rangers' single-goal victory in the final against Queen's

Park, although he had been injured ahead of this match. In fact, the title clincher at Fir Park would be Sam's last game for the Light Blues in his adopted homeland.

But while some supporters were still celebrating Rangers' title success, Sam and his team-mates set off from Glasgow in the middle of May: destination Germany. Rangers had been invited over to the continent for a five-match tour of the country, and a return game with Rapid Vienna in Austria. Being part of the tour may have been construed as Sam having a future at Ibrox, or a thank you for his efforts over the past couple of seasons. It could have been taken both ways.

The first match ended in a 5-1 victory for Rangers over a combined German team in Berlin, but English sat out the match as he still had a slight niggle. Smith notched a treble as Rangers were given a tremendous welcome by 30,000 spectators. Before kick-off, the German captain presented his opposite number with a bouquet of red tulips and white carnations – after which the German players lined up and gave the fascist salute. Victory meant Rangers were still undefeated outside of Great Britain.

The day after the game, the players visited the Berlin War Memorial, where skipper Davie Meiklejohn laid a wreath in memory of all those who had lost their lives in the First World War. The wreath bore the inscription 'In friendly remembrance' and after the short ceremony the touring party were guests of honour at a grand lunch.

The following day, Rangers were in Hamburg for their second match and lined up against a German national 11. The heat was oppressive when the players took the field and a crowd of around 18,000 were inside the ground, but Rangers won 3-1, and it's said the majority of those in attendance were completely taken by the visitors' ability to head the ball, an art form which hadn't yet made its way to central Europe. English was again a non-starter, and Rangers' scorers were Marshall and Smith, who netted twice.

The touring party moved on to Bochum for the third match, and English was back in his familiar position leading the attack against a German select. The kick-off was delayed half an hour due to torrential rain, and once it finally stopped, the German crowd were in for a real treat. Play was even during the first half but once again it was through the fine use of their heads that Rangers had the edge. Whenever a lofted ball arrived in the box, they looked favourites to win it, although it was a fine shot by McPhail which opened the scoring, after clever lead-up play by English.

Fleming scored just before the break to give the tourists a 2-0 half-time lead.

Rangers took the game by the scruff of the neck on the restart and English was quickly on the scoresheet, which effectively killed the game as a contest. Despite trailing 3-0, the sparse 2,000 crowd seemed delighted with the skills shown by the Scots, although their favourites did enjoy a spell of pressure near the end, but McPhail and English scored late on to give Rangers a 5-0 win.

Smith was on target three times in the fourth match, a 3-2 win in Dresden a couple of days later, although he had a bit of good fortune for his opening strike, which came back off the referee's head and fell at his feet. The Ibrox side definitely lacked a little cohesion up front, which could have been attributed to the absence of English, the glue that had so often held the side together.

The final match in Germany ended in defeat – Rangers' first loss on foreign soil, as a Bavarian Select won 2-1 in Munich. It's likely the defeat was down to fatigue, with the team being asked to play five games in just 14 days, and at the end of a long and tiring campaign. Marshall scored Rangers' goal.

Before heading home to Scotland, Rangers had agreed a return fixture with Rapid Vienna, following on from the success of the Austrians' visit to Glasgow. They took the train from Germany to Austria and on arrival at the West Station in Vienna, the players were given an enthusiastic welcome by more than 2,000 people. A band struck up 'God Save the King' as the players stepped on to the platform. Several local dignitaries were also there to meet the famous Glasgow Rangers.

The sides met on the Sunday afternoon in Vienna, and the winners were the 24,000 packed into the ground, who witnessed seven goals and a first-class match. President Miklas was among those who saw Rapid lead 3-2 at half-time and eventually win 4-3.

Rangers took the lead through Marshall who, after fine lead-up work by English, prodded home the opener. Their joy was short-lived, though, as Binder scored the first of his three first-half goals just moments later to equalise.

The second half was full of intrigue but Rangers came up just short, although after the game skipper Bob McPhail said that his players had enjoyed the challenge, and that while the Rapid players had played very well, he couldn't say the same thing for the referee, and left it at that.

That night, both teams enjoyed a lavish banquet in Vienna's Grant Hotel, and were joined by many prominent Austrians from the worlds of sport, politics and opera, for which the Austrians were famed.

Like his team-mates, Sam English would have enjoyed his night, although little did he know the match against Rapid would be his last in Rangers colours. It was going to be a rather interesting close season.

Eleven

IN THE lead-up to Christmas 1932, the phone rang in Bill Struth's office. It was a member of the Irish national football side's selection committee. Ireland were due to face a strong Wales in their final match of the British Home Championship and the selector was calling to find out if Rangers would agree to release Sam English for the match in Wrexham.

Struth listened intently before asking, 'Will English be listed at centre-forward?' The gentleman on the other end of the phone insisted he couldn't give any guarantees, which irked Struth. He was keen for his player to play where *he* wanted, as he felt Rangers were the club paying his wages but, as the selector pointed out, they also had to accommodate the great Jimmy Dunne, who was breaking all kinds of scoring records in the English First Division with Sheffield United.

A reporter from the *Belfast Telegraph* got wind of the conversation and ran a story in his paper criticising Rangers, and Struth in particular, for sticking his nose into the affairs of an international team. The reporter also accused Struth of double standards, adding, 'The only player asked from Glasgow

Rangers by the Irish selectors was Sam English. In releasing him the Rangers manager suggested he would like him to be played at centre-forward. This was rather impossible owing to Dunne being earmarked for this position, but one cannot quite follow the attitude of the famous Glasgow club in making any stipulation. Only a week ago that club played English at outside-right. In fact, English is considered the most versatile player in Scotland, and has been called a real two-footed player.'

Sam's international career extended to two matches and one goal. In truth, a man with his pedigree – Rangers' record goalscorer, Liverpool's biggest transfer fee – should have been given further recognition by the national side. He was a naturally talented footballer with a real eye for goal and, Dunne apart, the Irish side wasn't exactly awash with top-quality forward-thinking players.

After missing out on a place in the squad for one particular match, a respected newspaperman from Scotland remarked, 'If Ireland have a better centre-forward than Sam English, then I congratulate heartily my friends across the Channel.'

Granted, Irish football was a muddled commodity around this period, with politics playing a big part in the make-up of the different organisations running the game on the seemingly fractured island. In June 1921, the Football Association of Irish Free State (FAIFS) had created a new international team. Two years later, FIFA accepted their application to be allowed to compete in international competition.

Meanwhile, the IFA – the Irish Football Association – had been organising international football in the country since 1880, and included players from both sides of the political divide. That would continue until 1954, when they renamed their football team Northern Ireland.

But Sam played for Ireland when it was more or less an all-in team. The Irish Free State side picked players born in the south of the country, but Free State-born players were also free to play under the IFA banner, and it was agreed that if any of them were chosen to play, they would, on being picked, state their willingness to represent the international team run from Belfast.

It's thought that the beginning of the end of the IFA's domination arrived when the influential Leinster FA – which took in Dublin and virtually the entire south-east of the country – decided to leave the organisation. This was the climax of a series of disputes over what some footballing bodies in the south saw as an alleged Belfast bias within the IFA.

In 1920, all but two Irish League clubs were based in Ulster, the biggest part of which would become Northern Ireland the following year. While this largely reflected the balance of footballing strength within Ireland, southern clubs felt the IFA had been doing little to promote the game outside the professional clubs in its heartland, and they desired change.

A split was inevitable, and it duly arrived. For some time, players with a nationalist background had been grumbling about being picked to play for what they saw as a team steeped in the traditions of the north. In fact, no player epitomised that southern-based mentality more than the aforementioned Dunne, a record-breaking striker who was born in Dublin in 1905. As a teenager, he took part in the Irish War of Independence, siding with the IRA against the British, and was jailed for his actions. While interned in a prison in County Kildare, he chose to go on hunger strike.

Dunne had been a Gaelic football enthusiast, but honed his soccer skills while jailed and after being released, spent time with Shamrock Rovers before joining Sheffield United. Dunne's record of scoring in 12 successive English top-flight games was almost overtaken by Leicester City and England striker, Jamie Vardy, but he narrowly missed out and the record remained intact for an 89th year. Dunne also scored 167 goals in 190 Division One games, so he was a big rival of Sam's for the green centre-forward jersey of Ireland. And that is why the Irish selectors were keen to have the flexibility to deploy English in an alternative forward position.

However, one unanswered question remains the length of time it took for the selectors to actually invite Sam to be a part of the international set-up. The season before he won his first cap, he had been on target with incredible regularity but still there was no sign of him being picked to represent the country of his birth. It's difficult to recall another Rangers player who made such an impact in front of goal in his debut season, which makes it hard to understand why English was ignored by the selectors for almost 13 months.

Ireland played three British Home Championship matches during Sam's record-breaking 1931/32 season and he didn't feature in any. Still, he was present – along with 45,000 others – at Ibrox in September 1931, when Scotland hosted Ireland in the second of the three games, and he looked on as Dunne scored a consolation for the Irish in a 3-1 defeat.

But when the call eventually did come, the player answered it immediately and, as fate would have it, he was named at centre-forward. Sam made his international debut on Saturday, 17 September 1932 in a British Home Championship match, with Scotland providing the opposition. The Scots were hot favourites to triumph, and around 4,000 supporters from across the Irish Sea made the journey to Windsor Park, in Belfast, resplendent in tam o'shanters, and as the traditional manner in which to celebrate a goal in those days was to toss your cap in the air, the 'tams' spent a fair part of the afternoon in orbit.

In terms of footballing ability, Scotland were the superior side, and a couple of goals from Sam's Rangers team-mate Bob McPhail, one in either half, helped the Scots to a 4-0 victory. Shortly after kick-off, the Scottish half-backs began knocking the ball around in midfield, quickly exuding an air of confidence which somehow made the Irish feel inferior. In fact, with just two minutes on the clock, Hamilton Accies forward James King nodded the Scots in front.

McPhail scored either side of the break before Jimmy McGrory notched the final goal with an absolute thunderbolt that Liverpool keeper Elisha Scott had very little chance of saving. The majority of the 40,000 crowd had been forced to concede that the Scots were thoroughly deserving of their victory.

But it wasn't all one-way traffic. There were spells in the game when the hosts were on top. In fact, for a good 20 minutes in the first half, Ireland were undeniably the pick of the sides. The Scots were defending for their lives and it was only their goalkeeper, Sandy McLaren – the youngest ever custodian to be capped for Scotland – who kept them in the match. How he managed to stop a rocket shot from Sam English during Ireland's period of dominance only he knows. The ball looked destined for the back of the net until McLaren somehow clawed it to safety from under the crossbar. The final score of 4-0 made it look as though the visitors strolled to victory but the truth is, had McLaren not saved English's effort, things may have turned out rather differently.

McPhail's first goal was a definite turning point in the game as the hosts had just begun to assert their authority. If the big Ranger's goal didn't finish off Ireland, it certainly set them back somewhat. The hosts lost a good bit of their dash, and their supporters, heartened by an earlier change in domination, lost their voice.

After the break, Ireland once again took up the cudgel, although once again that man McPhail found the back of the net. It was all but game over, and the McGrory goal, scored late on, was the icing on the cake for the visitors.

Had there been a prize up for grabs for the home man of the match, then English would surely have taken it. His industry ensured the visiting defence never got a moment, and throughout he remained his side's best option for a goal. That he didn't score was through no fault of his own. English was joined by fellow Scots-based players Willie Cook, of Celtic, and Aberdeen's Eddie Falloon, while the remainder of the team was made up of three Anglo-Irish and five Northern Irish-based players.

A week before the next match in the British Home Championship, England versus Ireland, the Irish selectors met to discuss their options for the big game. The match was scheduled for a Monday evening at Blackpool's Bloomfield Road ground. In view of the disappointing result against Scotland at Windsor Park, their task would not be an easy one. In one way they were slightly fortunate, as the tie was being played on a Monday and therefore the objection of English clubs to allowing their players time off to play for Ireland would be removed on this occasion.

First on the agenda was the manner in which individual players had performed in the opening match against Scotland. Sam English ticked all the boxes and looked certain to win his second cap. The Irish committee had been delighted with his work rate, and he seemed one of the few to receive pass marks. Still, the committee sent a representative to Dundee to check up on the Rangers contingent of English, 'Whitey' McDonald and Alex Stevenson, the inside-left who had recently signed from Dublin Dolphins, and who would go on to make a name for himself as a player of real quality at Everton. It wouldn't be too long until Sam was locking horns with him in the Merseyside derby.

However, there was bad news for the Irish when English suffered an injury at Dens Park, which placed him in the doubtful category for the international. It was a blow because England were strong favourites, having won all but four of the tussles since the fixture was first played in Belfast in 1882.

English travelled with the party and they stayed at Blackpool's Imperial Hydro. The trainer put Sam through his paces the day before the game but it was decided his leg wasn't strong enough and a decision was taken to leave him out. English was gutted. The selection committee decided Jimmy Dunne would lead the line and be partnered up front by Dubliner Paddy Moore, who had been knocking in the goals for Aberdeen. Liverpool goalkeeper Elisha Scott was named as captain.

With kick-off fast approaching, Sam took his place in the Bloomfield Road stand alongside a couple of team-mates who hadn't made the starting 11. They were accompanied by a crowd of 28,000. On the night, though, Irish eyes weren't smiling as a blunder by goalkeeper Scott allowed England to win the match. Half an hour after the start he came out to collect a cross from Cunliffe, and instead of picking up, elected to kick, sending the ball straight to Sheffield United man Barclay, who shot into the empty goal. It proved the only goal of a game in which Ireland were the equal of their opponents in every department. They were unfortunate to lose and even after England had scored, there were occasions when Ireland could have equalised, for Dunne was always a danger to the home defence.

Sam looked on as his team-mates enjoyed their fair share of the game. The forward line, with four southern Irish-born players in Kelly, Dunne, Duggan and Moore, was a force to be reckoned with, and combined well together. They deserved at least a draw, and the fact they had played so well together would not have been lost on the Rangers centre-forward.

And so to the match in which Rangers boss Bill Struth had attempted to influence the Irish selection committee. Wales hosted an Irish side which, on this occasion, had plenty of choice up front. When the team was eventually named, English was listed at inside-right, forming a right-sided partnership with Linfield ace Billy Houston. Jimmy Dunne retained the centre-forward jersey – and Struth refrained from commenting on the selection. The players to make way were Moore, due to injury, and Harry Duggan, of Leeds United.

The match, played at Wrexham's Racecourse Ground in front of 12,000, was a thrill-a-minute affair, and despite losing 4-1 thanks to a late flurry of goals, the Irish felt the final score failed to reflect properly the overall 90 minutes. The result meant Wales were at least promised a share of the British Home Championship, with the remaining tie not due until after the new year.

An injury to Irish full-back Cook after just 15 minutes proved a handicap too much for the visitors, and although the Celtic man played on, the Welsh fully exploited the weakness on that side of the park. Elisha Scott was in fantastic form for Ireland, and more than made up for his gaffe in the previous game with some terrific stops. However, the Welsh won due to their superiority in the middle of the park. The visitors had no answer to the hard-working, and skilful, trio of Griffiths, Murphy and Richards, and their promptings of the Welsh strikers was a joy to behold.

Lacking support, the Irish forwards were ineffective in this period, and even the tireless English, who changed places with Dunne, could make little impression on the Welsh backs.

English, on the whole, was Ireland's most dangerous forward, and did everything asked of him. In fact, his toil and skill surely merited more than the single goal he scored. With 27 minutes on the clock, English, who had been shooting at every opportunity, got possession, and working over to the left, beat the goalkeeper with a shot which he reached but couldn't prevent hitting the back of the net, such was the force of the drive. He was overjoyed to score for his country. His partner, Houston, suffered badly from a lack of genuine opportunities in the second half, but still contributed much to the cause.

It was tough luck for Ireland that they came up against arguably the best Welsh team for many a year and one that fully deserved to win the championship, with Scotland eventually finishing second and England third.

The general standard of all four home international teams at that time was very good, and despite the Irish finishing bottom of the table, there wasn't a great deal between the sides. In fact, it seemed such a pity that as the football world was becoming a much smaller place – thanks mainly to the advent of the World Cup – many of the great players of the early 1930s would never get an opportunity to showcase their talents on the larger stage.

For Sam and his contemporaries in the Irish team, there would be no World Cup to look forward to. When the inaugural competition was staged, in Uruguay in 1930, Sam was turning out for Yoker against Pollok just three days after the hosts beat Argentina 4-2 in the final. There were no entrants from Great Britain for that competition as the home international countries had withdrawn from FIFA. There was no qualification for the tournament and only four European countries took part. Many cited travel as the main issue for non-participation, with a couple of the eventual participants only agreeing to travel after heads of state intervened.

Four years later the competition was staged in Italy, and this time reigning champions Uruguay decided not to take part in protest at several European countries refusing to travel to South America when they had staged the tournament. As a result, the 1934 World Cup is the only competition in which the holders didn't participate.

Once again the four British home nations refused to get involved, citing their self-imposed exile from FIFA, even though the sport's governing body had offered both England and Scotland direct entry into the finals. FA spokesman Charles Sutcliffe called the tournament 'a joke' and added, 'The national associations of England, Scotland, Wales and Ireland have quite enough to do in their own international championships, which seem to me a far better world championship than the one to be staged in Rome.'

And with those words went the hopes of guys like Sam English and Jimmy Dunne who, for all the talent they possessed, would never get the opportunity to show off those skills on a world stage.

Two international appearances might seem paltry recognition for a man with the talents of Sam English, and it should have been more, but bearing in mind the small number of representative games played in those days as compared to now, I suppose it isn't too great a surprise.

Twelve

THE 1932/33 season ended with Sam pocketing a league winners' medal. Rangers had edged Motherwell to the title, with Celtic a distant fourth. Individually, the campaign hadn't been as successful as the previous one for the Irishman. Sam had managed just ten league goals (from 25 starts) as opposed to the 33 scored by Jimmy Smith in 34 games. Bob McPhail had notched 30, and even Jimmy Marshall and Jimmy Fleming had outscored Sam.

But when the touring Rangers party arrived back on home soil from the continent, the players said their goodbyes and headed off to spend quality time with family. In Sam's case, there was only one possible destination – the Ayrshire resort of Girvan. Sam, Sadie and the two girls headed south and settled in their usual digs, close to the beach and all local amenities, but their annual holiday was cut short by a summons from Bill Struth: Sam was to return immediately to Ibrox.

There was little else for it but to comply, so he shrugged his shoulders and headed back to Glasgow. Approaching the main door at Ibrox, he thought back to the last time he had been ordered to the stadium – two years earlier for his midnight meeting with

Struth. Somehow this was different, though. It felt different. This time, trepidation replaced nervous anticipation. Struth wasn't calling him back to offer a pay rise or tell him what a wonderful season he'd had. No, something wasn't right, and there was only one way to find out.

He was ushered upstairs to the manager's office, and his heart pounded with every step he took up the marble staircase. He was a bag of nerves as he approached the office door. Another defining moment in the Sam English saga.

In his 1963 interview with the *Daily Express*, Sam recalled, 'I wanted to remain in the game – and with Rangers. But after two seasons the boss called me to Ibrox from a Girvan holiday. Bluntly, he told me Liverpool had made an offer and that I would be transferred.

'I admit that some of the edge had gone off my game. Goals came less readily. The heart had gone out of me. Still, it was a blow to leave Ibrox. There and then I thought I might as well give up the game, but when I spoke to Liverpool manager, George Patterson, he said to me, "Come and try it at Anfield. Maybe you'll find it different there."

'I cannot remember how the boss said goodbye, or even if he did. Struth was a distant man.'

There were few media announcements in the 1930s. If Struth wanted to get a story out, he would summon certain 'trusted' journalists to Ibrox and feed them a line. On this occasion, though, a few reporters had caught wind of this 'sensation' and one journalist in particular reported that Sam English was to leave Rangers – but that his destination was Dens Park, Dundee. Of course, the story was only half right. On Monday, 24 July 1933, Sam signed for Liverpool.

On the possible Dundee move, another journalist wrote, 'The idea that Sam would switch from Ibrox to Dens is completely ludicrous, to say the least, for the club with an admittedly lean purse is not the club to collar a Rangers star.'

They certainly were not. Indeed, the fee paid to Rangers from Liverpool was believed, initially, to be around £5,000. It was later confirmed that £8,000 had been transferred into the Ibrox coffers, the largest sum of money Rangers had ever received for a player. It was also a joint club record for Liverpool, equalling the amount they had paid to Bury for Scotsman Tom 'Tiny' Bradshaw in January 1930.

In fact, many learned gentlemen of the period reckon that had Liverpool purchased English at the end of the season previous, then the fee would surely have been five figures, and challenged the then British record transfer fee of £10,890, which saw David Jack move from Bolton Wanderers to Arsenal. 'Irish English' was tipped to do well south of the border, and it was hoped he would prove more of a success than the Scot named Ireland (Bob) who'd moved to Liverpool from Rangers in 1928.

Struth may have been the absolute authority at Ibrox but there were still a great many Rangers fans who lamented English's departure, and recalled with great fondness the considerable number of league goals he'd plundered in his debut season. The misfortune he'd encountered had surely been responsible for a reduced bag of goals, and had led to Struth rendering him surplus to requirements.

A change of scenery was perhaps what the player required and at just 24 years old, he had so much to offer the Anfield club.

It quickly emerged that Liverpool had been after Sam for quite some time. Mr Patterson had in fact travelled up to Ibrox as early as the previous November in a bid to sign the player, but at that point Struth had been reluctant to let him go, although he did promise Patterson that Liverpool would get first refusal on the player, should he become available.

Sam's de facto replacement at Rangers was Jimmy Smith, the ex-East Stirlingshire forward who had already been at Ibrox for four years. Ironically, Smith had also been a one-time Liverpool target, but they missed out on his signature by a few minutes. Rangers had been given a strong tip about this young lad and about Liverpool's interest, and when two Anfield scouts turned up at Firs Park one Saturday to sign Smith, who was still a teenager, they discovered he had just signed for Rangers. Smith was now more than ready to step straight into Sam's boots.

It was no secret that the Reds were in the market for a clever centre-forward. Gordon Hodgson, the South African, was extremely prolific in front of goal, but Patterson was keen for someone to share the goals burden. At their annual meeting, Liverpool directors promised shareholders they would sign a prominent front man before the season started, and they kept that promise. English was obtained in the face of strong competition, for it was common knowledge that several top clubs were also keen, but the Anfield board were convinced their supporters would be excited by English's amazing pace and terrific shot. And one pundit reckoned, 'English had the resource, decision and ability to transform Liverpool's front line into the unit it failed to be last season.'

But on the eve of the new season, a Liverpool supporter sent the following letter into his local paper, 'Surely it is too much to expect one good forward to convert our front line into championship contenders. As a unit, they failed last season. Too many times the defence was overworked. We need more cohesion between halves and forwards, and perhaps the signing of Sam English is just the beginning. We need new blood (but it must be good) and then we could see a winning team on the park. It is high time we loyal supporters saw games at Anfield in which we could honestly say, "Now we have a team who are masters of their craft."'

The arrival of English on Merseyside created a buzz among supporters, and when he alighted from his train at Exchange Station on the Sunday, the day before training was due to start, he was met by around 30 or 40 Pool supporters, despite the fact his arrival had not been publicised. But the warm reception made Sam feel he was among friends in a football-mad city.

He was met by Patterson, and his assistant Jack Rouse, new team-mate Gordon Hodgson and Sam McAllister, a new signing from Watford. Handshakes were no sooner over than the crowd were shouting, 'Good luck Sam!' while one wag yelled, 'Mind yourself Sam, don't let Gordon teach you any tricks,' a quip which was greeted with roars of laughter.

Sam was happy to talk to a local reporter, and said, 'I am looking forward to my first season in English football very keenly, and I hope to make my mark as speedily as some former club colleagues have done.

'I played with Willy Cook, of Everton FC, when he was with Port Glasgow. Cook was then an inside-left. Willy got his English cup medal in his first season in England, and I hope I am as lucky. I only want that to complete a very nice set. I got the Scottish Intermediate Cup medal at Yoker, and two seasons ago with Rangers I got the Scottish Cup medal. Wouldn't it be great if I could get the other this season?'

Mr Patterson laughed, and said, 'Yes, I'd like to see you complete the set. I celebrate a quarter of a century with Liverpool this year, and the English cup would be the best present you could give me.'

English said he was anxious to meet his new colleagues at Anfield, 'I know Elisha Scott very well, as I have met him while playing in the Ireland team at the international matches, but I don't think I have met any of the others before.

'Henderson, who was on Liverpool's books last season, is an old colleague of mine, but I believe he's gone to Clapton Orient.

Archie McPherson left Rangers the season I joined, so I don't know him. Incidentally, when I pull on that red jersey at Anfield it will be the first occasion in my football career that I have worn that colour. Blue has been my usual colour up to now, even in Junior teams.'

On the first day at training, the new men arrived almost in tandem, but first in was Sam, who confused all in the dressing room by speaking in a perfectly good Scottish brogue, despite being born in Ireland. The queer combination drew many quips and impromptu impersonations. Sam McAllister, an inside-right; Albert Gray, a left-half, and W.J. Tennant, a right-back, both from Torquay United, were the other new men to arrive shortly after. Prospects for the coming season were freely discussed between the new arrivals. Patterson, who doubled as secretary of the club, and Rouse were again on hand to make the new men feel at home.

Chairman Mr Cartwright also welcomed the players and in the dressing room made a short speech in which he expressed the hope that they would have a successful season, 'I hope you will soon become 100 per cent Liverpudlians and with your team-mates, assist in bringing honours to this club.'

Twenty-six players in total reported to trainer Wilson, who with Eph Longworth, his assistant, had them out on the road wearing huge sweaters within half an hour of starting. It was the last day of July; the hard work had begun.

The day after English signed for the Reds, a report in the *Liverpool Echo* read, 'This Irishman is a busybody at centre, strong and clever, too. He is the man Liverpool have been needing for 20 years. In fact, I consider it the biggest signing Liverpool have ever made outside of Bradshaw [Tom 'Tiny' Bradshaw – one of the famed 1928 Wembley Wizards].'

And Sam didn't have too long to wait until getting stripped for action. Liverpool staged their first practice match and he was in the Reds team. His inclusion saw a record attendance for a practice of 13,000, eclipsing the 10,000 who turned up at Goodison the night before for Everton's equivalent.

The match raised £330 for good causes and the Kop were reported to be 'as buoyant as they've been in years, and that is down to the purchase of Sam English'. Of course, the media attention was mainly focussed on English, and one reporter said, 'Sam keeps the ball on the ground, where it belongs, and he shoots hard and wheels about wisely. He has to form a companionship on the field with strange players and that can only come in time. He is not a giant, he is just a plain fellow like you and me, a man capable of delivering and taking charge, but his chief forte is his thought for team work, and he comes not a day too early in that direction. But do not let us be hasty to believe that a versatile man such as English can tumble into First Division football and become an instant hero. It is a question of time, there is no question about his ability.' Naturally, English scored a goal.

Liverpool had enjoyed a long and fruitful association with South Africa, and had signed their fair share of players from that country. And just as English was settling into his new surroundings, word came through that they had signed three more, with Berry 'Nivvy' Nieuwenhuys and Lance Carr expected to feature regularly. Liverpool had good contacts in South Africa, and pipped Motherwell to the trio. The cost of signing the players amounted only to air fares.

And so to the final trial match of pre-season, the Probables v the Possibles. Sam was lining up at centre-forward for the former. There was still a week until the season opened in earnest but Liverpool fans were already itching for action, and 16,900 saw Sam score a perfect goal with a grand shot after he had been off the field for a while with a damaged eye. He showed some excellent touches, and his overall display pleased the majority of the crowd.

His presence certainly pleased the *Liverpool Echo* reporter, who said, 'English showed how to head goals and crack them with a sharp shot. He has the experience and nous; the football brain and the quick feet to decide whether he shall shoot or pass. English has the first fine art of a forward, centre or otherwise, namely, the delaying of a pass until he has drawn an opponent. Today some players pass before anyone has crossed their path or thought of tackling them. Only by delayed passes can one get the defence out of position and outnumbered. The next best feature of English is his determination to play football rather than air-ball. There is now a greater hope for combination in attack at Anfield than we have had for years.'

The pressure was slowly mounting ahead of the opening game against Wolves, and the Anfield men were expecting a tough match against arguably the most improved side in the league. A crowd of 30,000 was inside Molineux and they saw Wolves take a two-goal lead and Liverpool lose two players to injury within the first 25 minutes. Hanson took the tally of walking wounded to three.

English made his league debut and went close with a first-half header, although chances for the Reds were few and far between owing to a shortage of personnel. They were forced to completely overhaul their tactics and their game seemed to improve as a result. Wright halved the deficit by the break and there was hope for Liverpool.

And that hope was multiplied on the hour when Gordon Hodgson converted a penalty, before the returning Hanson hit the bar with a fierce drive. Liverpool were now in the ascendancy and so keen was he to make an impression on his debut that English was spoken to by the referee – quite a thing in the 1930s – for a challenge that bordered on the boisterous.

There was heartbreak for Liverpool late on, though, as Barraclough got the winner for Wolves. The Liverpool players slumped to the turf on the final whistle. Defeat was hard to take but fans could take heart from seeing their favourites show great fighting spirit. One matter of concern, though, was the manner in which 'brutish' play had been allowed to permeate the game without the perpetrators being taken to task by the referee. In all, Liverpool had lost four players to injury at one time or another. The match official allowed far too much to go unpunished, especially the continued sliding tackle, the hack, the elbow, and the dangerous play, which should all have been punished long before it was. But Liverpool had played some good football, with English, although marked closely, keeping the balance of the line and playing like all great centre-forwards play.

The following midweek, English made his home debut against Stoke City in front of 35,000. The Potteries side took the lead but English, well marshalled throughout, scored from the second of his two chances to gain the Reds a point. Roberts shot, the ball cannoned against the underside of the bar, and English stooped to head home for a most spectacular goal.

As Liverpool prepared for a home match with Sheffield United, supporters made it known that after scoring his first goal for the club, they had taken Sam to their hearts. The local paper's Friday postbag was bulging with messages of congratulations, but all goodwill – on the pitch, at least – was about to take a dip.

First of all, though, it was important for the Reds to chalk up their maiden victory, and so 35,000 filed into Anfield looking for two points and a good performance, and they got both. Jimmy Dunne was up front for the Blades, which meant each side included an Irish international centre-forward. But it was a man making his debut for United, Peter Spooner, who got the game's opening goal, on seven minutes. English's second goal for Liverpool was a snap-shot effort 13 minutes later from a through pass by Hodgson. He beat Smith quite easily, and showed what an excellent opportunist he was when given the right kind of service. Hodgson was first to congratulate his club mate, before going on to score twice and ensure Liverpool's first win of the season.

English did have the ball in the net again but was incorrectly given offside as the referee was way behind play after running into Hanson in the middle of the park. It was unfortunate for Sam.

United reduced the leeway late on through Dunne but it was a mere consolation.

There was one incident in the second half which boiled over and earned English a caution. The Irishman was shielding the ball out wide when both Hooper and Holmes came steaming in. There was a moment directly afterwards when English forgot all about the ball and took up a fighting stance against Holmes. Hooper waded in and both he and Sam received a caution from the referee.

After the game, English told his manager that Holmes had called him a murderer, in reference to the incident with Celtic goalkeeper John Thomson. At once, Mr Patterson went to the referee's room and informed him that Liverpool would be reporting it to both the Football League and the Football Association first thing Monday morning. This was the reason English had adopted a fighting attitude. Liverpool insisted that not only was the remark indelicate, but also indecent.

While the type of incident involving English and Thomson had been uncommon, it was not unique. In 1899, Dan Doyle – a future Celtic player – was playing for Grimsby Town against Derby County when he came into contact with Derby player William Cropper, who was also a well-known cricketer. Cropper was carried off and died the following day. Like the case with English, there was no intention of hurt, and the challenge was fair according to the rules of the game. The coroner's jury ruled that death was due to injury, but also the poor state of medical attention at that time. In a cruel twist of fate, Cropper had asked to be left out that afternoon, while one can only imagine the impact it had on Doyle.

When Doyle signed for Everton, he turned up at Anfield for a game against Liverpool, and was abused from the terracing in a similar manner to which English had been abused by the Sheffield United player.

Meanwhile, there was an unsavoury sequel to Liverpool's match at Stoke. It took place at Crewe railway station and had its aftermath played out in the Police Court. Two Liverpool fans had stolen blackberries from a guard's van, and after being arrested by station police, were the subject of an attempted rescue by a crowd against whom the officers were compelled to draw their truncheons in self-defence. Two men were charged with stealing 4lb of blackberries, worth two shillings, which was the property of the station. Others were charged with assaulting police officers.

A police inspector said a special train had run from Liverpool to Stoke for the football match, and was timed to leave Stoke at 8.30pm. A large number of Liverpool men, however, remained in Stoke, apparently drinking, and returned by a later train, arriving in Crewe about midnight. 'There they behaved like hooligans,' the inspector added, 'smashed a quantity of crockery, and acted the fool generally.'

Two men entered the guard's van of the train, and Constable Popper, in plain clothes, saw them take the blackberries from a basket and eat them. The men were arrested but the crowd rushed in and there was a riot. Considerable difficulty was experienced in getting them to the police office. The two men were each fined 10s and 12s 6d costs.

A trip to Birmingham to face Aston Villa was next on the agenda for Sam and his colleagues, and they found Villa Park packed out with 30,000 supporters. The pitch was in fine shape, but so too, unfortunately, were the home men and Liverpool, playing in their change strip of white, were up against it from the start. That said, Gordon Hodgson edged Liverpool in front, but just minutes after Villa levelled, English thought he had gained his side an advantage, only for Morton in the Villa goal to pull off a stunning save.

There were 15 international players on view and the action was red hot. English was in the mood and was twice denied just before half-time, first with a well-placed header, and then with a firm drive. He was linking up the middle men and forwards well and looked as though he'd been a Liverpool stalwart for many years.

Villa scored again after the break but English rallied his side with a sparkling run and shot, which skimmed the bar on its way over. But he wasn't to be denied when Taylor sent over a teasing cross and he twisted his body into an unimaginable shape to head home. In fact, such was the complexity of the header the Villa crowd also cheered. It gave Liverpool renewed optimism and again English got through, but this time found the keeper impossible to beat. Villa scored late on to win 4-2.

The following morning, George Patterson drove from Birmingham to Southampton to welcome the club's new signings, Leslie Carr and Berry Niewenhuys, two forwards from the Transvaal, who had arrived from South Africa aboard the liner, *Edinburgh Castle*. Carr said they were eager to find out all about football in England, and added, 'We know we are joining a fine club and that we have a lot to learn, but we shall be among a lot of countrymen in Liverpool and will settle in quickly.'

English had started his Liverpool tenure so well that supporters looked on keenly as the Irish team was chosen to play Scotland the first Saturday in September. Their centre-forward looked certain to be involved, if he was given leave of absence by his club. The Irish Association had departed from their old policy of making known the players they wanted before contacting their clubs to ask for their release. But selectors made no secret of the fact they wanted Sam at inside-left, to play alongside Jimmy Dunne.

Liverpool were due to play Leicester City at Anfield on the same day as the international at Celtic Park, and after much deliberation they refused Ireland's request to release Sam. It was a blow for the player.

First of all, though, there was a tricky midweek Lancs Senior Cup tie against minnows Southport to negotiate. The ingredients for a shock result were all there; a sunny day, strong wind, and an early goal for the visitors – although it was chalked off due to an unfair charge on the Liverpool keeper.

Southport were on top before English made a 'drag' pass and Hanson was able to open the scoring in style. Hodgson followed up with a second, and English and Hanson netted before the break to put the tie to bed. After the break, Liverpool scored another four, with the pick of the bunch being a magnificent fifth by English, when he stooped to head home and ended up scraping his face along the dry turf. But after some quick treatment, he was back on the pitch and smiling broadly. The player was just a month or so into his tenure at Anfield but was already proving a big hit among fans, more so because of the type of goals he was scoring. In such a short space of time, English had shown how to balance an attack, and been commended for his overall play.

Comparisons were drawn with Dixie Dean of Everton, perhaps inevitably, given the start English had made to his Liverpool career, but they were somewhat premature. While many had seen fit to decry the comparison, there were certainly elements of his play which suggested that while he couldn't carry a side on his own, he could at least help make them move in reasonable formation. He had certainly made a positive impact in a short space of time.

Perhaps proof of Sam's Merseyside fame arrived when girls began writing into the local newspaper to ask if he was married.

Back came the answer, 'Yes, and he also has a couple of bonnie bairns!'

There was a further reminder of the English/Dean connection at White Hart Lane, at the end of September, when Liverpool secured the narrowest of victories thanks to a header of the highest quality. Up until the 1930s, heading the ball hadn't exactly been in vogue, but English and Dean were thought to be two of the most excellent proponents of this growing art. The winner against Spurs was described thus, 'This goal was a thing of beauty. English swirled his read round and made a goal typical of Dean, and made me marvel that we can have two of the best headers the game has ever known, and both at centre-forward.'

And continuing the theme, a couple of days after their fine win in London, Sam English and Gordon Hodgson visited a Liverpool nursing home to check up on the injured Everton striker. At his bedside, they found Alejandro Villanueva, known as the Peruvian Dixie Dean, comparing notes with the master striker himself. Dean had four pieces of loose bone taken from his ankle – and one as big as a nut, but he was doing well.

Ironically, Liverpool and Everton were due to meet on the Saturday afternoon, although the absence of the 'original' Dixie from the visiting line-up was a blow to the Goodison Park men. Still, the game was a corker. A crowd of 54,854 were present to see English make his derby debut.

Niewenhuys gave Liverpool the lead on the half-hour, but Everton levelled before the break. English missed a sitter at the start of the second half, but Hanson regained the Reds' advantage, before Sam atoned for that earlier miss to put the game beyond the Toffees. It was a tap-in, made by Hodgson and Hanson, but a vital one. Everton scored before the end but the majority of the big crowd went home happy, and Sam had his first derby bonus – and goal.

But despite the victory, it seems not everyone was happy. One supporter had a midweek letter published in the *Echo* asking 'when the heck Liverpool would have a clock installed at their ground'. Mind you, other points were of greater significance. Fans were furious that just one turnstile had been open at the Kemlyn Road stand. If you entered via the Anfield Road one shilling access, with thoughts of transferring to the 2s or 3s 6d stands, it was virtually impossible to do so, unless you pushed your way three parts round the ground. The Liverpool directors were accused of cost-cutting in the extreme, and several fans suggested they should be reported.

Equally as worrying, was the scene at the back of the Kop after the game when many youngsters were pressed against the exterior wall until they 'shrieked with fear'. There were calls for greater crowd control measures at Anfield.

Liverpool followed up their Merseyside win over Everton by beating Chelsea at Anfield. The Londoners were minus maverick striker Hughie Gallacher, and with the crowd down almost 25,000 from the derby match, the atmosphere was missing a beat. Still, Liverpool won comfortably and English scored the final goal of three with another tap-in.

The Emergency Committee of the Football Association met to discuss Liverpool's case against Holmes, of Sheffield United, regarding a remark he had made to English. After hearing that Holmes had apologised to English for his indiscretion, they expressed their strong disapproval of the player's conduct, but declared the matter closed.

Liverpool's form had slipped, and successive 4-1 defeats in the north-east, to Sunderland and Middlesbrough, were met with derision on Merseyside. English had a couple of good chances in the first half at Ayresome Park, although one of his shots is said to have been 'so high that the ball went into the nearby workhouse grounds'.

After the break, Niewenhuys swung in a corner and English headed magnificently, though not quite to the mark. English was having a lonely battle up front but stuck to his task and was rewarded with a fine consolation goal. Unlike his late effort at Sunderland – another tap-in – this time he took a pass from Bradshaw, beat three men and smashed it home.

A 'post-mortem' concluded that Liverpool had been the better team, but lacked the middle-to-front coordination of their supposedly inferior opponents. Play in the middle of the park had been eye-catching and zippy, but too often the inside men had chosen the wrong option going forward and English, who didn't have his best game, was ultimately left frustrated. It was a sign of things to come. Early-season optimism had been slowly replaced with a sense of dread.

But all was forgiven when Blackburn Rovers visited Anfield, and the Reds belied recent form to win comfortably. English failed to register but was the epitome of combination as the goals were shared around. The two points were welcome as Liverpool were just five places off bottom spot.

The Anfield side desperately needed something from their next game, against Birmingham at St Andrew's, and they got it, despite falling behind early on. English was in the mood and hunted down every ball with vigour – and just before the half-hour he got his reward. It was his customary goal a match, but what a quaint one. He beautifully controlled a stray ball, went sailing through, tricked the defence into thinking he was offside, and even looked as though he had lost control of the ball at a crucial moment. And then the finishing touch, which he gleefully provided. Many thought his light touch was skewing past the post, but English knew and watched the ball with a smile.

After the break, he was again through on goal but fell at the vital moment, prompting those around to ask, 'Did he fall or was he pushed?' Regardless, Hodgson scored late on to ensure win bonuses all round.

After the game, Liverpool chairman Mr W.H. Cartwright was a surprise visitor to the dressing room. First of all he congratulated his players on a fine win, before adding, 'In other news – all the way from Bonnie Scotland – our esteemed fellow Sam English has just become the proud father of a beautiful daughter!' He held up a telegram which had arrived during the game, looked at Sam and saw the emotion written all over the player's face. 'Congratulations, Sam,' came the cries from his team-mates. Mr Cartwright interrupted the back-slapping to say, 'Go on lad, get yourself ready and up the road. You've a new daughter to see.' It was a nervous, but ecstatic, Sam who headed straight home to Scotland to celebrate daughter number three – baby Eleanor Margaret – with his family.

And while the new dad was spending time with his extended family in Dalmuir, the Monday morning papers in Liverpool were hailing his performance against Birmingham, with one reporting, 'City suffered like most others, a goal to English; who should be commended for his constant endeavour and energy, unending, in trying to go through on his own. The centre's task is a difficult one these days. English might not have been in his best shooting form but he never gave up the ghost, preferring, instead, to continue to toil in the hope that it would create a breakthrough.'

The second Saturday in November saw Leeds United visit Anfield. It was a beautiful day, and as the teams lined up the band struck up the national anthem. Spectators respectfully removed all headwear and within minutes of the whistle both goals had witnessed terrific action. Niewenhuys was in electric form for the home side and his incredible pace caused Leeds all sorts of problems. Gordon Hodgson had several opportunities before English had the keeper beaten all ends up but took a coat of paint off the post. Leeds streaked into a 2-1 lead, but cometh the hour cometh the man, and English struck to level the scores. It was a well-taken goal, with a little help from Hodgson, but the strike which edged Liverpool in front was a thing of beauty. Seventy-seven minutes were on the clock when English outpaced Milburn, and when the keeper came out to block, Sam timed his shot to perfection and the accuracy was precise. The match finished 4-3 in favour of Liverpool, and fans had received their money's worth.

It was generally believed that the performance of English in the second half was the best individual show from a Liverpool player in a long time. The Reds roared up the table to joint fifth alongside Portsmouth, with leaders Tottenham five points in front.

However, Liverpool's run of three straight wins – with ten goals scored – came to an abrupt end at the Baseball Ground as Derby beat them 3-1. English headed a fine goal but despite some incessant Liverpool pressure, they simply couldn't add to their tally. It was a step backwards.

West Bromwich Albion proved stubborn visitors to Anfield seven days later, and it required a fine goal by English to secure a point for the home side. But then with time running out, English sprinted clear of the West Brom defence and was hacked down just inside the penalty area. To a man the Kop roared at the referee for a penalty. Mr Crew refused, and for a moment a degree of crowd disorder seemed likely, so the referee ran across the field and asked for two policemen to patrol the Kop for the remainder of the match. It was an unfortunate scene, but the late foul on English was simply the latest in a long line on the Irishman. He was rapidly becoming the most fouled player in the English top flight.

Next up was a trip to the bright lights of London, and the theatre that was Highbury. Had Arsenal boss Herbert Chapman managed to usurp Rangers for the transfer of Sam from Yoker then the talented centre-forward might have been lining up against

Liverpool, not for them. Sam might also have been known purely for his goals rather than the most unfortunate of football accidents.

Before the match, Mr Cartwright took advantage of being in the capital to hold talks with Sir Frederick Wall, of the Football Association, with a view to bringing the touring Austrian national side to Anfield for a grand challenge match. The FA rubber-stamped the proposal and the Liverpool public rubbed their hands in anticipation.

It was a stormy game at Highbury, and once English had headed home to draw the sides level, Arsenal grabbed the winner. It was undeserved as Liverpool had played some great football. Just before half-time, Arsenal were awarded a free kick in a dangerous area. English was furious at the award and told the referee so. Backchat to the match official was virtually unheard of in those days and Sam was given a lecture so stern that he stood with head bowed.

Late in the game, English looked to have rescued a point but Hapgood pulled off an astonishing save from a shot which looked a goal all the way. So good was the save that fans of both clubs cheered. And it wouldn't have been the first time that afternoon that a home supporter had shouted, 'Watch that English feller!'

There is no doubt English was enjoying a purple patch in front of goal and had scored in ten of Liverpool's previous 11 league games. He had also scored on every English ground he had visited, bar Wolverhampton. That season, English had scored more goals than Dixie Dean and was undoubtedly the hottest property on Merseyside. Of course, Dean had been laid up for a while, and would score an incredible 379 goals in 438 games, but in later years, Rangers legend Bob McPhail would say, 'Dixie Dean was a great striker, but I rate Sam English as the best I ever played with.'

We had just entered December and already English had 15 league goals. Sam was also being tipped by many to smash Gordon

Hodgson's Liverpool record of 35 league goals in a single season. He was already looking great value for the £8,000 fee, and was playing with a real air of confidence.

But as with most other things involving Sam English, life was never straightforward or simple.

Saturday, 9 December began the goal drought, certainly in the league. It was also the beginning of the end for Liverpool's slim title hopes. Hard to believe, but fourth from the top entering December, the Anfield side would end the campaign in a dogfight to avoid relegation following an incredible 15-match winless run – which included a 9-2 loss at Newcastle.

It all started with the visit of Sheffield Wednesday, and an icy wind which 'helped' the visitors take the lead. English then equalised, but the goal was controversially ruled offside. Just before the break, English again thought he'd levelled, but the ball hit a rut in the turf, bounced up, hit the goalkeeper's outstretched leg and snaked wide of the post. Brown, the visiting keeper, then pulled off an astonishing stop from the same player. Liverpool had another goal ruled out for an infringement, and when the final whistle sounded, Wednesday were 3-1 winners. Still, Kopites trooped out of Anfield content that their favourites had given everything, and assured that no visiting team could ever again enjoy so many lucky breaks.

Despite Liverpool grinding out some very positive results – and playing some excellent football at times – there was also a train of thought that the system deployed by the manager wasn't bearing fruit. It was felt their variation, or exaggeration, of the 'W' formation was bound to sooner or later isolate English up front, and render him ineffective as he was being man-marked by two centre-backs. Many also felt the two inside-forwards lay far too deep. While English was adept in the air, the majority of goals came courtesy of either foot. His obvious strengths lay on the ground, yet most crosses delivered into the box were far too high for a man of no more than 5ft 8in. It was a source of frustration for many that the team didn't seem to be playing to its obvious strengths, but up until the Sheffield Wednesday game, results had been positive so there had been no real case for the management to answer.

And then the Austrians arrived at Anfield a week or so before Christmas, and brought a few inches of snow with them. They also brought a piece of attire alien to Anfield – black woollen gloves!

Snow had been falling all day and by teatime the game was in some doubt. It took a massive effort by volunteers to clear the pitch before the referee would pass it playable, and when the Austrians emerged from the tunnel, silence instead of cheers greeted their arrival. For the Anfield crowd had never before seen football players wearing gloves during a match. Yet here were the Austrians, to a man sporting this rather natty line in hand wear!

Once 20,000 Liverpudlians had recovered from the shock, they settled down to enjoy two completely different halves of football. In the first period, Liverpool were sensational. They simply blew their visitors away with a tantalising display of football, and scored four times.

Football players in the 1930s tended to be on the slight side, apart from Liverpool's 'Tiny' Bradshaw, of course, but the guy marking English was quite a brute. Weighing in at some 97kg, he was a wall of solid muscle, but Sam wasn't put off by his size.

The first half was a whirlwind for fans – with Liverpool leading 4-1 – and momentous for Sam as he notched his first hat-trick in English football. He scored with his head and either foot before the break: in fact, he scored all three goals in 20 minutes.

It was a fine night's entertainment for the crowd and merely served to enhance English's growing reputation south of the border, especially after the game when the Austrian manager, and one or two of his players, insisted Sam was the best 'English' centre-forward they had ever seen.

The match finished 4-2 in Liverpool's favour, but near the end, one of the Austrians, Kait, was knocked out when he stopped a shot with his head. Several Liverpool players had a remedy, though. They rubbed snow on his face and the player recovered instantly!

After the game, the Lord Mayor of Liverpool hosted a banquet for the players and officials of both sides and Sam was much in demand. The Austrian manager spoke of how the English had introduced football to Vienna in 1900, and of how the city had also used the British idea of electric trams and running water. While the elements may have been against the Austrians, they had proved a popular attraction and made many friends with their football craft.

Next up for Liverpool was Manchester City away, although when the players arrived at Maine Road they were told the match was in danger due to a thick pall of fog covering the playing surface. It had cleared by the time Liverpool had named four South Africans in their starting line-up for the first time. It was said that English was Liverpool's main hope, because he 'usually gets a goal a game', but despite having a couple of decent chances he was off colour and Pool lost 2-1.

That said, the issue of playing the inside-forwards well adrift of the attacking region had once again reared its head. The reason behind the lateral deployment of the pair was to counter-effect their opposite numbers, but all the 'tactic' succeeded in achieving was to leave English up top on his own, and it was surely no coincidence that the downturn in results arrived around this time. It seemed a strange philosophy to adapt given Liverpool's lofty league position in the first half of the season, and their obvious qualities going forward. No one was suggesting the entire team and system had suddenly become poor, but English's isolation seemed to be taking an edge off the team. But despite the frustration Sam must have been feeling, he still found the time to give a resting shoulder to the injured Manchester City goalkeeper, Langford, a gesture which did not go unnoticed by the City support.

With Christmas on the horizon, Liverpool were facing a double header with Newcastle United, and knew that positive results were required to give supporters a lift. Newcastle were also struggling in the bottom half of the table and required a boost of their own, but Anfield patrons would be disappointed following a narrow home loss; a match that could easily have gone Liverpool's way had Sam remembered his shooting boots. He provided the opening goal for Niewenhuys, working his way out to the left wing before sending in a beauty of a cross to the far post, which the South African headed home.

Minutes later, Sam had the opportunity to double the lead when he was sent clean through on goal, but shot straight at the Newcastle keeper, before squandering the rebound. Newcastle equalised before the break and found a winner ten minutes into the second half, straight after Hodgson was carried off injured. It wasn't Liverpool's day.

English had picked up a knock and missed out on the next fixture, at home to Wolves, who were kicking around the top ten. Bush took over from Sam at centre, but the best the home men could muster was a draw, which left them fifth from bottom.

Indeed, it would be an unhappy New Year for followers of the Anfield club, and even more so for those who made the cross-country journey to St James' Park for the return fixture. With an hour on the clock it was 2-2 and the visitors could consider themselves unfortunate not to have been in front. And then the roof collapsed. The Reds lost seven goals in the last half hour, with goalkeeper Elisha Scott still managing to keep the score down. Sam was absent, but present, and it must have made for

X-rated viewing. The fall-out from the match on Merseyside was venomous.

Liverpool were at Bramall Lane on the first Saturday of 1934, and the players wore black armbands as a mark of respect for Arsenal's famous manager, Herbert Chapman, who had sadly passed away from pneumonia earlier that morning. Once more, English was forced to watch from the stand as David Wright deputised. Liverpool were also missing Hodgson and did well to leave with a draw.

Ahead of their FA Cup tie against Fulham, the manager took his players to the pantomime at the Empire Theatre, starring Liverpool fan Jack Edge. It was hoped it would give a boost to a squad down to the bare bones following an exceptionally unlucky run of injuries, but one reporter reckoned the rot had set in long before the injury epidemic, in a match against West Brom. He explained, 'English was subdued by a centre-half nearly twice his size, yet his changing places with Hodgson was vetoed. English rarely got a good ground pass.

'Liverpool refused to score more than three goals against Chelsea but let other clubs rattle nine into our net, but we will not take revenge – hence our weak goal average.' The mood was changing.

English and Hodgson were back in place for the cup tie against Fulham at Anfield, and it was a perfect day for the match, but a murmur went round the field when the home fans saw the height and weight of the Fulham side. They were a hefty lot, but soon showed this wasn't their only asset.

Hodgson scored a cracker for Liverpool and then Sam should have had a penalty when he was barged in the back by Gibbons, just as he was about to shoot.

It was all square at the break, and the 51st minute produced one of the biggest thrills of the game. Had it not been for a super save by Toothill, Liverpool would surely have taken the lead, and the work which led up to English's shot was of such good quality that it was worth a goal. There was superb movement between English and Hodgson, the ball passing from one to the other three times before English struck the ball so hard and true that a goal seemed inevitable. Toothill saved superbly, but then an almighty tussle involving eight players ended with English being carried off injured. The match finished one apiece, with Hodgson and English doubtful for the replay in London.

As the Mersey Tunnel neared completion, it was hoped that the King and Queen would be present at the grand opening to celebrate such a true feat of engineering. Before that, though, Liverpool had a replay just a few miles along the Thames from Buckingham Palace. The players travelled down to London by train and were two goals down inside eight minutes. There was no Sam, but Hanson and 'Tiny' Bradshaw were on hand to equalise, and Roberts scored an extra-time winner to set up a Merseyside cup derby against Tranmere Rovers at Prenton Park.

At the beginning of FA Cup week, the Liverpool players travelled to Harrogate for some rest after the exertions of their win over Fulham, but one commentator wrote: 'The club is in league distress, and this is of more importance than the possibility of cup success. If either Hodgson or English, or both, could come back to give the attack some bodily strength there might be a change of fortune. But Liverpool have not won a league game for so long their position is now perilous.'

Hodgson had a leg injury and was rated 50/50 to play against Tranmere, but the position with English was entirely different. He had been advised to stay at home under doctor's orders. He wasn't suffering from any break or displacement, but club officials reckoned he had taken so much physical abuse during the first half of the season that he desperately required rest. Given the club's predicament, it must have been serious as no board would have given the green light for their star signing to rest during a time of crisis.

A couple of days before the big match, English joined the squad in Harrogate, as a tool to aid his recovery. The cup tie represented Liverpool's best hope of saving a disastrous season, but following the statement put out by Liverpool about English's condition, no one in the ground expected him to play against Tranmere. But when the teams were announced over the public address system, the majority of the 61,036 packed into Anfield – with a few thousand more paying their entrance fee but seeing none of the action – gasped as his name was read out. The attendance was a new Anfield record but the inevitable swaying of the crowd brought numerous casualties of crushing at the angle of the Kemlyn Road and Kop stands, and police quickly ushered fans down to the pitch to form in orderly fashion around the touchline.

Within a minute of kick-off, Liverpool almost scored – and English was carried from the field. Morrison began the move, which also involved Hanson and Sam, and when the latter swivelled to make a pass to Hodgson – who almost scored – he hit the ground with a thud and was helped off. It looked like his afternoon was over, but no sooner had he disappeared up the tunnel than he was back on the touchline receiving words of instruction from his trainer! And just moments after returning to the field, he and Hodgson homed in on the Tranmere goalkeeper, Gray, the Welsh international. The ball seemed to hang in the air for an eternity before being caught, and promptly dropped, and both players bundled the ball over the line at the same moment.

But who got the vital touch? As they ran off celebrating in unison, a tete-a-tete emerged as to who had scored. Hodgson was keen to take the credit, although it was English who had knocked the ball home. That was all forgotten a few minutes later when the visitors equalised, and then Niewenhuys shot through Gray's legs to restore Liverpool's advantage.

The second half began with an incredible solo run by English which deserved a goal, but brought only a close thing. Moments later, English was again in the wars. He was running at full pelt to reach a through pass, which he did, but his momentum carried him on past the goal and straight into the crowd. Supporters helped Sam back on to the park and the game was soon under way again.

It was a cracking cup tie and the final outcome was still in doubt until five minutes from the end when Hodgson's cross-cum-shot landed at the feet of English, who barged home his second of the afternoon. Game over. At full time, both sets of supporters showed their appreciation as the players left the field, tired but satisfied.

One welcome spin-off from the cup tie came in Liverpool's next league game, against Spurs. It was a dry, foggy day and supporters caught sight of a Liverpool win – for the first time in 14 league outings. English had plenty of the ball early on but the Spurs defenders were on top of their game, and the Londoners led by a solitary goal at the break. English almost equalised at the start of the second half when Niewenhuys centred and it smacked Sam square on the face, and flew inches wide of the goal. But just moments later Liverpool were level. English was sent crashing inside the box and Hodgson scored from 12 yards. The Spurs players argued that English had gone down through weight and not by foul means, but to no avail.

In their next attack, Pool had two players knocked out – English and Hodgson – and both had to receive treatment. In fact, English was probably still dazed moments after play resumed and he was presented with a chance in front of goal. Niewenhuys passed back to him and his shot struck the crossbar when he was expected to score. However, Sam moved out to the left wing and a super run and cross set up Niewenhuys to fire home the clinching third goal. It was a welcome victory.

On the Monday morning, a supporter penned the following letter to the *Liverpool Echo*: 'Since 1925 Liverpool have found themselves wandering around at the bottom of the table. What is the cause of this? I will tell you: Injuries and bad positional play. The real trouble is in attack. We possess a genius centre-forward in English, but he doesn't get support. If all five forwards were to work together, keeping the ball on the ground instead of in the air, Liverpool would get somewhere and English would score in every match.'

However, on the same page, another reader, 'Curious Bootle', moaned, 'I do wish our clubs would not go to Glasgow Rangers for players!'

And to complete the set, a journalist suggested, 'At times Liverpool play as if they are total strangers and one wonders if they receive any coaching on play according to their own individual ideas. It is ridiculous to talk about signing new players when it is common knowledge they haven't any money, therefore they must make the best of the players they have. It appears to me that what's required is management. The directors are playing men in unsuitable positions.'

Next up was the Merseyside derby, and with Dixie Dean still absent, the Reds had a great chance of victory. Sam was in his usual place, and opposed by his former Rangers team-mate Alex Stevenson, making his Goodison Park debut. The Lord and Lady Mayor of Liverpool led out the teams and there was a moment of real sportsmanship at the start when English and Stevenson warmly shook hands.

But a few seconds after the first whistle there was little sportsmanship in sight when English was hacked to the ground by

Everton's Cook, a former Port Glasgow team-mate from Coleraine. The crude foul set the tone for a rough encounter, although that didn't deter English from making a nuisance of himself to the Everton defence. He didn't give them a moment's peace, and had a couple of decent chances to break the deadlock.

Midway through the second half, English had the ball in the net, but it was disallowed for offside. It gave the Reds renewed optimism and they pushed forward at every opportunity.

There was a curious incident near the end of the match when Niewenhuys sprinted to prevent a long ball from going out of play. He eventually won a corner, and when the ball was played into the box, English was on to it in a flash, but he stopped, hesitated, and pulled back as there was a chance that he might have injured the Everton keeper had he followed through. It was a great opportunity to score, but he put the welfare of the Everton man before the needs of his team.

Once again, 'where to play English' was stirring in the newspapers. One correspondent wrote, 'Make English inside-left, where his dribbling and manoeuvring will be of more benefit to the side, and move Barton to centre.'

Next up was the FA Cup fifth-round tie against Bolton Wanderers, and one journalist wrote, 'If Bolton leave the middle open, as is their wont, then English will return to his best form – providing he gets a centre from left or right, or a through pass. Centres cannot play without the ball. English has had a poor spell but it's hard to blame him. I blame the style of the other members of the line.'

When the teams walked out on to the hallowed Anfield turf, to the rousing 'March of the Gladiators', 54,000 fans were exercising their vocal chords, and the gladiators were ready for battle.

The cup tie, while not a formality, was seen as Liverpool's to lose, and the way they set about Bolton at the start seemed to suggest exactly that. Hodgson and English were causing havoc and had the South African been on top form, the tie could have been won in the opening minutes. English then made a defence-splitting pass to Taylor, but the latter slipped when through on goal.

When Bolton took the lead midway through the first half it was against the run of play. And if that wasn't bad enough, disaster struck when English picked up the ball midway inside the opposition half and drove forward. He tried to play the ball back to Bradshaw, but it was loose and picked up by an opponent. Seconds later, the visitors were two up and English slumped to the ground with his head in his hands. There was no way back.

Liverpool turned their attention back to the league – and their fight for survival. There were a dozen games remaining and the Anfield men were third from bottom.

Meanwhile, the war of words was heating up in the press. After one wag suggested, 'Liverpool shouldn't buy any more Scottish failures', even though English was Irish, 'Blue Red' hit back, saying, 'English is still top scorer of both local teams, and no centre could do better with the support – or lack of it – he has been receiving.'

Opinion was split. More than half were in the Sam camp, while the others were less convinced.

One journalist reckoned, 'Anfield was the graveyard of the centre-forward,' although he suggested that a remedy was easy – to play as a team and not as a group of individuals. A theme was emerging.

Another reader had the answer, 'When the team lose at home, they should have £2 deducted from their wages. Why send them to Harrogate? Why not Hell's Gate?'

A 1-1 draw with high-flying Sunderland, at Anfield, left the Reds perilously close to the foot of the table, with just Sheffield

United and Chelsea keeping them off the bottom. During the match, English was knocked out from a goal kick taken by his own goalkeeper, but was able to resume after treatment.

There was a real frustration among the support that the team continued to lump high balls into the box at every opportunity. They realised that at 5ft 8in Sam had virtually no chance of winning them against central defenders of six foot plus – despite possessing a tremendous leap.

Meanwhile, there was talk of another Rangers player joining up at Anfield, although this one came with 'baggage'. Dr Jamie Marshall had set his sights on a new career south of the border and was also looking for a medical practice. The Anfield club spoke to the player, and Rangers, and made initial arrangements for the purchase of a suitable location for a surgery, such was their keenness to land the good doctor. Marshall deferred his decision, but would eventually choose Arsenal.

The first Saturday in March was judgement day. Mid-table Middlesbrough were in town, and it was a must-win game for Liverpool. And boy, how they responded. The Reds were fantastic and at the end of a tremendous 90 minutes had slammed six past their shell-shocked visitors.

The score was 2-2 at the break, but a couple of well-taken efforts from English put Liverpool on easy street and despite picking up a late knock, and moving out to the wing, he was the star man as the home side got back on track.

Sam's return to form had coincided with his wife, Sarah, and the girls, who were still living in Scotland, coming down to Liverpool for an extended visit. It was great to see Sam again playing with a smile on his face.

Following a terrific result against Middlesbrough, Liverpool journeyed to the coastal resort of Cleveleys to prepare for their next match, at Blackburn Rovers. When they got to Ewood Park, the weather was pleasant but the ground heavy, and within 20 minutes both English and Niewenhuys had been carried off after taking heavy knocks. English limped back on, and had a good chance to score, but while in the act of shooting his leg gave way and he was again forced to leave the field.

It was goalless at the break, and with only a couple of minutes of the second half played, English re-emerged to great cheers from the travelling Reds – and within 30 seconds had beautifully set up the opener for Hodgson. However, with seven Liverpool players carrying knocks, Blackburn ran out 3-1 winners.

A couple of days after this latest defeat, Sam was sent for a scan on his damaged ankle, and while the result was that no bones were broken, the X-ray revealed a joint so badly damaged that the only remedy for the Irish international was rest. He had been kicked from pillar to post in England and the physical abuse had finally taken its toll.

As Liverpool battled to beat the drop, stories started to emerge of dressing-room disharmony. It was claimed a boot had been thrown by one player at a team-mate after a recent defeat. There was also unrest on the terraces – the Kop, especially – and an appeal was made through the pages of the *Liverpool Echo* for the bad language to be toned down.

Describing the forthcoming match against Birmingham as 'the most important match on Merseyside since the beginning of time' was perhaps something of an exaggeration, but nevertheless it was vital for Liverpool as their top league status was at risk. Birmingham were a good side but were blown away by a four-goal salvo from Hodgson. Two points were heaven sent. English missed the game, and also matches against Leeds United, in which the Reds lost 5-1, Arsenal and West Brom. At the very time when Liverpool needed all hands on deck, the centre-forward was sidelined.

Nearing the end of April, Liverpool travelled to Hillsborough – still minus their Irish international – and put up a great fight, eventually winning by the odd goal in three. The points went a long way to ensuring Sam would be playing top-flight football on his return to the team.

On the last Saturday of the month, the great amateur side, Corinthians, visited Anfield for a friendly and English was fit enough to play. He was back in his usual position and had a couple of decent chances as Liverpool ended the half 2-0 up. On the day Manchester City beat Portsmouth to win the FA Cup, English set up a third for the Reds moments into the second period and scored a magnificent goal himself to end the scoring at six late in the game. It had been a triumphant return for the Irishman who, apart from the goal, had led the line superbly.

And to add a touch of gloss on a tremendous day for Reds fans, Stoke beat Newcastle United 2-1 to confirm that Liverpool would not be relegated. There was a collective sigh of relief on Merseyside.

In his first 25 competitive games for Liverpool, Sam had scored 18 goals. In more than 120 years, only three players – Fred Pagnan (22 goals in 1914), Ronald Orr (19 in 1908] and Daniel Sturridge (19 in 2013) – managed more English top flight goals in their first 25 games, which puts Sam's achievement into some sort of perspective.

Thirteen

AFTER A season in which Liverpool had gone from riches to rags in a few short months, Sam English was ready for a holiday. He had also picked up the unenviable tag of the most fouled player in the English top flight. His bones had taken a battering and there was no better close-season remedy than the clean air and inviting Irish Sea off the coast of Girvan. It was baby Eleanor's first visit to the Ayrshire resort, but she was well loved and looked after by her big sisters and mum and dad. Sam was delighted to get away from the rigours of professional football – even for a week or so. He had scored his fair share of goals in his debut campaign, but had been just as shocked as everyone else at the team's alarming form slump.

There's no doubt that Sam had been a little out of sorts in the closing weeks of the campaign, but his injuries had stacked up and had taken a terrible toll on his body. There were also times when he looked short on confidence, but there was no way he could have prepared himself for the furore which accompanied his arrival back on Merseyside ahead of pre-season training.

Most of the close-season chat had centred on one position – the centre-forward berth. Despite Sam being Liverpool's joint-record signing, apparently his place in the starting 11 wasn't guaranteed. Truth is, there were few who deserved a regular jersey after being part of the season from hell.

One player who was tipped to start the campaign leading the line was Gordon Hodgson. He was ready to begin his tenth season at Anfield, and after a tentative first campaign in Liverpool colours, he had averaged more than 25 goals a season for the next decade. The dependable and consistent forward had played international football for both England and his native South Africa.

While at Liverpool, he also held down a successful second career as an extremely gifted, right-arm fast bowler who once took all ten wickets in a match. He played 56 times for Lancashire, once taking 6-77 against Middlesex at Lord's, and was twice a County Championship winner.

When English joined Liverpool, Hodgson was moved to outside-right to accommodate the Irishman, but had still managed 25 goals. Sam's barren run towards the end of the campaign would lead to manager George Patterson dropping him and restoring Hodgson to centre.

But what to do with Sam was the dilemma facing Patterson ahead of the new season. The manager had two options – he could switch Sam to one of the inside positions, or he could drop him into the reserves. The second option was obviously far more radical than the first, but both were up for review, which was, quite frankly, ridiculous, given English had scored 20 competitive goals in a season in which he had been fouled consistently. Patterson himself had been criticised for tactics which had often isolated English, so to even suggest demotion as a possibility was poor.

Meanwhile, season tickets were put on sale, and for a little over £2.50 supporters could have a seat in the New Stand (centre portion).

The Upton Horticultural Show had a special attraction in the summer of 1934 – a game of cricket between the footballers of Liverpool and Everton, and the event attracted a fantastic crowd. It was also a novel attraction for the players and, with Hodgson in their ranks there was only ever going to be one winner, but in the end it was fine margins and just five runs separated the teams. Sam decided, rather wisely, that it would be far safer to watch from the sidelines as his cricket experience was extremely limited.

When the football restarted, on Saturday, 11 August, Anfield hosted the club's prospective first and second teams. Liverpool's Central League team was important to the club as good individual and team performances kept those in possession of first-team jerseys on their toes. But when the respective teams were announced for the Anfield trial, Patterson's selections raised a few eyebrows, more so because Sam was named in the 'Whites' – the Central League 11. As had been predicted, Hodgson was centre-forward for the 'Reds'. While the bulk of the pre-match press coverage centred on the first-team players, one correspondent urged supporters 'not to forget Sam English, especially his goals-per-game ratio of the previous season, nor his "picture goal" against Rapid'.

The trial match was a big success, and 11,000 attended, contributing more than £270 to charity. And they were treated to a fine match consisting of 11 goals and a 7-4 win for the Reds. Apart from the Kop being heavily criticised for their barracking of a young goalkeeper, the highlight of the afternoon was an effort from English, which was described as 'the prettiest goal of the 11'. The report added, 'Sam has lost his injuries and found his confidence. He held the ball neatly and securely, and scored the best of the lot when he lofted the ball over Riley's body. English on such form could hardly be left out of the senior side.'

But for the second trial, English again lined up for the stiffs, and once again the theme of the evening appeared to be Hodgson v English. Both were on target, and while the former netted a hat-trick, the match report stated, 'The support of the crowd for the very popular Sam English was a big feature of the game.'

Off the field, the local council had the answer to one of the country's fastest-growing problems – the scourge of the motor car. Usage was up, which was causing major headaches for the immediate areas around Anfield and Goodison Park. Stanley Park split the grounds so the forward-thinking council built a car park right in the middle, with paths leading to both stadiums. A parking charge of sixpence was the price motorists would have to pay, and those living in the vicinity of both grounds would get a little more peace and quiet.

On the eve of the opening league game of the season, against Blackburn Rovers at Anfield, there was something of a backlash in the letters pages of the press regarding English's omission from the starting 11. Instead, he played at Blackburn in the corresponding Central League reserve fixture, and scored the only goal of the afternoon in front of 5,000 spectators.

Once again, the football correspondent of the *Liverpool Echo* was championing Sam for a first-team recall. He said, 'Sam played inside-right for Rangers on many occasions – very successfully, too – but his true position is centre-forward. Sam is the fastest centre-forward in England and, given the right support from his inside-forwards, would be the finest centre-forward in Great Britain. The man who broke the Scottish goal-scoring record in his first season as a Senior is worthy of his place. The one-time idol of Ibrox Park should be given the opportunity to become the idol of Anfield.'

Liverpool beat Blackburn 2-0, with a double from inside-right Vic Wright.

A couple of days later, they were due at Maine Road to face Manchester City, and there was a shock recall for Sam. On the eve of the game, one correspondent said, 'Tom Johnson is a doubt, and Sam English may be brought into the attack – a popular choice, as in this city I find English has made an enormous ring of friends even as far as Goodison Park!' Sam filled the inside-right position and linked up well with Hodgson, although a 3-1 loss was a disappointment, if not entirely unexpected.

It was Liverpool's next league game which was far from third time lucky. They travelled to Highbury, with English occupying the inside-left position, and might not have bothered turning up as the Gunners ran riot. In fact, it was just 1-0 for the home side after 40 minutes, and then the heavens opened and the home side added another seven. It was 21 years to the day that Highbury had opened, and the Londoners celebrated in style, with home legends Alex James, Ted Drake and Cliff Bastin leading the rout. There was little point in a post-mortem, and so the Liverpool party vanished from the capital immediately after the game.

Just four days before their next match, against Manchester City at home, manager Patterson had a big job on his hands to lift his players. It was time for them to earn their corn and against a team who, it was said, were playing the best football in the country.

There was a concern within the corridors of power at Anfield that the gate would be affected for the match after the team had suffered such a hiding against the Gunners. It was also a midweek match, and traditionally they weren't as well patronised as weekend fixtures. Before the match, skipper Ernie Blenkinsop had said, 'I would love to win this game.'

Well, he needn't have worried, because 32,000 supporters got behind the Reds from the first whistle. Of course, there were blips along the way, such as Gordon Hodgson missing out on creeping ever closer to his 200th Liverpool goal (his first was against Manchester City, and he now sat on 198) when he failed from the penalty spot.

The following day, a newspaper correspondent wrote, 'Fortunately, Sam English put the hallmark on the result by scoring a great goal, taken very beautifully after Hanson's first-class gliding pass. Sam, chatting with me on Saturday, said, "I'm afraid there are two bad lads – you are one and I am certainly the other." We keep smiling, and English showed sufficient form and tasty football bite to prove he is *the* centre-forward for the club.'

Players rarely went on the record in those days, so a rare insight into perhaps how 'left out' he was feeling. After being first pick for the centre-forward's jersey the season previous, he had clearly slipped down the pecking order, and he was feeling it.

The correspondent also noted that asides from a standout individual performance from City's prompting Scot, Matt Busby, the revival of Liverpool, just when they needed it, was in large part down to the performance of English, who was responsible for a big improvement in the forward line through his holding of the ball and his ability to bring the wingers into play. 'Something the team had been lacking in recent weeks,' he added. 'Yesterday they played as if they had known one another for a great number of years!' Oh, and Hodgson managed his 199th goal.

English retained his place for the next game, at home to Portsmouth, but a shock 1-0 loss meant it was back to square one for the Reds. Liverpool had started the game well, and English picked up where he left off against City by spraying some bonny passes around and linking up the forward play with great intelligence, and had one headed effort beautifully saved by Gilfillan when it looked destined for the net.

Pompey had obviously done their homework and English had a shadow the entire game, Salmond, who put in a shift and a half. Still, English found space after the break and once again his shot seemed destined to find its target, until Gilfillan clawed away the effort. And that was the cue for the visitors to run up the park and score the only goal of the game, which looked offside.

Next port of call was Goodison Park, home of arch-rivals Everton, and with 45,000 inside the ground at kick-off, the noise was off the scale as the teams took to the field. There were chances at both ends early on, and it was clear that Everton were looking to *their* former Rangers star, Alex Stevenson, to pull the strings in the middle of the park. But English was pivotal in the second period, after a goalless first 45 minutes, although he should have done much better than shoot wide when presented with a golden opportunity shortly after the restart.

Undeterred, he took up a fantastic position at the near post, and when Hanson centred, English whipped the ball past Sagar and into the back of the net. However, his joy was short-lived when the referee insisted the goal was offside, a decision which brought fury from Reds fans, who were convinced the goal was good.

There was no doubt the visitors were on top and when Taylor delivered a pinpoint corner, English met it perfectly and guided his header towards the top corner. Surely a goal, although he hadn't reckoned on the cat-like athleticism of Sagar, who leapt from his line to tip the ball over the bar. It was a world-class save.

There had been pre-match talk of the game being possibly decided by the two centre-forwards: Dixie Dean and Sam English. With time ticking away, English picked up the ball 12 yards out and looked to place it out of the keeper's reach, but Sagar's elasticity saw him again reach the ball and this time turn it round the post. In contrast, Dean had hardly been in the game – until the last minute, when he rose majestically to bullet a header past Riley. It was the only goal of the game and took Everton to the heady heights of fourth in the table. For Liverpool, though, it was a completely different story: they remained third-bottom.

Monday's *Liverpool Echo* had the following to say, 'The Liverpool side in general, and the forward line in particular, surprised everyone. Here was craft, speed and endeavour without mere rushing and dashing; here was movement. Liverpool complain the goal scored by English was not offside. Perhaps not, but the elbow bored into the back of one of the home side was definitely "offside" and was on the blind side of the referee. It was safe to say, though, that the gesture of Sagar in seeking out English after the game to offer his hand in friendship showed exactly what the Everton goalkeeper thought of Sam's first-class performance.'

Next up for Sam and Liverpool was a trip to Elland Road to face a Leeds United side just a point better off. The blustery, wet conditions belied the mood of the Reds, who started well, no doubt feeling a sense of injustice that their previous two matches had ended in single-goal defeats despite dominating both fixtures. In fact, an early, sweeping move brought Gordon Hodgson's 200th Liverpool goal, although the talented South African miskicked the ball before watching it loop over the keeper's head. Then, an incredible English solo run took him past four defenders before the keeper stuck out a leg to save his shot. Mind you, the ball fell kindly to Hanson who promptly made it 2-0. The same player finished the scoring nine minutes after the break and Liverpool had two precious points.

Hanson and Hodgson might have scored the goals but there was no doubt that once again English had been the lynchpin between middle and front. He had shown many times in the past that he knew the best way to goal, but he was certainly no one-trick pony.

Liverpool's next league match, at home to West Brom, was a bitter-sweet affair. The game opened with the playing of 'Abide with Me', as a mark of respect for the victims of the Gresford Colliery disaster, when an explosion and underground fire killed

266 men. It had been a busy night shift, with many miners 'doubling up' so they would be free to watch Wrexham play Tranmere Rovers the following afternoon. As the Christian hymn rang out around Anfield, the crowd of 20,000 stood bareheaded and the players lined up alongside one another.

Liverpool opened the scoring when English uncharacteristically missed the ball completely in front of goal, but he was saved by quick-thinking Hanson who fired home. English atoned for his error when he gratefully accepted a pass from Hodgson and steered the ball past Pearson in the West Brom goal. Liverpool scored a third soon after, with a high-tempo move. Wright sent Taylor away with a raking pass. Taylor played over a perfect cross and there was English to control the ball and back-heel it to Hodgson in a single movement and the South African shot home. The visitors pulled back a couple of goals but Liverpool took the points. There was a collection at the game for the Gresford Fund, with fans of both sides contributing £155 10s.

Supporters who turned up at Anfield for the match against Birmingham City were treated to a nine-goal thriller. In the first half, Wright and McDougall scored for the home side before Booton reduced the deficit from the penalty spot, an award which led to the referee calling a policeman to help restore order in the Oakfield Road end. English soon restored the hosts' two-goal advantage with a fine header before Hodgson scored either side of half-time to hand Pool an unassailable 5-1 lead. But they hadn't reckoned on Mangnall registering a six-minute hat-trick, and the final minutes of the match were spent with Liverpool hanging on for dear life.

In their next two matches, the Reds drew against Grimsby Town and Preston North End. In the second of these, English picked up a nasty leg injury and missed the next game, against Wolves at Anfield. Hs replacement, Vic Wright, who had been moved from an inside berth, was on target, and the victory helped propel the Reds up to mid-table. The experiment of moving Wright to the centre was hailed a success, and the former Rotherham man retained the jersey for the trip to Leeds Road, Huddersfield, to play the league's bottom side. However, the game was a disaster, with the hosts scoring four in each half to register Liverpool's second eight-goal defeat of the campaign.

There was a backlash in the media after the embarrassing reverse and some fans were calling for radical changes to the team. One correspondent, called 'Some Reds who are Blue', said, 'Liverpool's faults this season have mainly been in the defence. It needs to be fixed, and then the selectors can rectify their biggest blunder, by putting English back in the team. Also, our inside-forwards require lessons on the art of giving the ball to the centre-forward, so that he can make some use of it. At present they seem to pass the ball to "the invisible man" who, apparently, stands about 20 yards away from the centre-forward and who is about 20 feet tall. The only snag is he doesn't score goals!' Within the sarcasm there was truth.

Sadly the selectors weren't interested in reinstating English to the first team. Sam's leg injury had kept him out of action for a single week. In that time, Wright had been 'elevated' to centre-forward and the selectors seemed happy enough with his contribution. Quite what they learned in the 8-0 defeat to Huddersfield is anyone's guess but English was out of the picture and it was something he would have to get used to. He spent the month of November playing Central League football, but was praised for a headed winning goal against Aston Villa at Anfield that apparently 'defied gravity'.

That said, Vic Wright went quietly about his business in the first team and by the end of the month had scored seven league goals, appearing to justify the selectors' decision.

December brought much of the same and Liverpool excelled three days before Christmas when they won 3-2 at league leaders Sunderland, after being two goals down. The win propelled the Reds up to joint fifth, although the Black Cats held on to their mantle as top dogs under pressure from Arsenal.

The one downside was an injury to top scorer Gordon Hodgson, but one man's loss is another's gain, and English was recalled for the 29 December clash at Blackburn Rovers. He had been scoring for fun in the Central League, to such an extent that the Reds' second string were being touted as possible champions. Now he was keen to keep that record going on his reintroduction to the first team – and he didn't disappoint.

He was in the thick of things from the off, and as well as having a hand in Liverpool's opening goal – which was scored by South African ace Niewenhuys – he forced the Rovers keeper into several very good saves. Ten minutes before the break, Wright hit the byline and after beating two men centred for Sam, who fired home from around ten yards. It was a comprehensive win for the Anfield men and Sam could be proud of his contribution.

Just a few days before being returned to the first-team fold, a rumour was circulating that Sam could be set for a dramatic move back to Scotland. One journalist wrote, 'George Stevenson, the Motherwell inside-left, is one of the men under review by Liverpool. Maybe he will be included in an exchange for English, whom Motherwell have in mind.'

The correspondent continued, 'It is quite possible that Sam English, Liverpool's international leader, may return to Scotland to take up the centre-forward berth at Fir Park. The Anfielders are anxious to recuperate after the heavy expenditure on Tom Cooper of Derby County.'

Mention of the transfer raised eyebrows, especially in the steel-making town of Motherwell. Centre-forward Willie MacFadyen was playing so well, and there was the possibility that if English did move to Fir Park he might have some difficulty finding a place in the team.

The English–McClory incident of a few years previous was also still fresh in the minds: the day goalkeeper Alan was ordered off at Ibrox, therefore the sight of Sam English in a Motherwell jersey would be one of the sensations of the season.

The first Saturday in January brought the great Arsenal side to Anfield, and English retained his place in the line-up, which was a great way to start to 1935. There was also a place for Wright, as Hodgson, who was now fit, was forced to sit in the stand. The Liverpool selectors realised that English and Wright were both excellent ball players, with an ability to bring team-mates into play.

The match was played in front of 57,000 frenzied spectators – with thousands more locked outside – the majority of whom were desperate to see if their favourites could carry on their good form with victory over the star-studded Londoners. It was exactly a year since legendary Arsenal manager Herbert Chapman had passed, but the Reds were in no mood to be charitable and set about their illustrious opponents from the start. But it was Arsenal who were the more clinical and their two-goal interval lead remained intact until the end. The Liverpool manager ordered Niewenhuys and English to swap positions near the end, but the pay-off was negligible. If anything, Sam seemed more like his old self out wide, probably as a result of being able to throw off the shackles of Herby Roberts, the commanding Arsenal centre-back who'd hardly allowed the Irishman a kick while he was playing through the middle.

The day after the game, the actions of the Liverpool manager were roundly criticised in the pages of the *Echo*. One reader said, 'During the match, a Liverpool official came on to the pitch and ordered English and Niewenhuys to switch positions. Is that action allowed? Surely it is contrary to the spirit of the game. Surely the Liverpool captain, on seeing that English (like a good many centre-forwards) was being outclassed by Roberts (the best centre-half in the game today) has the power to change the forward formation without the interference of club officials. It's also the way the Arsenal operates.'

Next up for Liverpool was a trip to the West Country for an FA Cup tie against Yeovil, but after three games in succession, Sam wasn't on the south-bound train. Instead, he was at Stoke for a reserve fixture, and while the top team were winning 6-2, the Central League men were losing ignominiously by the same scoreline. It was like a dagger to English's heart.

The match against Arsenal would be the only appearance of a cold January for Sam, but he knuckled down and worked hard while playing for the second string. He scored a couple of goals as Leeds United and Liverpool racked up seven between them (the Yorkshire side edged it), and when talented young centre-forward Fred Howe was introduced to the reserves, Sam switched to outside-right to accommodate him. Instead of sulking, he offered the young man the benefit of his experience. When Liverpool reserves beat Sheffield United 3-1 at Anfield, Howe scored a hat-trick, and English had a hand in all three goals. It was a similar story when the Reds beat Oldham 3-1 and Sam made a couple for hat-trick hero Alf Hanson. Sam certainly appeared to take as much pleasure from creating goals for his team-mates as he did scoring them himself.

With his contract up at the end of the season, it looked to all intents and purposes that he would be seeing out the remainder of his time with the stiffs. But during a league match at the Hawthorns, Vic Wright pulled a leg muscle against West Brom, and then aggravated it when he was asked to play at outside-right. That meant a recall for Sam, and he was ready and willing to take the call. He started in the midweek match against Sheffield Wednesday at Anfield. It was a cracking game and but for Brown, in the Wednesday goal, English may have had a genuine contender for goal of the season, but somehow the agile keeper plucked the ball to safety and English was thwarted. Pool lost 2-1 but English had shown up well enough to retain his place in the side for the prickly visit to St Andrew's to face relegation-threatened Birmingham City a few days later, despite the directors making changes.

Liverpool were in startling form and it looked like Hodgson and English had been playing together their whole lives. Their understanding was uncanny and it came as no surprise when English opened the scoring in the 13th minute, with the help of the South African inside-right. The England goalkeeper, Hibbs, was well beaten. Hodgson also scored a couple as the Reds moved up to joint sixth in the table, level on points with their great foes, Everton. As a postscript, English was credited with keeping the wings working fluently; the oil in the Liverpool forward line, so to speak.

A third appearance in a row for Sam came when Liverpool travelled to the east coast to face Grimsby Town seven days later. And he was on target again, this time picking the pocket of a defender before beautifully lobbing the ball over the keeper. It was a thrilling contest but Grimsby snatched victory late on to deny the Anfield men a point.

The beginning of March brought Preston North End to Anfield and once again English was leading the line. Preston had enjoyed an unbeaten start to 1935, and a dogged, determined display would ensure such an impressive stat remained intact. Midway through the first half, English raced away with the ball and as he bore down on Holdcroft in the North End goal, he seemed certain to score. But just as he was about to pull the trigger,

Lowe put in a tackle and down went English. It was inside the box and all eyes turned to the referee. Penalty kick? Mr Clark decided it was a perfectly legitimate tackle and play continued. In that case, it was a wonderful challenge.

It remained goalless at the break, and with just 30 seconds on the second-half clock, Hanson crossed for English to make a perfect header; one that Dixie Dean would have been proud of. Holdcroft, the former Everton keeper, looked well beaten, but just as the ball was about to pass him, a hand shot out to turn the ball round the post. It was the highlight of the match, but the game ended goalless.

English had done all that was expected of him, bar score, but that exquisite header would be the final piece of great play he would offer up to his Anfield admirers, for Vic Wright was fit again, and despite English showing a renewed vigour for first-team football – and scoring a couple of goals – the selectors shoehorned Wright straight back into the team for the trip to Wolverhampton, which Liverpool lost 5-3.

When the team was announced for the impending midweek derby match against Everton at Anfield, Wright kept his place, which meant fans were denied one last clash of the titans: English v Dean. This prompted one correspondent to write to his local paper with the following, 'Surely our loyal supporters deserve a better class of football than we are currently getting. As for Sam English, I'm afraid he is too clever for Anfield. Perhaps had he played with better players around him he would have been more of a success. I think he would make a first-class outside-right, and would like to see the following forward line play against Everton; English, Hodgson, Wright, Johnson and Taylor. That line would beat the Everton.'

Liverpool did indeed win the Merseyside clash but Sam looked on from the Anfield stand. And when Wright suffered another injury, and young Fred Howe was promoted into the first team for a league match against Derby County, Sam knew his time was up. Pool lost the match but Howe showed up well and was certainly 'one for the future'.

The season was drawing to an ignominious close for English and as he viewed the crowning of Arsenal as champions, perhaps he looked back on his late-night meeting with Herbert Chapman with a degree of regret. And so it was with a deep sense of irony that with just two fixtures remaining, English was granted a swansong in the north of London, at White Hart Lane, just 15 minutes from Highbury.

Tottenham were already relegated, so they had little to play for bar lost pride, while Liverpool were all but guaranteed to finish in the top six. Perhaps someone forgot to tell the Spurs players it was a dead rubber, for within 20 minutes, Carr had been stretchered off and English badly fouled, thus curtailing his final competitive appearance in red. Sam was still able to provide an assist for Niewenhuys to score, but he suffered two further heavy fouls against him and was limping badly by the time the final whistle had sounded and Spurs had won 5-1.

The match report read, 'I do not mind robust football, and neither do the Liverpool players, but they were very sore about the treatment meted out to English, who was black and blue after the match. Liverpool were undoubtedly the more polished side; Spurs were not.'

Mind you, English was fit enough to take his place in the Liverpool line-up for a benefit match at St James Park, Exeter, just four days after the battle at White Hart Lane, and scored a hat-trick in Liverpool's 3-1 win. A crowd of 5,000 turned up to pay tribute to Exeter's Scottish left-back Jimmy Gray, who had enjoyed a short spell at Anfield. English's finishing was described as 'lethal'.

For the match, Liverpool named Stanley Kane, understudy to Arthur Riley, as their goalkeeper, but he had received a nasty hand injury in a friendly at Torquay a couple of days before the Exeter game, and when Liverpool asked the Football Association for permission to play a different goalkeeper in the benefit match, the FA refused, and Kane was forced to play with the damaged hand.

The curtain was brought down on Liverpool's season with a 2-2 draw at home to Sunderland, in which young Howe filled the centre-forward jersey, and the day after the match their first signing for the following season was another centre-forward.

So that was that. Another part of Sam's footballing adventure was over, and while he had enjoyed a prolific debut season in front of goal, his second was something of an anti-climax. He had become such a popular figure on Merseyside that the goodbyes would take a considerable time. When he collected his belongings from Anfield and headed home to Scotland, he was joined on the journey north by his strike partner, Gordon Hodgson, who had signed for Forfar. Not the Athletic, but the cricket variety, and the talented South African scored 80 on his debut as club professional.

Sam was looking forward to a complete break from football and a holiday in Girvan with his wife and children. He would ponder his next move while enjoying the beautiful Ayrshire coast.

For the remaining Liverpool players, they were off on a close-season tour of the Canary Islands, where they would play a couple of friendly matches and recharge the batteries for another season of hope.

Fourteen

THE ENGLISH family had enjoyed their holiday in South Ayrshire and were heading home to Dalmuir. On the journey up the road, Sam reflected on how much his life had changed in just a couple of years. From his time at Yoker Athletic, when he more or less played football for fun and a few pounds in his back pocket, to his move to Ibrox where scoring goals was his job. And then on to Anfield. In four years he had witnessed all sorts of emotions. He'd hoped his spell at Liverpool might have offered a fresh start, but the demons, both physical and mental, had followed him to Merseyside.

It looked to all intents and purposes that his time at Anfield had come to an end. He was unlikely to be asked back, and therefore had a decision to make. He was on the verge of turning 27 and should have been reaching the peak of his career. There was interest from clubs on both sides of the border, but the roll call was starkly different from his final days at Yoker, when the cream of British football actively pursued his signature. Now, the list contained more modest names.

When leaving Ibrox, England was the only plausible destination. He'd wanted to get out of Scotland and escape the spectre of September 1931, which hung over him like a dark cloud. But his time at Anfield hadn't exactly been a bed of roses, and taunts from rival players and spectators had made it pretty miserable. His initial hopes, that he might be allowed to get on with playing football, had proved disappointingly wide of the mark. Perhaps Liverpool, with its close connections to the south of Ireland, both politically and geographically, had been an unwise choice of destination. Regardless, there was plenty to think about.

Meanwhile, 70 miles south of Glasgow, George McLachlan had just been appointed manager of Queen of the South, and he wasted no time in hinting that Sam English was the man he wanted to lead the line. Few people in the game took him seriously, but the former Manchester United captain had high hopes for the Doonhamers. He was a big hitter and was keen to raise his new club's profile, and what better way to do that than with a marquee signing as his first for the club?

Meanwhile, Sam discussed his future with Sarah, and made no secret of his desire to leave Liverpool. He believed the Anfield club wouldn't stand in his way. Theoretically, as his last port of call, he was still attached to Liverpool and was due to report back to Anfield for pre-season training at the start of August. He was keen to sort out his future beforehand but realised the major stumbling block would be the transfer fee. A sum of £8,000 had changed hands between Liverpool and Rangers just two years previous and Liverpool would be keen to recoup as much of it as possible.

Sam was only back in Scotland a matter of days when George McLachlan paid him a visit. The personal touch impressed the Irishman and he agreed to sign for Queens if both they and Liverpool could come to a financial arrangement. Knowing Queens would be unable to stump up anything like the sum Liverpool had paid Rangers, he travelled down to Merseyside to speak to the Liverpool manager. He intimated his desire to return to Scotland to play his football, citing 'family reasons', and leaving the ball firmly in Liverpool's court.

Truth is, George Patterson didn't want Sam back so he wasted no time in starting negotiations with McLachlan. Liverpool listed English at £4,000 and while talks were tough, they were concluded after a couple of days and the Queens boss was delighted to get his man. In the end, Queens paid £1,600 for Sam, which was believed to be a record for the club. With two seasons at both Rangers and Liverpool on his CV, English was a good catch and it made others in the Scottish First Division sit up and take notice, especially those who hadn't taken McLachlan seriously.

Sam was back up the road, and while it was a bold speculation on the part of the Palmerston people, the player was also putting his reputation on the line by dropping down a few notches on the career ladder. It was no secret he had been unhappy for a while at Liverpool, and even before the 1934/35 season had concluded, he had spoken to Patterson of his desire to return to Scotland.

Queen of the South had been keeping tabs on developments and were, of course, keen to entice a centre-forward to Palmerston after encountering all sorts of issues with various 'number nines' the previous season. It was the club's second big transfer of the close season, coming hot on the heels of Johnny Bell rejoining the Doonhamers from Preston North End for the princely sum of £1,000. That a provincial club like Queen of the South, with a following which didn't ever exceed five or six thousand at most, should splash out to this extent was enterprise with a capital E.

Both signings instigated a rush for season tickets, which meant a re-think by directors of how they would distribute their limited number of briefs. They decided to offer them to existing season ticket holders, and that left them a surplus of 40. There were 70 bidders for the remaining season books, and that was when secretary Jimmy McKinnell's bowler hat came in useful. The

70 names went in and 40 were drawn out. It was hoped a new stand would be built for the following season to help alleviate this problem. Mind you, there would be no problem with comfort, as a group of supporters had undertaken the task of making cushions for season ticket holders, and they were sold for a tidy profit along with the tickets themselves.

Sam was delighted with the move, especially as it meant he could live at the family home in Dalmuir and travel to Dumfries specifically for matches. An arrangement with McLachlan allowed him to train nearer home, and he quickly struck up a deal with Yoker Athletic to train there Monday to Friday.

He didn't take part in the pre-season trial games but was keen to get started when the action began for real, and there were just over 11,000 – approximately double Queens' average home attendance – inside Palmerston Park when the Doonhamers hosted Hibernian on the opening day of the season.

As the players warmed up before the start of the match, it was noticeable that Sam was carrying a few extra pounds. Of course, he had only managed a week's training beforehand, but should still have been looking after himself a little better. Nothing escaped the newspaper reporters, though, and one said, rather jauntily, 'Sam will come on a ton once he gets really fit, for at the moment he is carrying some avoirdupois!'

The crowd were in their usual good spirits and prior to kick-off there was a buzz of anticipation, the likes of which is normally reserved only for opening day. But that gleeful anticipation disappeared momentarily before kick-off when half a dozen Hibs fans jumped the perimeter fence and ran on to the pitch. They made straight for English. There was genuine concern in the ground, and also on the face of the player, but the local police needn't have worried as the green-clad fans only wanted to shake hands with Sam and wish him all the best. After the game, English said, 'The incident took me completely by surprise, but when they told me they were glad to see me back in Scottish football I couldn't speak at first. I was overwhelmed. It was a lovely thing for them to do.'

As for the football itself, it was something of an anti-climax. It was by no means a classic match, with the fast and slippery surface, and strong wind, making it impossible for the finer points of the game to be displayed. English found the conditions against him, but did well. He was in direct opposition to the great Hibs centre-back, Willie Watson, and the strongly built defender got many balls intended for the new Palmerston leader, simply because of the fiery turf.

Sam, however, was involved in Queens' goal, and his great footballing brain allowed him to get to a ball ahead of Johnny Egan, and when he nicked it past his adversary it caught the hand of the Hibs player and Queens scored from the penalty spot.

The game ended one apiece and a point on his debut wasn't too bad. After the game, English was given a rousing cheer by the home supporters.

The following Saturday, Queens suffered a heavy defeat at Dunfermline's East End Park. They got the ball forward quickly on many an occasion but English wasn't anywhere near as quick off the mark as he had been in his Rangers days. In fact, he appeared laboured in his movements at times, and a contemporary match report stated, 'Sam English is not the quick, darting type of old. Occasionally he had openings which, in his Ibrox days, would have been easy.' There was no doubt Queens had the foundations of a good side, and it was hoped that once English got up to speed, defences would have many sleepless nights. He did get his name on the scoresheet with a grand header but Queens lost 4-1.

The next home game, against Partick Thistle, was played in temperatures more suited to the Caribbean than Dumfries, but that didn't prevent Queens notching their first win of the campaign. In fact, George Cummings, the Scottish international, thought he'd seen it all while playing on the national side's close-season tour of America, when the sweat was pouring off himself and his team-mates, but insisted Palmerston was far hotter.

Chances were few and far between, but midway through the second half, English had a great opportunity in front of goal but saw his shot saved at point-blank range. He was still the pick of the forward line, though, and got the only goal of the game when he headed home a Bell cross. He had repaid another little chunk of his transfer fee.

The Irish international was on target again the following Saturday, this time from the penalty spot, but no doubt he would have remembered the 3-1 defeat at Arbroath for a bizarre incident in which the home side's Johnny Duff got him in a headlock when Queens were awarded a corner, and didn't let go for what seemed like a couple of minutes – and all in front of the referee. Sam had never been one to succumb to bullying on the field but even he seemed more than a little taken aback – and subdued – after that incident.

There was no doubt that English still possessed the skills and ball control that had made him a standout at Rangers and earned the big-money move to Liverpool, but there was another issue that needed dealing with. It was the thorny subject of Sam's weight. He had put on a few pounds in the close season and struggled to shed them in time for the new campaign. Supporters loved having Sam in the team but were well aware that the extra baggage was having an adverse effect on his ability to remain competitive in Scotland's top flight.

The Queens management, who had initially been happy for their star striker to train with Yoker, suggested a change of tack. They contacted St Mirren and spoke to the Paisley club's well-known trainer, Di Allison. Mr Allison's methods were legendary, if not a little unconventional, and he agreed to take Sam under his wing and help get him fit.

One of his more curious approaches concerned Saints' reserve keeper Bill MacKay. The young man was tipped for the top, but Allison thought him a shade on the small side to be an effective keeper, so he purchased stretching equipment and would leave MacKay hanging from it for hours on end in an attempt to make him taller.

It was only the end of August but it was glaringly obvious there was something wrong with the Palmerston side. Many suggested change was required if they were to avoid another long and ultimately unsuccessful campaign, but the club refused to press the panic button.

And then the contest that we knew had to come: English's first match against Celtic since leaving Rangers. It was played at Palmerston and while Celtic won 3-1, Queens made a real game of it. The attendance of 12,000 was just 160 short of the Palmerston record and the excitement on the terraces frequently hit fever pitch.

It was real end-to-end stuff and Celtic, through superior repose and skill, deserved to win, but they had to fight every inch of the way against opponents who were inspired by the occasion. Indeed, a draw wasn't beyond them, and the visitors' third goal was scored when play had run five minutes over.

Queens' inside-forwards, Burns and McKay, played some great football, but it was clear that both had still to come to an understanding with English. Too often an attacking link was lost due to a lack of combination. The Celtic back line was solid, and English's goal – the equaliser a minute before half-time – was claimed as offside. Certainly he had a clear run in, but it was believed that Hogg, on the right, had played him on. The goal was English's first against Celtic, and with the score at 2-1 to the

Celts, he headed against the bar, and Kennaway caught his second attempt from the rebound.

A match report included the following passage, 'English was not quite the Sam I knew at Ibrox. Football across the border does not seem to have given his play more lustre. He led with class, but not with the old skill and understanding. At times he struggled to shake off his shadow, Willie Lyon, as the Celts paid him the ultimate compliment of allocating him a minder.

'Two minutes from half-time English found himself with the ball and only the keeper to beat. Sam hesitated. He thought he was offside, with the Celts vociferously protesting. But the referee heeded not the protesters, and Sam raced on to score.'

Next up was a match against Hearts, and it's generally accepted that English played his best game since arriving at Palmerston. It was a thriller from start to finish and although Hearts played cleverly, they were beaten by a very determined Queens, despite the loss of an early goal. They were soon on the front foot and only a miraculous save by Harkness prevented English heading an equaliser. After the break, Harkness pulled off fine saves from English and Cummings, but was powerless to prevent the Doonhamers scoring twice. English might have failed to get on the scoresheet, but he led the line superbly.

However, he did grab a goal seven days later in a 2-1 home win over Ayr, although once again it was suggested he was labouring in front of goal and in desperate need of greater fitness.

When Motherwell visited Dumfries at the beginning of October, they were, while perhaps not in their prime, still a very good side. Once again English was heckled for being overweight, but he silenced the critics with his seventh league goal of the season on the stroke of half-time, which earned the Blues a good point.

Moving into November, Queens were starting to slip worryingly into the relegation zone, and it was hoped the visit of Hamilton Accies would see them arrest the slide. Sadly, they suffered another home defeat, and once again the critics in the press knew exactly who to blame. One report read, 'Queen of the South's forwards let them down in this game. They had a real bad day and could do little right. English is only a shadow of his former self, being slow in movement and clumsy in his footwork, but it must be said he did not receive a great deal of support from his inside men. They were posted missing. McKay scored for Queens and English missed a great chance to draw level.'

Queens fans who travelled to Pittodrie a week later would have been entertained by seven goals, four penalties and end-to-end football, but ultimately the marathon return journey to Dumfries would be one of great disappointment.

English played a pivotal role in the game, winning an early penalty after being fouled, and setting up Cummings with a beautiful back-heel. It was a cracking game, but with time running out, and the Dons leading 4-3, Queens thought they had equalised deep into stoppage time, but the referee had spotted an infringement and by the time the game restarted, he had sounded the final whistle. After a few weeks of taking the flak for a string of disappointing results, one report included the line, 'The home defence could not play "Slippery Sam" – not this fair-haired one!'

On Saturday, 9 November Rangers were in town, and it would be the only time that English lined up against his former employers. When the teams took to the field, Sam was given a rousing reception by the Light Blues followers, and he looked a little choked. But if ever a team chucked away the points through faulty finishing it was Queen of the South. Surprisingly, they had most of the game, but they could've played until midnight and still not scored, which must have been frustrating for the home supporters due to the apparent ease with which Bob McPhail scored both Rangers goals.

As for English, he gave the impression of being more suited to the inside game than the leadership, but perhaps that was due to a lack of understanding with some of his team-mates, which was still an issue almost four months into the season. One dribbling flash of the old dashing Sam brought out the very best in Jerry Dawson, and it prevented an equaliser just before Rangers got their second. Queens should have had a penalty early on, when Dawson pulled English down, and later Davie Meiklejohn kicked off the line with his keeper beaten.

English's main problem was a struggle for consistency. One week he was outstanding, the next, lethargic, but it was as frustrating for the player as it was for those around him, as each disappointment seemed to take its toll, judging by the manner in which he slumped off the pitch after a poor individual performance.

For a match against Clyde at home, four weeks before Christmas, manager McLachlan moved English to inside-right, and it seemed to work as he opened the scoring in just three minutes. But it proved a false dawn and in the end the home side were fortunate to salvage a draw.

A fortnight later at Tynecastle, English was back at centre-forward, but opportunities were in short supply. He managed just one effort on goal, which beat keeper Harkness, but was cleared off the line. Queens were third bottom with just Hibs and Ayr below them. It was a worry, especially for a provincial club who had shelled out so much cash in the close season for very little return.

After much soul searching, McLachlan decided he needed a new centre-forward, and quickly. English was nowhere near as fast, or active, as he had been in his Rangers days. He was a good deal cleverer, and his footwork was still a treat, so McLachlan decided he would make Sam's transition to inside-forward a permanent one.

English had led the Queens attack in all but one of their 21 league games, in which they had scored just 25 goals. Eight of those stood against the centre's name. The man being touted as his replacement was the big and powerful Englishman, James Bartram.

Four days before Christmas, English started against Hibs at Easter Road in the inside-right berth. Queens were awful and lost 3-0, thus slipping a spot to joint second-bottom. It was clear something had to be done, and the decision to drop English was followed by their first victory in 13 weeks. Bartram led the line as the Doonhamers beat Dunfermline Athletic 3-1.

The day after the game, the following story appeared in the *Sunday Post*:

> Yesterday, Sam English, Queens' costliest player, was dropped from the team. The football community gasped when it heard the news. Sam, who probably cost more than the entire Queen of the South team! Sam, whose Rangers goals are things that can't be forgotten! Dropped in an hour of Queens' crisis!
>
> But Sam English asked to be dropped!
>
> He made the request to manager McLachlan. Told his chief he considered he wasn't doing himself or the club justice. Somehow he felt a couple of weeks' rest would make all the difference; would give him the required tone.
>
> And Sam's request was granted in the spirit in which it was asked. Queen of the South have no doubt that their English deal was a splendid one. They considered he was the man for them, and they still do.
>
> But they realise that the switching from England to Scotland means more than just a railway journey. When Sammy is tuned in he will be the sparkling Ranger he once

was, say Queens. Here's hoping. We can do with all the
Sams we can get.

Queens' good fortunes continued over the festive period as they
beat both Ayr United and Arbroath with, it was said, the heaviest
strike force in Scottish football. Norman Haywood – the ex-
Peebles Rovers centre-forward – weighed in at 13st 4lb, while it
was said that Bartram was just a pound or so lighter.

In the middle of February, it seemed that English was ready to
make a comeback, and McLachlan chose a Scottish Cup tie away
at Highland League club Elgin City as the match to re-introduce
his record buy. English played at outside-right and scored in a
relatively straightforward 3-0 win.

He retained his position at outside-right for the following
Saturday's trip to Fir Park, Motherwell, and played well as Queens
pulled off a great 2-0 success. However, apart from a Scottish Cup
third-round tie at Cappielow (a 2-0 loss to Morton) and an away
league defeat at Hamilton Accies, Sam wouldn't feature for Queen
of the South again. In fact, he was placed on the club's 'open-to-
transfer' list in the middle of April. Sam hadn't re-emerged as the
sparkling Ranger he once was, as the club had hoped.

Was it a shock to anyone? Probably not. Truth is, the player
had been largely inconsistent and had never really struck up any
kind of understanding with the players around him. Goals had
been thin on the ground and the bottom line is Queens didn't get
value for money – even at the reduced fee they'd negotiated. What
the club initially thought was a great piece of transfer business
quickly turned sour. The player had also failed to properly address
the issue of his fluctuating weight.

And then came the bombshell news, released through the
pages of the newspapers, that Sam felt he was once again being
hounded out of his adopted country. He claimed that unscrupulous

opponents continued to goad him about the part he had played in the death of John Thomson. 'Some players,' he insisted, 'were just not prepared to let it go.'

Once again, a topic which many thought had been put to bed had reared its ugly head. For Sam English, though, it had never gone away. However, an article entitled 'SFA Chief and Sam English' which ran in the *Sunday Mail* on 17 May 1936, was less than generous to the player. It stated:

> Two years ago Sam English said to me, 'If I could tell you of the threats and taunts thrown at me on the field since the accident to John Thomson you would wonder how I've managed to keep playing!'
>
> I told him he'd be better to forget that incident.
>
> Unfortunately he hasn't. And his recent outburst to the effect that he has been forced out of Scottish football is all the more regrettable.
>
> In short, his declamation is little less than a denouncement of Scottish League players.
>
> 'I was considerably perturbed when I heard about it' said Mr James Fleming, the SFA president, to me. Allegations like these, which cannot be proved or disproved, cast an unwarranted reflection on the game and the players whose livelihood it is. The game was never in a cleaner state than it is today. The present-day player is an intelligent and often highly cultured young man. In any case, if English was made the object of any unfortunate remark he had the remedy in his own hands. It was his duty to report the matter to the referee, who would immediately have taken action.
>
> 'It is extremely deplorable that after so much work has been done by the SFA to raise the standard of playing field

behaviour, accusations such as these should discredit the result of that work in the public mind.'

One national defender said to me, 'I was really astounded when I read it. The whole thing is so preposterous. It suggests that Scottish players are no better than hooligans. I've played against English often, and as recently as the season just past, and never at any time heard the slightest mention of the Ibrox incident.

'Indeed, it is a subject players would naturally make a point of avoiding, for no body of people had more sympathy for English in consequence of the Ibrox tragedy than his fellow players. For English to make wholesale accusations as he does against the sportsmanship of his opponents is definitely hitting below the belt.

'The present-day footballer is no gangster. There never was a better type of fellow in the game than now. To represent him as a vindictive rotter who attempts to take advantage of a circumstance which might find any player its victim is as lamentable as it is untrue.'

Harsh words, but several folk immediately sprung to Sam's defence, and one reader, from Mosspark in Glasgow, wrote, 'In reference to the article about the statements made by Sam English against opposing teams and some individual players, I myself believe English's statements to be true.

'I have never heard players on the field making remarks to this player but if we could maybe get closer to the ground these remarks could be heard. I am an Englishman living here a few years and do not support any particular team, but being near Ibrox I have seen quite a few games.

'Myself, I used to think English was a very capable player and always seemed to conduct himself quite as well as the average leader does. But after the tragic way John Thomson was fatally injured, I myself witnessed incidents which left me cold, with regards to the way this player was treated.

'I saw a defender who is now out of football altogether, deliberately kick English viciously. This was after clearing the ball. He was passing English. The crowd roared disapproval and English complained to the referee, but no action was taken.

'I quite agree with English that he has been forced out of the game of football by the very bad sportsmanship of opposing players who could easily have had the same misfortune that unfortunately befell a very fine player in Sam English.'

Another reader said, 'It was with amazement and disgust that I read of the statement Sam English has made to the press with regard to the remarks passed to him by opponents on the field of play, referring to the late John Thomson's tragic end.

'Sam says that he will never kick another ball in Scotland. Now, Waverley, you have always been an outspoken critic of rough play and unsportsmanlike tactics, and I hope that you will give every publicity to this letter. Any player who is low enough to behave as English alleges should be hounded out of the game, because he is not fit to wear a football strip.

'I suggest the SFA make a full enquiry into this matter. We are proud of Scottish football but we cannot remain so if this sort of thing is going on. I believe it is up to Sam English to carry on playing in Scotland, and any player who tries to bait him in this way should be reported to the referee immediately.

'This baiting of English is a menace to Scottish football and I for one am finished with First League football unless a full enquiry is made. I shall watch only Schools and BB football in future.'

The *Daily Record* reporter, Waverley, had this to say on the matter, 'I agree that such behaviour as English complains of is as near sportsmanship as a lion is related to a louse, and it is one of my regrets that there is far too much of the talkee-talkee on the football field.

'After a recent international, I asked one of the younger players why he had fallen off so much during the second-half. He told me he had been upset by being subjected to vocal abuse even unto the questioning of his parentage and being a complete stranger to such tactics, especially in the international arena, he was dreadfully upset.

'"My first inclination was to shove the man's words down his throat with my fist," he commented, "but I knew that would bring shame on my mates, if not actual ruin to my own career."

'I remember [former Ranger] Jimmy Gordon telling me of a similar experience many years ago. It was in an Inter-League game in England, and an opponent became most profligate with words of profanity. Jimmy asked him twice to "chuck" it, but the player persisted. He must have been sorry afterwards, for he was carried off with a severe leg injury, and Gordon was not the man who caused it. An older member of the team had been listening in.

'Frankly, I think referees permit far too much latitude in the manner in which a certain type of player addresses another. Indeed, it's been going on so long that some officials seem to take it as part of the game.'

Sam didn't kick another ball for Queens that season; his time in Scotland was over. At the club's annual meeting, held at the end of the campaign, chairman James S. Steel commented on the club's debit balance of £2,698 and said that the players upon whom they had spent most at the start of the season, and from whom they expected so much, had been the biggest disappointments. It might have been unprecedented for a chairman to speak personally about individual players, but the season just finished had been so costly, and disappointing, that he felt it necessary to give shareholders a brief statement on the policy the board had adopted and carried through.

At the previous year's annual meeting, the then chairman mentioned they had tried eight centre-forwards, and in place of spending sums of money, such as £250, £150, £100 and £50, it was resolved by a vote of the board that a centre of repute be purchased – one who, to the best of their knowledge, would settle this key position for a few seasons to come. The board thus secured English from Liverpool. It was a bold policy for a provincial Scottish First Division club to undertake, but it was a gamble they felt worth taking.

In the first part of the season, the football, from an artistic point of view, might have been quite satisfactory, but it did not keep them in the position on the league table which they all so much desired. In the middle of the season, to make good deficiencies, they were again in the market for players, and they purchased another three – bringing their total of new players to ten. Again the results of the gamble were disappointing but Mr Steel did at least report an increase in attendances.

At the close of the 1935/36 season, Queen of the South manager George McLachlan took 16 players off to France, Luxembourg and Algeria on a glamour 11-match tour. Queens returned home with the Algiers Invitational Tournament trophy after beating Racing Santander in the final, but English didn't make the trip. By that time, his mind was once again on pastures new.

Fifteen

SAM ENGLISH was 27 when he slid down the divisions to sign for Hartlepools United; an age when most successful players are reaching their prime. Therefore, banging in any number of goals in the bottom tier of English football shouldn't have presented such a talented player with too many problems. But it didn't work out that way. Perhaps it wouldn't have mattered who he'd signed for. Perhaps the damage had already been done and in his head the curtain had fallen: career over. Still, his signing provoked a fanfare in the town most famous for, as the myth goes, the hanging of a French monkey back in the 19th century, during the Napoleonic Wars.

Each time Sam moved clubs, his options became more limited and less glamorous. It would have been difficult to stay in the Senior game and slip any lower than Hartlepools, given where he'd already been. The season before Sam joined, Pools had finished eighth in the Third Division North – the joint bottom tier of English football – 18 points adrift of top spot, but just five points above fifth from bottom. Up until 1936, the club had just two Durham Challenge Cups to show for almost 30 years of football history.

But on the day Sam put pen to paper, and committed himself to the north-east club, the headline in the *Northern Daily Mail* boasted, 'International signs for Pools – Famous Centre-forward is Here!' And no wonder.

It was 1 July 1936, and this signing, it was said, would help drag Hartlepools up from the depths of despair and into the realms of respectability. Pools had made an important capture on the eve of the new season and they were looking to the stockily built centre-forward to bring class, goals and a change in their fortunes.

Negotiations for English had been ongoing for some time, with one report suggesting Pools had been trying to get their man for several months. The respective club managers, Jimmy Hamilton of Hartlepools and George McLachlan of Queens, were involved in the talks. As usual, the stumbling block was the transfer fee and Pools would not make their move until the Doonhamers had significantly reduced the asking price. Initial reports suggest the fee for the Irish international was a substantial one. However, the day after the move it emerged that English – who had cost Queens the best part of £1,600 – had been on the Palmerston club's transfer list at £1,000. The fee paid to QOS was not divulged, although it was believed to be considerably less at just £275. It was a measure of just how much his value had fallen. Still, McLachlan insisted his board were satisfied with the transfer, as was he, and the fee was still a record for Hartlepools.

English had been at Palmerston for just a single season, and hadn't exactly set the heather on fire. Great things had been expected, but only occasionally did he produce flashes of the form that had made him the darling of the Rangers support. He had filled several positions in the forward line but still struggled to find any real consistency.

But he swapped the blue and white of Queens for the same colours at Pools, and was determined to help his new club maintain the progress they had made the previous season. The transfer fee paid to QOS would swallow up a large chunk of their player budget, but they hoped such enterprise would be met with due reward in the form of increased pressure on the turnstiles.

Pools signed six new players that close season to take their squad up to 21. Of the six, it was said that E.R. Self (from Bury), John Scott (Exeter) and English were the most important acquisitions, and if they came up trumps, Pools would have one of the best forward lines in Third Division North.

At the club's annual general meeting, vice-chairman W.J. Coates expressed appreciation of the chairman's effort in securing the services of English. He said that if Sam played up to his reputation, and the others maintained the standard of the season previous, they would be virtually assured of continued success. The season before they had lacked a regular centre-forward, otherwise they would have finished even higher up the league.

Pre-season training started during the first week in August and the players had three weeks of tough work ahead. They trained every day; morning and afternoon, and in spite of the bad weather, the routine carried on as normal. In the morning the players would walk to the nearby seaside resort of Seaton Carew and back, a round trip of just over six miles. The afternoons would consist mainly of ball work as the new trainer, Jimmy Cartwright, got to know the players under his charge. When assessing their general fitness on day one of pre-season, Mr Cartwright could find no fault with the condition of his protégés, although he did reckon a few of them were a trifle heavier than they ought to have been after the close season, but that steady training should shift any extra pounds without too many problems.

Pools arranged their first public practice match, very much the trend in those days, for the middle Saturday of August, and while this type of fixture rarely revealed much that wasn't already known regarding a team's prospects, they were often of interest to supporters, especially when new players were on view for the first time.

The teams selected for the practice brought into opposition the players considered the best defenders and attackers at the club. They included six of the seven new professionals, with English named as centre-forward for the 'Reds', who were opposing the side in Blue and White.

On the day of the match, the sun was splitting the sky. A sign of things to come for Sam in the north-east? Certainly that day it was as he treated the 4,000 spectators to a commanding performance, and the goal he scored had them purring in anticipation.

Before the match, and with supporters flocking through the turnstiles, the players didn't need a frenzied workout to break sweat. Instead, there was a life-saving gentle breeze to help. Anyway, all eyes were on groundsman Frank Hewitt, who lapped up compliments about his pitch resembling a bowling green. The playing surface was in tip-top condition, and almost instantly it witnessed some deft touches by English, who finished off a sizzling team move by hitting the bar in the first minute. When his goal did eventually arrive, it was the cutest of lobs over the advancing goalkeeper which drew much applause. Thereafter, English's every touch was admired as the players put on an exhibition of fine football for the paying customer.

There was no further scoring but gate receipts totalled £61, which was a big improvement on previous years, and a welcome boost for charity. The crowd was the greatest Pools had ever attracted for a practice match, also beating many league matches in recent years. It was also a thumbs-up to the board for the enterprise they had shown in the close-season transfer market. Sam English, in particular, had proved that not only did he know the quickest route to goal, but that he also had the touch and skill to supplement his marksmanship.

Of course, folk were advised not to get too carried away as it was only the first practice match. But had they attended the second, they would've been quite entitled to get carried away, as Sam was in glorious form. The Victoria Ground looked magnificent as a similar amount of supporters watched the Probable league 11 take on the Possibles. English lined up for the former, as did a player called Johnny Wigham, a man Sam would strike up a feared partnership with over the next two seasons. Wigham, who had signed for Pools in 1931, was a real fans' favourite, and while he remains one of the club's all-time leading scorers, he was also a skilled creator of goals. That said, Sam was on target four times in this match, and all were scored without the help or assistance of Wigham.

For his first, he whipped the ball home from the most awkward of angles. A furious drive moments later took the paint off the crossbar, before he accepted a pass and beat the keeper with a neat shot with a little swerve. His third was picture perfect. Think Maradona against England at the 1986 World Cup. He picked up the ball near the centre circle, out on the left, dribbled past six or seven players and fired a fierce shot past the keeper, which earned a standing ovation from supporters. His fourth goal arrived late on, a relatively ordinary strike from inside the box. While filtering out of the ground, Sam English was the talk of the small town.

But the time for 'practising' was over, and with the opening league match – a tricky tie at Southport – looming, it was important for Hartlepools to start the season well and take something from the contest. English would be in direct competition to Southport's new centre-half, Tom Frame, the big Scotsman who had made more than 80 appearances in four seasons at Manchester United. The former Cowdenbeath pivot was a formidable opponent.

He would also be up against inside-forward Tommy McKay, a colleague at Queen of the South the season previous.

Southport's highest attendance for two years, just over 6,000, looked on under an intense and beating sun and witnessed a terrific game between two very committed sides. The game finished 1-1 and the man who emerged with most credibility was trainer Jimmy Cartwright, whose players proved they were super fit by lasting the 90 energy-sapping minutes with a bit to spare.

The fact that Pools forwards English, Scott and Robertson should have had at least one goal each might not have been entirely down to their shooting boots. The English Football League was trialling a new lightweight ball that seemed to duck, dive and swerve with every connection and none of the forwards seemed able to fully control it.

English, though receiving flattering attention from Frame, was always a menace when he got a reasonable chance. His ball control and shrewd distribution were features of the forward play that augured well for the future.

He didn't have long to wait for his first league goal, which arrived in the opening home fixture, against Accrington Stanley. A crowd in excess of 7,000 were present, full of early-season excitement, as were half a dozen workers who were supposed to be busy on the roof of the new cinema in nearby Hart Lane, and they were treated to an entertaining contest.

The first half was an even affair, but the destination of the points was decided ten minutes after the break when English snapped up a chance with a grin of gratitude after a cross had been missed by two defenders. It was the type of goal the centre had made a career out of scoring and it was sufficient to give Pools both points.

The win was all the more appreciated given Pools were without Wigham. The little school teacher had sent a telegram to say that he was busy at work and unable to play. It was felt English would miss his creative play the most, but still did enough to be voted man of the match.

English was on target again in Pools' next game – a 2-1 win over Tranmere Rovers – and afterwards a local journalist had the following to say about the Northern Irishman: 'The most pleasing feature of the game from the point of view of the 8,500 spectators was the continued success of English at centre-forward. English is a footballer who bears the stamp of class, and what is perhaps equally important is that he is not afraid of work.

'Under the circumstances many in his position would have taken matters more or less easily in the second half, but English took on a roving commission and led his depleted attack with redoubled energy. A little more support from his fellow forwards and English might easily have put a Tranmere revival out of the question. Unfortunately all members of the side were not up to English's standard.'

The attendance was the best at a Victoria Ground league match for 14 years, and that had been a derby between Pools and Darlington.

It seemed Pools, or rather English, had become pure box office in the Yorkshire town of Halifax, as the forthcoming match had been billed locally as 'an event of unusual importance'. The report in a Halifax paper went on to say, 'The clubs have met regularly in cup football recently, but the big box office attraction will be Sam English, the former Rangers and Ireland centre-forward. I am looking forward to seeing this dashing leader in action.'

Sadly for the visitors they suffered their first defeat of the season, although the home crowd not only got their wish of two points, but also looked on in awe as English took the game to their favourites almost single-handedly. He hit the bar, had two fierce drives brilliantly saved, and never stopped trying to find a route to goal.

But he was back on the goal trail in a derby match against Darlington in the semi-finals of the Durham Senior Cup a couple of days later. The crowd of 5,000 were delighted with the 3-0 win, but even more ecstatic about the manner in which it was achieved. It was the brightest and best exhibition of football seen at the Victoria Ground in years.

English was outstanding. Besides scoring one of the three goals, he made the other two and did so many clever and unexpected things that one couldn't help but feel sympathy towards Strang, whose duty it was to mark the cleverest and most dangerous forward on the field. The Irishman supplied the icing for the cake with a thunderbolt free kick late on.

Things were going well for Pools, and that was reflected in the numbers coming through the gates. It seems English had provided the missing link, and when Mansfield Town visited The Vic in September, more than 7,000 clicks of the old turnstiles helped keep them rust-free. There weren't many still alive in the old town who could remember such crowds, but it proved that 'give them what they want and the crowds will come'. And the majority went home with a smile as they watched Pools cruise to a 3-0 win. Good times lay ahead if they could maintain their promising start.

But their next test would be the toughest. Chester were due at the Victoria Ground. Dubbed 'the Arsenal of the Northern Section', because of their drawing power, they would present a tough nut to crack. Something had to give as Pools were unbeaten on their own ground, and Chester on any ground.

Days before the game, though, Sam English unwittingly caused a storm in his adopted home town. He was the subject of a newspaper article titled, 'The best player Hartlepools United have ever had on their books'.

Supporters were annoyed. Not because they didn't agree with the main theme of the piece, but because the author of the article went on to ask, 'Why do fans keep on crying for more and more goals from him? In their curious blindness they do not see that English has provided most of the openings for all the goals scored to date.'

Supporters took exception to this text and bombarded the newspaper with complaints. Sure, most agreed that English was an exceptional talent, and perhaps the best Hartlepools had indeed been fortunate enough to have, but many considered it 'an insult', 'perfectly ridiculous' and 'a gross misstatement' that they should be portrayed in that way.

One reply stated, 'Nine out of ten spectators would be perfectly satisfied if English never scored at all. We are all fully alive to the fact that English as a footballer is perhaps the greatest Pools have had, that has been admitted ever since the fans first saw him. His touches are dreams, and not even a rugger international could sell the dummy as well as Sam does. But to say the crowd are only impatient to see him score goals is a lie, and should be scotched right away. Spectators are perfectly happy with English in every way.'

And so to the battle of the form sides; Pools v Chester, on the first Saturday of October 1936. A record league attendance of 12,200 expectantly filed into the Victoria Ground and they were treated to an excellent game of football, but ultimately the result – a 1-0 defeat – disappointed a great many. There were no quarters asked, and none given. With so much at stake, the tackles were flying in and both sides gave everything they had.

The Chester officials agreed that in few previous games had their players been required to fight harder for the points. It was touch and go up until the final whistle and Pools certainly had their chances.

It was no exaggeration to say that English's side were on the attack for 70 of the 90 minutes but when Chester went down to ten men, and then scored on the break, they defended in numbers for the remainder of the game, and did so very successfully.

Despite the defeat, Pools still had the distinction of having conceded the fewest goals of the 88 teams in the four English leagues – a record they shared with Chester.

A goal by English against Oldham Athletic, the only one of the game, got Pools back on track and once again in among the leading pack. The game would be remembered for an incredible number of offside decisions against a player in a single game – 17 – and that player was Sam English.

Thankfully, Sam remained onside sufficiently to help his new side land the Durham Senior Cup against top-flight Sunderland, who would finish eighth in the First Division that season. Pools turned in a monumental performance to upset the odds, and it was all the more pleasing as the match took place at Roker Park. It must have been a severe blow to Sunderland's ego, but Pools won on merit. Sure, Sunderland had a few injuries but were still able to include the bulk of their top team and by the end of the 90 minutes, the Black Cats were simply no match for their visitors.

Hartlepools were also without three of their top men, and this was acknowledged by John Cochrane, the Sunderland secretary, after the game when he presented the handsome trophy to Reg Hill. He declared Pools the better team and insisted no one should grudge them the congratulations they fully deserved on winning the competition for the first time.

As was to be expected, Pools had their backs to the wall early on, but once English realised the home defence weren't as secure as first thought, he set about putting his stamp on the game. He quite clearly enjoyed the match as only an old international could, so when Hornby headed the ball the right way for him and the wrong way for Sunderland, the centre-forward showed his gratitude for this unexpected assistance by scoring as simple a goal as anybody had seen at Roker in a long time.

Later on, when the game was safely won, English took the opportunity of showing Sunderland folk that Roker Park didn't boast a monopoly of all the football craft in the north-east. He sent some First Division players one way while he and the ball went the other, and even found the time to test the home keeper with one or two cracking shots.

But the wheels came off the wagon slightly when Pools lost at Port Vale. If anything, it highlighted a deficiency in the attacking department. English had more or less been working up top on his own for a few weeks and as the issue finally came home to roost there were calls for the club to bring in extra firepower to support him. Fans wanted the issue remedied as quickly as possible to ensure their good start to the season wasn't wasted.

The defence and midfield were doing their jobs satisfactorily but inventive play was breaking down when it reached the forwards. The problem was merely compounded when Rotherham – without an away win all season – turned up at the Victoria Ground and left with both points. It was Pools' most disappointing home display of the season, and the supporters let the players know exactly how they felt. These failings had once again been clearly demonstrated, and to make matters worse the defence developed unexpected flaws once they began to neglect their own job in the interests of attack.

English must have realised his luck was out when three fierce drives rocked the framework of the Rotherham goal with the keeper well beaten. Not for the first time, he and Wigham were the only forwards to inspire any degree of confidence and, lacking adequate support, were generally outnumbered in the shooting line. Twelve goals in as many games from the forwards simply wasn't good enough.

As usual, Pools supporters picked up their pens and fired off letters to the local paper. The tone of the majority was similar. The forward line was letting the team down and the game of Sam English was suffering. As a result he was being man-marked out of most games. Some suggested switching English to inside-left where much of the heat would be taken off. They reasoned that as he was such a clever footballer he would be able to create chances for another centre.

The manager took the advice, and a point at Stockport County was followed up with an excellent 2-0 win over high-flying Wrexham – with English in the thick of the action. The Welsh side played well but came up against a Pools XI desperate to get back on track. And they made sure of both points when English scored his second goal four minutes from time. The Irishman was in great form despite being marked by two defenders, but the big difference was in the support he received, and the team was rewarded with two first-class goals. He showed what a fine footballer he could be when given assistance, and also created several opportunities for those around him.

When the draw for the first round of the FA Cup was made, Pools once again missed out on a home tie. A rather unattractive draw against Rotherham was their tenth FA Cup road trip in 11 seasons, and their sixth successive away tie at the opening stage. Yet in spite of this, Pools had reached the second round four times in their last five attempts, and it wasn't beyond them to do it again. It would be the first meeting of the clubs in a cup tie.

It might have been a few years since Sam had felt the thrill of the derby match with either Liverpool or Rangers, but the league meeting between Darlington and Pools was one he, and everyone in attendance, would remember for a long time. There were goals aplenty, names taken, boots flying in and enough excitement to keep fans enthralled from the first minute to the last. As the players trooped off the field at the end, they were covered in either mud or blood – or both – and each had a story to tell. They had just played out an incredible 5-5 draw.

Certainly no one could grudge Pools their point after the manner in which they fought back against repeated setbacks. Three times Darlington held the lead, twice by a margin of two goals, yet each time Pools drew something from their reserve tanks.

When Towers scored Darlington's fifth 15 minutes from the end, most thought Pools were done for, but where there is time there is hope, especially with Wigham around. With two minutes to go the little school teacher defied all Darlington by heading a goal that was a lesson in opportunism.

The playing surface had the variable qualities of a skating rink and a quagmire, and defenders were constantly at a disadvantage. English and his team-mates realised this. They also realised that quick passing and prompt shooting was the stuff that was needed under such conditions, and their shooting was of such high quality that the score might have been doubled but for some great defending.

There was a marked improvement in their forward play. Wigham had his best game of the season, while English, as usual, was the link that held the line together. His tireless leadership was all the more remarkable given he suffered a bad cut to the side of the head after just five minutes, and which troubled him for the rest of the afternoon.

'Pools for thrills' could have been the club's new motto as they followed up the ten-goal thriller against Darlington with a cracking cup tie at Rotherham, but they had to fight tremendously hard to force a replay, despite looking a beaten side several times over. Sheer grit and good spirit, aided by a little luck, earned the desired reward. Twenty minutes from time, Rotherham led 4-2, yet Jimmy Hamilton's team of triers not only levelled the game, but almost won it in the dying minutes, and if the game had run on a few minutes more, they would have as Rotherham were on the ropes.

The scene when Park scored the eighth and final goal will remain perhaps the most vivid memory of a match whose every moment was electric, thrilling and critical. In a last desperate rally, John Scott sent in a corner kick which Park, standing on the outskirts of a jostling crowd of players, swung his boot at where he thought it would drop, and before goalkeeper Greaves could even guess what was happening, through a thicket of hostile legs it flashed into the back of the net.

Five hundred Pools fans went crazy. The noise they made – with voices, bells, rattles and various other 'weapons' of cup-tie warfare – certainly belied their numbers. Suddenly blue and white seemed more in vogue than Rotherham red in the closing minutes.

English had been one of the most industrious as well as the cleverest forward on view. His goal, which was the outcome of a beautiful header following another of Scott's flag kicks, offered inspiration to his side at a critical stage.

It was only after the game the manager realised his star signing had played a large part of the game with a pulled thigh muscle, which made him a doubt for the replay. The wheels also started turning in an effort to have Johnny Wigham released from his scholastic duties. But imagine the surprise, and delight, Sam felt when he received a telegram of congratulations after the game from none other than Al Capone. Mind you, this Al was no Chicago mobster offering prohibition liquor to the Pools forward, but a champion boxer from West Hartlepool with the same name. This Al Capone fought successfully between 1932 and 1942 and was a big supporter of his local football team.

There were two interested spectators at the cup tie in Rotherham: a couple of Luton Town directors, and they were on a mission – to open the cheque book and return south with the name of Sam English on a contract. Apparently they were impressed by what they saw, but when they enquired as to his availability after the match they were told that he was not for sale – at any price!

English was indeed ruled out of the replay, although the club managed to secure the release of Wigham, and he took on the role of centre-forward with relish. The match kicked off at 2pm on the Wednesday afternoon and the Victoria Ground was packed out. What they witnessed was a stuffy contest, fought out mainly in the middle of the park, but a 2-0 win sent the vast majority home happy. However, seven Pools players were injured in the process and all but one subsequently missed the weekend visit to Hull, as did English who still hadn't fully recovered from the thigh injury.

But Pools were in the second round and, you guessed it, another away tie awaited – this time at Crewe. In the lead-up to the big game, the players followed their usual routine – morning walks to Seaton Carew and light ball exercise on the beach followed by baths and massage in the afternoons. Pools' seaweed baths had become legendary in the lead-up to big matches. They were perfectly simple and inexpensive, and the benefit derived was highly rated at the Victoria Ground.

Pools travelled to Crewe in fine fettle, but when they arrived at Gresty Road, they found the pitch resembling a mud bath. Oh, and a blanket of fog sat happily on top of the boggy surface. Once the game was given the go-ahead, and Jimmy Hamilton had offered up a rousing pre-match team-talk, the players sprinted out to do their stuff. Roared on by a vociferous following, Pools looked up for the fight. Thanks to several inches of mud, which made controlling their own feet a difficult enough job for the players, never mind trying to control and pass a ball, the fog increased in density, and so too did the anxiety on the terracing. Players slithered and skidded about on the sloppy surface in the most inelegant way, while the ball behaved like a lump of wet soap let loose in a bath tub. It was common to see a player coax the ball into a favourable position, and then find, when he tried to do something serious, that he had suddenly lost control of his limbs or that the ball had become so firmly fixed in the mud it refused to budge.

No player was more sorely tried in this respect than Wigham. Frequently this frail-looking forward beat three or four opponents by exquisite dribbles down the muddy middle only to discover that, when he decided to part with the ball, he hadn't the strength to shift it. It really was that bad.

Fit-again English scored an excellent goal, and it was just the tonic his team needed at a time when the going was tough. It put Hartlepools one up at the break. However, Crewe came out all guns blazing for the second half and immediately equalised. For most of the second half Pools fought hard for FA Cup survival, and they were forced to endure a couple of real scares, but when the final whistle sounded, they were still in the cup.

Once again, the replay was set for a Wednesday afternoon and so it was off to Seaton Carew to assess the walking wounded. English was among a string of minor casualties but he wasn't about to allow a leg knock to sideline him.

Manager Jimmy Hamilton decided on a slight change of preparation and booked the entire squad into a matinee performance at the Picture House on the Tuesday night. After that, it was a light snack at the Marine Hotel, in Seaton Carew, and an early night.

Crewe had yet to win at The Vic, with Pools prevailing in each of their last nine visits.

The prize for the victor was a home tie against Plymouth Argyle on 16 January. But there was a real shock in store for the

8,000 who attended the game when the teams were read out prior to kick-off, and English was missing from the line-up. Sadly, Sam had suffered a recurrence of his thigh strain. And the afternoon went from bad to worse when Crewe – no doubt taking heart from the absence of Pools' star man – won 2-1. A dejected Sam sat in the main stand looking on as a boisterous wind completely spoiled the game. It must have been heartbreaking to watch Scott hit the bar with the goal gaping, or when his replacement, Hardy, missed an easy cross. Admittedly one player does not make a winning team, but English would surely have made a difference.

It was decided that Sam should also sit out the next game, on Boxing Day, at York City, as the icy pitch might affect his thigh. With a heavy festive programme coming up, the manager didn't want to lose his prize asset for any great length of time. However, a 4-1 defeat saw Pools slump to 13th in the table with just 17 points from 18 games. Two days later, they made some seasonable atonement for recent failures by beating Southport 2-0.

It was their first league win since defeating Wrexham by the same score in the middle of November, and it was no coincidence that English was back in the side. The centre-forward was on top form and his clever and altogether unselfish leadership encouraged his colleagues just as surely as it distressed the Southport defence. And his goal, which proved the turning point in the game, was the best seen at the Victoria Ground since the same player had scored against Wrexham earlier in the season. The other forwards expressed their pleasure at English's return in fitting style. Wigham, whose slight shoulders bore the main burden as well as most of the criticism during English's absence, was happily restored to his proper position. Pools also hit the woodwork three times, and forced the Southport keeper into a string of fantastic saves.

And they followed up with a 2-0 win over York City on the afternoon of Monday, 28 December. English scored from the spot towards the end of the first half, and six minutes after the change of ends, Hardy grabbed a second direct from a free kick.

York, who fielded the team that had defeated Halifax so easily on the Saturday, arrived at the Victoria Ground just ten minutes before kick-off. The London–Edinburgh express which they were due to catch at York was an hour late, and at the last minute, a motor-coach had to be hired for the journey, with the players changing en route.

On New Year's Day, Pools completed a hat-trick of holiday victories by defeating Barrow 3-1 before 6,700 at the Victoria Ground. However, the match was marred by an injury to English, who retired with a damaged ankle ten minutes before the interval and missed the entire second half.

Despite playing for just 35 minutes, he still managed to influence the game. He was instrumental in setting up goals for both Robertson and Wigham. In fact, English almost scored himself, with only a desperate intervention by Nixon robbing the forward as he was about to shoot.

And then with half an hour played, Pools won a corner. Scott took the set piece and English met the ball perfectly with his head, only to see it scrambled off the line by the keeper. However, momentum saw him fall full length in the goalmouth and come down heavily on his right ankle. The trainer was immediately called on but English was still limping after treatment. He decided to play on, and while the injury evidently proved a big handicap, his head was still very useful in distributing the ball. He moved out to the right wing for a spell but hobbled off shortly after.

Both English and Wigham missed the trip to Tranmere, and allied with the strain of five games in eight days, Pools did well to limit the margin of defeat at Prenton Park to a single goal.

The next game, against Halifax Town at the Victoria Ground, threw up an interesting scenario. With English still missing, Pools signed Jimmy McCambridge from Sheffield Wednesday. The striker – who also hailed from the north of Ireland – was seen as a stop-gap, but scored a hat-trick against the Yorkshire side in a thrilling 5-3 win. His goals might not have been spectacular, but they were vital, which left the manager with a dilemma. Sam would be fit to play in the next game against Gateshead, and McCambridge had one ever so well, but Jimmy Hamilton was quoted in the run-up to the game as saying, 'Sam isn't exactly the type of player one can afford to leave out.'

Hamilton's decision to reinstate English to centre-forward and move McCambridge to inside-left seemed a winner. It would be the first time the club had listed two internationals in their forward line. Or would it, because with a healthy attendance already inside the Victoria Ground, the tannoy announcer read out the teams … and there was no Sam English.

Supporters were furious and made their feelings known to the directors in the main stand.

There were also many grumbles in the direction of the local correspondent for the *Northern Daily Mail*, who had announced in midweek that Sam would play. He fended off a barrage of complaints on the Monday morning by insisting he had merely imparted the news given to him by the club.

The official reason offered for his absence was that he was given a fitness test on the Saturday morning – which included kicking a heavy ball – and that he felt his ankle injury hadn't healed sufficiently. As it transpired, Pools completely trounced Gateshead 6-1 and therefore English wasn't missed, although at the end of the game, one supporter asked the question, 'Would it have been a cricket score had Sammy been playing?'

He made his comeback in a reserve match against North Shields in a North Eastern League Cup tie; his first run-out since New Year's Day, and three times the normal reserve crowd turned up, such was English's pulling power.

Just moments after West put Pools in front, English tested his injured ankle with a drive which caused spectators behind the goal to duck hurriedly and remove their bowler hats. Yes, it was just slightly off target, but the forward felt no ill effects on the ankle.

That wasn't the case a couple of days later, though, and English was out of the weekend match at Mansfield. With the team scoring 11 goals in their previous two league matches, it was hoped he wouldn't be too much of a miss. Sadly Pools lost heavily.

It's perhaps too simplistic to suggest that when English was fit again, Hartlepools won. FA Cup conquerors Crewe Alexandra visited the Victoria Ground and were easily despatched with a few goals to spare. Sam was on target but his greatest contribution was his eagerness to link play between the midfield and forwards. The weather was atrocious and only 2,000 people (by far the lowest attendance of the season) made the effort, obviously seeing a greater attraction in the fireside and wireless. Perhaps many felt the snow-covered pitch would be unplayable, but while treacherous in parts, it seemed fine, and English made light of the conditions.

Seven days later, and a trip to Chester brought completely contrasting fortunes weather wise. The old world city was bathed in glorious sunshine, but there would be nothing but gloom for the visitors as Chester won 3-0.

But Pools were a different animal altogether at The Vic, and when Rochdale visited, they clocked up another comfortable home league victory. A 4-1 success meant that in their latest winning run they had scored 28 goals and conceded just seven. Naturally, English got his goal.

Once again the weather proved a more formidable opponent than Port Vale at the beginning of March. The crowd was well down and it seemed that only those stout-hearted gentlemen who stuck to football in defiance of the best wishes of their wives, and the worst warnings of weather experts, were huddled together in the main stand for the visit of the promotion challengers.

The playing surface resembled a swamp in which webbed feet and oil skins would have been more useful than normal football attire. Yet both sides made light of their heavy task and fans were treated to an excellent game worthy of a far bigger audience.

English scored both goals, by using the head, and Pools claimed both points. It was a personal success for Sam, as it was the first time he had scored twice in one game for Pools; and his total stood at 14 in 22 league games.

Easter is traditionally a busy period in the English football calendar. Three matches in four days was a tough physical challenge for the players, as well as a big financial commitment for supporters, but depending on results it could make or break your season. Pools' itinerary started with a trip to Carlisle, followed by a home game against Darlington and the return fixture with the Cumbrians.

Pools got nothing from the match at Carlisle, which was expected. But the long-awaited north-east derby match the following day brought arguably the biggest disappointment of the season. Darlington were bottom of the table and Pools were fully expected to win, comfortably, but they lost comprehensively to their opponents. English did little else apart from scoring, and while Pools dillied and dallied, Darlington took the plaudits.

The final match brought the only success of the holiday period – and also the most glaring miss of the season. Hartlepools won 3-0, but it should have been four. English set up McCambridge four yards out and with the Carlisle keeper on the deck, he blazed high over the bar, straight over the *Football Mail* scoreboard, and into a nearby rugby field.

With the season coming to an end, Pools travelled to Gateshead looking to win at Redheugh Park for the first time. And given the fact they skipped into an early 2-0 lead they really should have left with both points, but a change of ends brought a change of fortunes and Sam and his mates had to settle for a draw. There was a can collection in aid of players' wages at half-time and had the home supporters known the extra effort their favourites would make in the second half, they may have chipped in a few extra coppers.

English missed a chance late on to win the game but he was limping long before the spot kick after being the victim of yet another heavy challenge.

It had been a long and arduous campaign for Pools but there was still a chance for them to finish fifth in the table, although first they had to beat Hull City. Despite English bagging his 16th of the season, Pools could only muster a disappointing 2-2 draw.

An interesting feature of the afternoon was the fans' attitude to the updates they received on the scoreboard from the Millwall v Sunderland FA Cup semi-final. Despite being big rivals of the Roker Park side, the enthusiasm with which they greeted news of Sunderland's recovery and ultimate success was indicative of the keen interest the entire district had in the game. But even the announcement of Sunderland's triumph, welcomed though it was by almost everyone in the ground, failed to inspire Pools to a similar recovery against Hull.

With just a couple of games remaining, Pools had little to play for bar pride. Their penultimate league match was against Lincoln City, who were locked in a titanic struggle with Stockport County for the title. And with the teams due to meet on the final day of the season, Lincoln needed a result at the Victoria Ground. But by close of play, the pendulum had swung firmly in favour of Stockport as Hartlepools defied logic to dump the title contenders 3-0.

After the game, Pools announced their retained players for the following season, and it was little surprise to find Sam topping the list. Eleven players would be kept on, with ten released.

In the final home game of the season, Pools thumped New Brighton 5-0, with English on target twice. Proctor maintained his 100 per cent record from the spot by scoring his eighth penalty of the campaign. The win put Hartlepools on 45 points for the season, which equalled their highest ever return, set in season 1929/30. In contrast, both north-east rivals Gateshead and Darlington finished in the basement and would have to apply for re-election.

It had been a mixed campaign for English, but while he seemed to be enjoying life in the coastal English town, things would unravel a little the following season. For now, though, he was on the first train north, back to the bosom of his family in Dalmuir.

Sam struts his stuff in a Liverpool jersey

Sam, front row, centre, pictured in the Liverpool team of 1933

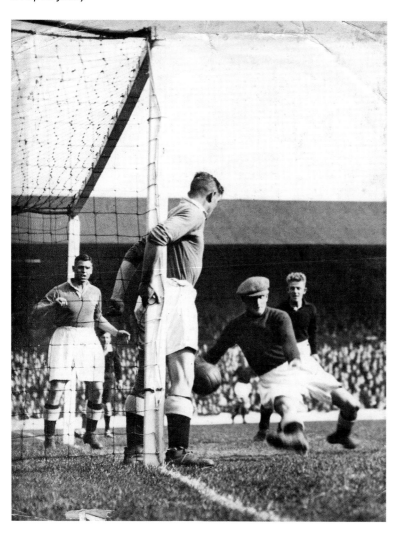

Sam, right, in action for Liverpool (courtesy of Liverpool FC)

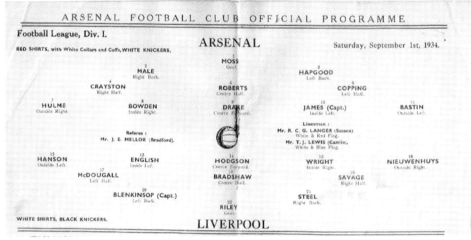

ARSENAL FOOTBALL CLUB OFFICIAL PROGRAMME

Football League, Div. I.

ARSENAL

Saturday, September 1st, 1934.

RED SHIRTS, with White Collars and Cuffs, WHITE KNICKERS.

MOSS
Goal

MALE
Right Back

HAPGOOD
Left Back

CRAYSTON
Right Half

ROBERTS
Centre Half

COPPING
Left Half

HULME
Outside Right

BOWDEN
Inside Right

DRAKE
Centre Forward

JAMES (Capt.)
Inside Left

BASTIN
Outside Left

Referee :
Mr. J. E. MELLOR (Bradford).

Linesmen :
Mr. R. C. G. LANGER (Sussex)
White & Red Flag.
Mr. T. J. LEWIS (Cardiff).
White & Blue Flag.

HANSON
Outside Left

ENGLISH
Inside Left

HODGSON
Centre Forward

WRIGHT
Inside Right

NIEUWENHUYS
Outside Right

McDOUGALL
Left Half

BRADSHAW
Centre Half

SAVAGE
Right Half

BLENKINSOP (Capt.)
Left Back

STEEL
Right Back

RILEY
Goal

WHITE SHIRTS, BLACK KNICKERS.

LIVERPOOL

Sam lines up for Liverpool at Highbury, Arsenal. Sadly, Liverpool were thrashed 8-1!

Sam English was one of English football's most fouled players during his time with Liverpool

A kick in the ankle for Sam by a young Tranmere player!

This caricature of Sam is made up with the letters of his name!

Sam got no change out of Roberts, the towering Arsenal defender

The feared Liverpool trio of Hodgson, English and Taylor

Sam was KOd by the goalkeeper!

A 1930s depiction of Sam English

Sam, as depicted by a Liverpool cartoonist

Shaking hands with Jimmy Dunne, his Irish international team-mate, before the Liverpool v Sheffield United match

Sam pictured on his first day at the Victoria Ground, Hartlepools

Sam finished top scorer in both of his seasons at Hartlepools United

Sam, centre, in action for Hartlepools against Gateshead at the Victoria Ground

September, 1937. Sam, in Hartlepools colours, jumps up with the Accrington Stanley goalkeeper

Sam dropped down the leagues to sign for Hartlepools United

A goalmouth incident during a Hartlepools match. Sam is pictured right

Sam and his wife Sarah sitting out in the garden at their Dalmuir home

Far left: Sitting happily in his garden despite rumours of his impending death!

Left: Sam with his wife Sarah

Sam and his wife Sarah with two of their daughters and grandchildren

Sam English, left, looking as dapper as ever

The Belfast mural featuring Sam was a true work of art

Eleanor Cree alongside Helen Runciman's painting of her father, Sam

Former referee Bobby Tait, left, with ex-Ranger Davie Wilson, and John Gilligan, right, the former Rangers director

The Sam English Rose Bowl started out as a circle of silver!

Silversmith Cara
Murphy hard at it in
her workshop

The beautiful Sam English Rose Bowl
(picture by David Pauley)

The Sam English rose
bowl takes pride of
place in the Ibrox
trophy room

Cara Murphy presents the Sam English Rose
Bowl to Rangers FC historian David Mason

Andy Little, Rangers FC, proudly shows off
the Sam English Rose Bowl

On the table at the Sam
English Centenary Dinner at
Ibrox

Sam English plaque: Back row, from left, Lloyd Gailey; Mr
H Moore, Chief Executive of Coleraine Borough Council;
Mark Dingwall (Rangers Supporters Trust). Front row, from
left, Ronnie Cree, Deputy Mayor Barney Fitzpatrick, Dawn
McKellar (Sam's granddaughter). Photo taken at Coleraine
Borough Council

Sam's son-in-law Ronnie Cree meets Coleraine's deputy mayor, Barney Fitzpatrick

A plaque commemorating Sam English at his birthplace in Crevolea, Aghadowey

Deputy Mayor Barney Fitzpatrick welcomes Mark Dingwall to Coleraine. Mark was one of the driving forces behind the Sam English centenary celebrations in August, 2008

Sam English takes his place on the famous Hall of Fame board at Ibrox Stadium (pic by Michael Allan)

Gregor Cree: Following in his great-grandfather's footsteps (Image by Colin Poultney – Collarge Images – Photography & Art)

Gregor Cree scores for Yoker Athletic (Image by Colin Poultney – Collarge Images – Photography & Art)

Sixteen

THE SUMMER holidays were over; Sam had played his last round of golf, and the English family had enjoyed their annual break in Girvan. It was back to Hartlepools for pre-season training, and several of the senior players had agreed to return a week earlier than planned, although it was optional.

The end of the August bank holiday traditionally signalled the end of the professional footballer's close-season rest. It meant three weeks of training instead of the usual fortnight, and also an extra week's wages to those who had come back early, but the club deemed it money well spent if it would give the players an extra yard on their opponents.

Sam was one of those who reported back early and, as he had been installed as vice-captain of the side, it was good leadership on his part. Nothing at all to do with the fact that he had been enjoying some nice family meals, and a few refreshments, while back home in Scotland for the close season.

In the 1930s, there was a wage scale in operation, with players receiving a regular weekly wage during the season and reduced 'retained' terms during the summer. The maximum weekly wage set by the Football League was £8 in the winter and £6 in the summer.

Pools were scheduled to play their first eight matches in the space of a month, so manager Jimmy Hamilton was keen for his players to be as fit as possible. However, he wasn't a believer in the 'old school' way of training, with players wearing three sweaters, knocking off a few laps of the track and then having a nice bath to complete their day's work, but he was also careful not to tread too firmly on his trainer Jimmy Cartwright's toes. There had to be a balance, and once the initial gruelling fitness training was out the way, Mr Hamilton would have the players involved in lots of ball work with methodical exercises, interspersed with occasional sprints, and followed each afternoon by massage treatment. A real visionary, good use was also made of the long stretch of beach at Seaton Carew.

Jimmy Cartwright had a tough job on his hands as the first public practice match was scheduled for Wednesday, 18 August, and the second just three days later. The clock was ticking. The ground staff had also been busy during the close season with improvements including the installation of electric light in the press box.

For the first practice, the Probable first-team attack would once again oppose the Probable first-team defence. The manager had signed 12 new players, with cover for every position in the team, except centre-forward.

The new signings were given a good run-out in the opening practice, and 3,400 paid to get in, with charities benefitting to the tune of £56. Although the result was immaterial, fans saw the teams share six goals. The second game drew a similar crowd and English was then selected, unopposed, for the opening league match of the season, against Lincoln City at Sincil Bank. Lincoln were one of the early favourites to win the division, but the neutral may have had trouble distinguishing between the sides as it took a controversial penalty to separate them, and it was Lincoln who benefitted. English, closely marked by a grand centre-half in Meacock, was at his best only in flashes. His shooting, too, was below par otherwise the home keeper would have been a much busier man.

Still, there was little rest for the players and Accrington Stanley opened the Victoria Ground action a couple of days later. It wasn't a great game, for several reasons. It seems the 7,700 crowd weren't too enamoured with yet another prototype light ball, which proved a heavy handicap for both teams. There was also little cohesion to the home side, and the opening goal came about when a shot rebounded off the bar, hit English on the back of the head and ended up in the net.

English then played a sublime, defence-splitting pass, and following a clash with the Accrington keeper, Scott was hauled down and Proctor calmly despatched the penalty. And then came the miss of the season, despite it being so early in the campaign. Scott returned the favour by sending in a beauty of a cross. The keeper completely missed the ball and there was English, four yards out, with time to light his pipe before shooting – and he stuck it over the bar. He buried his head in the turf, refusing to be comforted, even when Wigham offered him a sympathetic hand. English was again below par, though some of his moves were wasted because the others failed to anticipate them.

Hull City were next in town and 8,000 turned out for the contest, although it didn't start well for the home side as they were two goals down in the opening minutes. The collective sigh around the ground could be heard as the second bulged the net. But thank goodness for Wigham, who scored twice to earn Pools a deserved point. English was disappointing, but was cut some slack by supporters as they knew their centre-forward possessed all the tricks of the trade.

Another midweek trip loomed, this time to Peel Park, Accrington, for a quick return match against Stanley. And there was an immediate setback as it took the players five hours to get there by road – normally a two-hour journey at best. Pools were also without several key players and so it was no surprise they lost.

But when they shipped a staggering ten goals at surprise packages New Brighton and Wrexham it was time to hit the panic button, especially as league leaders Gateshead were next to visit the Victoria Ground. Hopes had been high that Pools could build on their sixth-place finish of the previous season and mount a challenge for honours, but they had gone in the opposite direction. Manager Hamilton reshuffled the middle line to seek out a winning formula but it was all to no avail as the match ran true to form and an away win was marked on pools coupons up and down the country.

At the risk of sounding like a broken record, English was again off colour, and serious questions were now being asked about how such an incredible lapse in form was possible. Here was a man with the talent to play at the top level, although it was no use showing it in flashes. Others in the team looked to him for inspiration, but when little was forthcoming then collective performance levels fell way below expectation. It was worrying for the hierarchy. Perhaps those who had followed English's career noticed this grave lapse in form as some sort of second-season syndrome; a condition which had prevailed to some extent at both Rangers and Liverpool, although it didn't take as long to surface at Queen of the South.

There was some respite, though, in the shape of a semi-final win over a strong Sunderland side in the Durham Senior Cup. Sure, it wasn't exactly Sunderland's FA Cup-winning team, but still a strong side nevertheless. A single-goal win belied Pools' dominance, and it was hoped the team could take heart from this and kick on in the league. English played a big part in the build-up to the goal.

But it was the same old story when Pools visited Oldham, although the opening paragraph of the match report read like something from Charles Dickens's *Oliver Twist*.

'Oldham, in the heart of industrial Lancashire, is not a place to captivate the casual visitor. On a dull day it is even less prepossessing than usual. Fog was hanging above its gaunt grey streets when I was there on Saturday. Nor is the situation of the association football ground calculated to inspire the other fellows. You get to Boundary Park via an unusually long, straight thoroughfare which seems to be full of barbers' poles and pawn shops – and elderly women wearing clogs. Follow the tramlines until you come to an imposing building, which is the workhouse, and then turn down an allotment-flanked lane and there is Boundary Park, which it is difficult to believe once held 48,000 people.'

There was certainly something quite painful about having to play a game of football next door to the workhouse, especially if you were bottom of the league. Pools were three down before a late rally provided a consolation, but ultimately it was another afternoon to forget.

Thus the derby showdown with Darlington seven days later took on greater significance. Win, and there was a chance Pools would leapfrog their troubled rivals at the foot of the table. Lose, and the basement berth would be consolidated. As it was, Pools won 2-1 – with English and Wigham on target – but results elsewhere conspired to keep them at the bottom. The manager was happy enough but there were still some temper tantrums to sort out as the latter part of the match was marred by rather unsavoury shows of faux masculinity.

Pools travelled to Port Vale the following Saturday and were on the wrong end of a 5-1 drubbing. They were due to play Hull

City in the Northern Section Cup five days after the Port Vale debacle and selectors vowed to mix things up. Meanwhile, the club cancelled the contract of skipper David Davidson, the former Liverpool and Newcastle United centre-half, and threatened that others would follow him out the door. Sam English was asked to take over the captaincy.

But they say nothing goes right when you're down on your luck and that was certainly the case when high-flying Chester visited the Victoria Ground. Fewer than 6,000 turned up, more than 50 per cent down on the same fixture 12 months previous. They gave Chester a good run for their money but couldn't score. Had football been decided on points, like a boxing match, then Pools may have won easily, but they had no luck at all and English's early injury proved a heavy handicap. He started off in grand style, but was only as good as a wonky knee would allow in the second half.

The malaise continued with another defeat at Rotherham, and the only thing missing – apart from a victory – was the manager, who had decided enough was enough and gone off to watch prospective new players. He was back in the dugout for the next home match, against Rochdale, and the home supporters in the disappointing – but understandable – crowd of under 4,000 must have been rubbing their eyes in amazement when they saw their team race into a three-goal, first-half lead. For the first time that season, Pools fans had witnessed their favourites score three times in a league match – and it was only half-time. But what's that they say about complacency? If the first half had been a pleasant dream, the second was the stuff of nightmares, and Rochdale scored three times to save a point.

By the latter part of November, Pools had recorded just a single victory in 12 matches, and needed something against Southport. English appeared in the mood, and set up a couple of early chances for Wigham, the second of which he scored to earn a half-time lead. But the second half was almost a carbon copy of the match against Rochdale. Pools faded after a bright opening and lost two goals.

While the defence had to accept responsibility, the forwards were equally culpable. There was far too much messing around in front of goal and English was as guilty as the rest. In fact, a letter sent into the local paper said as much. It read, 'We need a centre-forward who can take the chances given to him by his colleagues. Don't think I do not appreciate Sam English, I think he is a clever footballer, but he belongs to the old and stylish class.'

A trip to Bradford City's Valley Parade proved equally disastrous and a 4-1 reverse kept Pools rooted to the bottom. To compound matters, Pools lost Proctor with a twisted ankle while Wigham was laid up in bed with flu.

But FA Cup weekend was looming and the players were up for some extra training. The usual morning walks to Seaton Carew, ball practice, massage treatment, and the inevitable seaweed baths were a welcome distraction from the usual routine. This match had the potential to put smiles back on faces. Hartlepools had at last received a home draw in the first round of the FA Cup, against Southport, and given their awful form in the league, this was their one shot at glory. For many of the bigger sides, getting to the final, or even winning it, was success. For Pools, reaching round two was the extent of their ambition.

Win and attendances would start to rise again. Losing was too depressing to even contemplate. Jimmy Hamilton once again rung the changes with Wigham named centre-forward, and English filling the inside-right position.

There was a worry that the players might be overwhelmed by the importance of the occasion, and that over-eagerness could lead to panicky play, which would of course be fatal, especially as the visitors had already won the league clash with a bit to spare.

Come kick-off, Pools were decked out in unfamiliar colours of all-white shirts and black pants. It was hoped the change might give the players a psychological boost with white apparently giving the impression the players were bigger and stronger. Earlier in the season they had lost at home to Gateshead and Chester, both of whom had changed to white shirts for the day. Could it work for Pools?

The weather was mild as supporters queued to get into the ground. A sense of anticipation was building. There were 5,000 inside The Vic a few minutes before kick-off, but the early start was responsible for a last-minute rush on the turnstiles, so the crowd was much higher.

The home side started brightly and a smart move by English, Self and Wigham gave Scott an opening, but Grainger cleared. When Pools took the lead in ten minutes, it was said the roar could be heard in Newcastle. English pounced on a cross by Self, and played in Scott, who lobbed the ball beautifully over the head of the Southport keeper. This was a different Pools from that earlier league encounter, one which was revelling in the special atmosphere of the FA Cup. They would go on to win 3-0 and the majority of the 7,415 crowd was delighted. The biggest difference in the side was a noticeable improvement in attack. If Pools had been four up at half-time, it wouldn't have been a surprise. Apart from English's penalty miss, the Southport goal had some astonishing escapes.

English was still very much a discerning tactician, as well as a clever ball player, whether at inside-left or centre-forward. Against Southport he made up for what he lacked in speed by the skill with which he worked the ball, with both the first and third goals attributed to his passes.

Jimmy Hamilton hoped the cup win might prove the catalyst for an improved second half of the season. Sadly the answer was in the negative – and it was down to a moment of real indiscipline on the part of the captain. Instead of basking in the glory of the cup success, Hamilton was forced to attend a hastily convened board meeting on the evening of Monday, 6 December. After the meeting, Hamilton phoned the local *Northern Daily Mail* reporter to announce a fortnight's suspension for English due to a 'breach of training regulations', although it would appear there was a bit more to the story than a training ground breach.

Sam had been drinking in the Crown Bar, in the town's Stockton Street, which was just a stone's throw from the ground. He had consumed a few pints before being asked by the manager to return to his lodgings. The manager of the pub was thinking of Sam's reputation, and being seen out and about drunk wasn't particularly clever. But Sam refused, and continued to drink. He was still in the alehouse some 40 minutes later and the club was duly informed. They immediately convened to discuss the situation and decided on their punishment of a two-week suspension, preferring to cite the reason as a breach of training ground regulations in order to protect the club's reputation.

Sam was at a low ebb and, having failed to score in his last six league games, was feeling a severe dent to both his pride and confidence. Unbelievably, he was still dealing with barracking by so-called supporters for his part in the John Thomson tragedy, which had taken place six years previous. There seemed no escape, and so he sought temporary refuge in the bottle. It would transpire many years after he finished his playing career that the boos and catcalls had never actually gone away, and that it was just the aggressive accents that had changed.

But on this occasion, his timing was lousy. Pools were due to face Tranmere Rovers at Prenton Park in the second round of the FA Cup and the town was buzzing – but mostly with rumours about their star player's indiscretions. English had previously missed five games that season, but only through injury, although his absence against the Birkenhead side would be sorely felt. English missed the walks to Seaton Carew and the seaweed baths, and the overnight stay in Liverpool on the Friday evening. Tranmere's players prepared for the match by taking brine baths and playing an impromptu golf tournament in Birkenhead.

It was the second match on successive Saturdays against Rovers in the Wirral. Pools had lost 4-0 the previous weekend in a league match, so their prospects for cup glory were grim, especially without their star man. Sadly they fared little better in the cup tie and lost 3-1.

When his suspension was up, Sam reported to the Victoria Ground and was ushered into manager Jimmy Hamilton's office for a long chat. The manager was worried about Sam, and asked about his welfare. Hamilton was desperate to ensure his star player was in the best possible frame of mind for the battle that lay ahead, but he was also genuinely concerned about the individual who sat before him. Sam assured his gaffer he was fine and wouldn't let him down again. The player left the office promising to knuckle down in training, and started to prepare for the visit of Crewe Alexandra to The Vic on Christmas Day. He was almost certain to be reinstated to the team.

Meanwhile, one correspondent from the *Northern Daily Mail* suggested that Sam should be tried in the outside-left position, which didn't seem likely. Neither did his forecast of English repaying the supporters for his misdemeanour with a hat-trick. As prolific as he had once been, those days seemed buried in a dim and distant past.

It was Pools' first home match in a month and two points were a must if they were to mount a genuine ascent up the league table. Pools fans were also in dire need of some Christmas cheer.

Sadly there would be no festive win, but a point was secured in an entertaining 2-2 draw – although it should have been two, as English scored a beauty of a goal after being sent clean through. His shot from all of 25 yards zipped past the keeper, but the referee stopped the game for offside. After a quick rethink, he apologised to Sam for making a mistake but still disallowed the goal and restarted the game with a drop ball in the middle of the park.

English played well but received far more than his fair share of robust treatment – on and off the ball – and came off at the end nursing a pile of bruises and no win bonus, both due to the ineptness of Mr Mellor, the referee.

Early in the New Year, a flu epidemic swept through the Victoria Ground. Even the manager was forced to stay at home while a skeleton squad were put through their paces by the trainer. Sam was given permission to train alone in the stand, away from the other potential carriers. But it mattered little as he fell victim to the virus on the eve of the final of the Durham Senior Cup against Darlington at The Vic. Pools had a few players missing but still did enough to land the trophy, although there would be no medals for those who missed the big game.

English returned to the side in time for the trip to York, and while he couldn't help steer Pools to a rare away success, he did provide his team-mates with one of the funniest moments of the season. The players travelled by train and stopped to change 'locomotives' in the North Yorkshire town of Selby. As they walked to a cafe on the outskirts of the town, they passed two goats being loaded on to a truck. This was the cue for Sam to tell his mates about his time growing up on a farm, even though he had been a mere bairn when he left. Nevertheless, he cheerfully proceeded to demonstrate how one would go about milking a goat – until one of the chaps loading up the goats pointed out that these 'weren't the type of goats you milked'. His team-mates fell about laughing.

When Pools travelled to Humberside to face Hull, they didn't pick up the point their play deserved. To start with, conditions were awful. The pitch wasn't just muddy; it was a mud bath. In each of the goal areas there was a large pool of water, and in the centre of the field the mud was ankle deep, which led to the hosts hitting the front early on, as they seemed to know where all the thick, gooey patches lay. Hull led by three at the break, but Pools gave a good account of themselves in the second period. And well to the forefront was English, who, as in the York match, played a fine game. He suffered a bang on the ankle in the latter stages which curbed his activities somewhat, but up until then had been alternately raiding and defending.

Another match, this time against New Brighton, came and went without victory. The situation was grim. Pools had loads of chances; English worked his socks off, but the re-instated captain and centre-forward was often beaten for speed by his marker. Still, Sam showed some neat touches, which, although resulting in nothing tangible, were nice to watch.

Seven days later, English had a clinching goal to show for his efforts as Pools beat Oldham Athletic 2-0 at The Vic. The visitors controlled the match, but hadn't got a striker capable of putting the ball in the net. With Pools, it was the reverse, as their forwards fired in more shots than they had done for weeks, and the score might have been even greater. On one occasion, for instance, English showed skill and trickery way beyond Division Three level to completely bamboozle a couple of defenders before turning and crashing a 20-yard drive off the bar.

Sam had one of his best games in weeks, even though he was well watched by Ratcliffe. He showed everybody he could still shoot, which was something many supporters had started to doubt. The victory appeared to galvanise the supporters and suddenly there was an appetite to run a special train to Darlington for the big Third Division North derby. Even the most negative fan now had the belief that Pools could drag themselves away from the need to apply for re-election at the end of the season.

Sam's picture-book goal seemed to have earned him something of a reprieve from a section of the Pools support which, perhaps, was not as vocal as the rest. A letter to the local paper, under the heading of 'The Feminine View', stated, 'In view of the recent controversy over the formation of the Pools' team, we thought it might interest you to have the opinion of the fairer sex on this matter. We had originally written this letter days ago, but didn't get it sent off, and after seeing Saturday's match have revised our opinion of certain players. Before, we had put Sam English off the team, but as he played very well against Oldham, we would leave him at centre-forward. I hope you won't think we've got an awful nerve writing to you like this, but we thought you might find reading it as amusing as we did writing it.'

The next game was against Port Vale and Sam proved his female supporters were correct to leave him in the team as he was on target in a 2-1 win. However, he showed his Jekyll and Hyde side in the second half when he missed an absolute sitter from a yard out.

And the team, collectively, showed the other side of their character the following Saturday when they lost 6-0 at Chester. Jimmy Hamilton promised to ring the changes for the visit of league leaders Rotherham seven days later, and he introduced youngsters Mackie and Nevin to the attack. Both scored as Pools romped to a 4-0 win. What is that they say about keeping your home fans happy?

Before the game, supporters were surprised to see such a radical change to one department of the team, and afterwards they were hailing Sam English for helping make it a game to remember for the kids. His unselfishness was almost without precedence in an era when very rarely did one see an older player so clearly encourage youngsters as did Pools' international ace. No young players could have had a better colleague and a more considerate guide, because it was thoughtful and unselfish play by English which gave these kids encouragement. And the Irishman also found the time and space to score the finest goal of the four. Mackie's effort may have been the more spectacular, but it was infinitely less difficult than English's counter.

For a team languishing in the lower reaches of the division, Pools appeared to have an on/off switch, as the top three teams – Lincoln, Oldham and Rotherham – had now been sent packing from The Vic. The win against the latter moved Pools off the bottom of the table.

Spring is supposed to be a joyful time of year, marking the prelude to the grand symphony of summer, and the time of year when the sun starts to shine in earnest. For Pools supporters, though, with the club in a state of flux, it marked the commencement of a period of desperate anxiety which they hoped would culminate in their club reaching the promised land of league safety.

Before that could happen, they needed hope, and a point from a 0-0 draw against Doncaster was all very well, but they really needed to be winning home games. That said, Doncaster were a smart side and played well, but once again English was the victim of some heavy challenges, with one in the opening moments of the match seeming to hamper him throughout. It was frustrating that the creative players were given little protection by match officials, and with the advent of substitutes still some way off, it was a hindrance to those teams that tried to play football.

Yet again, Sam was the topic of conversation in the letters page of the *Northern Daily Mail*, with 'Disgusted No 1' saying, 'I wrote a few weeks ago advocating team changes, particularly at centre-forward, and I still think we should persevere with young Nevin in that position. English is a far better schemer at inside-left and gets more scope than he does at centre. I consider Sam has lost a lot of his dash, but he is still a fine footballer.'

For their next match, at York City, Hamilton again rang the changes, with his most notable switch coming up front. English was moved to inside-left, with Wigham at centre-forward. Who says managers don't read papers? Pools played well but lost 1-0. It was the one that got away, but they were now two points adrift of both Darlington and Accrington.

The busy Easter holiday period – with three matches in four days, two of which were at home – was make or break time. It would seal their fate one way or the other. Barrow would visit The Vic on Good Friday, and 24 hours later Tranmere Rovers were in town. Pools were scheduled to travel to Barrow for the return fixture on Easter Monday. The games were also important for the opposition. Barrow were near the foot of the table, while Tranmere were promotion contenders.

As there hadn't been any rain for a couple of weeks prior to the weekend, Pools asked the West Hartlepool Fire Brigade to give the ground a good soaking. But supporters had that sinking feeling for the majority of the opening game as they trailed Barrow 1-0, and it wasn't until five minutes from time that Wigham headed a goal to earn a point. It was something. The biggest disappointment for the majority of the crowd wasn't the final result, but the manner in which the home players seemed to capitulate rather than show some fight.

The game against Tranmere was a huge improvement on the display against Barrow, but the result was the same. Pools were two goals up in 15 minutes, with English and Proctor on target, but once again managed to snatch a draw from the jaws of victory.

Five successive home draws was Hartlepools' season in miniature. Having to apply for re-election was the devil itself, as there was no guarantee the football authorities would look favourably upon your application. It was home points that counted in those hard times and Pools were conceding them with frustrating regularity. A scoreless game at Barrow on Easter Monday made it three draws from three weekend fixtures.

On the Monday night, while Pools were at Barrow, back in Hartlepool (the football club was known as Hartlepools until 1965, but the town itself has always been Hartlepool), two small boys could be seen running around in the sand. At first glance, they looked like two ordinary schoolboys having fun. On closer inspection, they could be identified as 11-year-old Raymond Craggs, son of the well-known local sportsman Tommy Craggs, and Austin Taylerson. Both were promising local footballers and Raymond was helping Austin prepare for his big test a couple of nights later for Durham County against the Kent County Schoolboys at the Victoria Ground. Both boys were also protégés of Sam English. It was said that Sam was as happy as a sand boy when passing his craft on to youngsters, and to these two laddies in particular the Pools crack was a true hero. They hardly ever missed a home match and to them Sam could do no wrong.

In Pools' next league match, they did everything bar score at Halifax. In fact they might have secured their one and only away win of the campaign had their big players stepped up to the mark. That seemed to be that, but while there was hope they had to battle on. They had a game in hand over their basement rivals, but to survive bottom spot, they more or less had to win their remaining three games, all of which were at home – and something they hadn't achieved all season.

The first of these was against Carlisle United and English opened the scoring as the home side started brightly. Pools were rampant and didn't once take the foot off the gas. They won 4-1, firing a warning shot to the others battling to avoid re-election.

And when supporters turned up for the home match against Halifax, there was an audible gasp when they learned that English and Wigham were missing. It was a blow, but the 11 named players showed a resolve that had been missing for months and a 2-0 success was just reward for a fantastic display.

And months of groaning, complaining and agitating were all but forgotten when the final whistle sounded in the final match of the season against Wrexham, and Pools walked off the field happy that they had saved the club from the ignominy of finishing rock bottom. Once again Pools were without the injured English, but they deserved the win. They fought grimly against a side which played the better football and seemed inclined, like Halifax the previous Wednesday, to score every time they neared Pools' goal. But the home side prevailed and there were joyous scenes at the final whistle.

In the end, Barrow finished bottom of the table.

Pools had completed the season with the unenviable distinction of being the only side in the four leagues without an away win, but they had achieved their goal of avoiding re-election. And one week after the final ball was kicked, manager Jimmy Hamilton had his contract renewed for a further two years, while Jimmy Cartwright, the trainer, was also kept on. Sam English was joint top scorer with 11 goals from 36 appearances. It wasn't a fantastic return for a player of his calibre, but perhaps no great surprise as seven different players had worn the centre-forward jersey during the campaign.

But there was still sporting success to celebrate within the family as Sam's older brother Davie was crowned Scottish Champion cyclist. He was a member of the Loch Lomond Cycling Club, and was also in charge of the joiner's shop at the John Brown shipyard.

Player recruitment for the new season was slow, and it didn't look too good for Sam being kept on when chairman Mr W.J.

Yeats announced, 'It's always been my ambition that United should consist entirely of Hartlepool boys, or at any rate, drawn from a radius of 20 miles. I should like to see it the ambition of every young player to be able one day to say he played for Hartlepools United.'

A few days later, at the club's AGM, he added, 'We have made up our minds to have a young side. We are taking a risk but our manager will guarantee at least a team of triers.'

Jimmy Hamilton offered Sam a new contract, but on vastly reduced terms. Understandably, the player asked for time to consider, which he was granted, although he eventually declined the offer, as he believed it to be borderline insulting. Perhaps he thought the club would increase the offer, but they didn't.

Seven years after the clash in which John Thomson had lost his life, English was still being haunted by terracing taunts and decided it wasn't worth the hassle any more. He parted company with Hartlepools and moved back up to Scotland, and even if he had wanted to try and find a new club north of the border, his hands were tied as Hartlepools rubbed salt deeper into his wounds by effectively putting him out of the game at the age of 28. They had signed him for £275 24 months previously, but shamefully placed a £500 transfer bounty on his head, which scared off any would-be suitors.

They refused to lift their demands for the full transfer fee until after the Second World War, but Sam was by then 37 years old and effectively finished. It was an inglorious end to his career, and an awful way to be treated by a club which Sam had served well: a reprehensible decision by Pools' board.

Seventeen

SAM PLAYED his last game of professional football on 15 April 1938, and just a little over a year later Britain was at war with Germany. By then, he was back living permanently in Dalmuir and back earning a living in the shipyards.

Just six weeks after appearing for the last time in a Hartlepools jersey, however, Coleraine made an audacious attempt to sign the famous centre-forward. They wanted him to lead the line at The Showgrounds for the 1938/39 season, but Hartlepools refused to sanction any transfer unless they were paid the £500 fee in full. They wouldn't budge, and Coleraine couldn't afford such a fee, so the Irish League club swiftly dropped their interest. Coleraine played their football just 20 minutes up the road from Sam's birthplace, but sadly there would be no homecoming, and no emotional swansong.

Sam had been a professional footballer for seven seasons; a period during which his talents had presented his family with a comfortable lifestyle. After just a few weeks at Ibrox, he had looked destined for the very top, seemingly with the football world at his feet. He had seamlessly made the step up from Junior football to the Senior ranks, and possessed all the attributes required to take him to the very top of his profession. He was also a hard-working centre-forward, and more often than not the link man between his inside men and the forwards.

But here he was, back home in Dalmuir and on the football scrapheap in his late 20s. It was heartbreaking, but Hartlepools held all the aces so Sam went back to earning a wage the only way he knew how. Just prior to his final season at the Victoria Ground, during the close season, he had been enjoying a game of golf one day with friends, although what awaited him on his arrival home rocked him to his very core.

Sam recalled during an interview with the *Daily Express* in 1963, 'I had just parked the car when I was told my three daughters all wanted to see me. Seriously they lined up like a neat row of jugs – Charlotte, the eldest, on the outside; May in the middle; then little Eleanor.

'Charlotte explained, "It's Eleanor, daddy, she wants to ask you something." My youngest girl looked troubled but intent. "Daddy, did you kill a man?" she blurted out. "Why did you do it, daddy?"

'She was five years old. Minutes earlier she had been playing in the park, her blonde curls flying. Now this. "Did you shoot him, daddy? Did he hurt you?"

'Heavily it came to me that the sadness and insult of my life were to be visited upon my children as well.

'At Ibrox Park on the afternoon of 5 September 1931, I was playing centre-forward for Rangers. Celtic goalkeeper John Thomson fell at my legs. That evening he died of his injuries. So, six years later a stranger stops Eleanor in the park to tell her that her father is a killer. So even today my persecutors never sleep.

'Charlotte, May and Eleanor now have families of their own. Before anyone else approached them, my daughter decided to tell them the simple truth about their grandfather. "But we know, mummy," they choroused. "We've known it for ages.'"

During the Second World War, Sam and his family – like thousands of others – were directly in the firing line of Hitler's feared Luftwaffe. When the war was 18 months old, Nazi Germany decided to target the Clydebank and Dalmuir areas. Devastating air raids on the evenings of 13 and 14 March 1941 decimated many square miles. The Germans had targeted Clydebank due to its worldwide shipbuilding reputation, and the Dalmuir Royal Ordnance Factory, one of Scotland's major munitions depots, was included on the hit list. Other targets included the John Brown shipyard, where Sam worked, and the Singer sewing machine factory in Clydebank.

At the time there were approximately 12,000 homes in Clydebank and the number that remained undamaged after two nights of almost constant bombardment could be counted in single figures. It was a terrible time for the country, but unimaginable for those who were directly in the sights of the skilled, but ruthless, pilots dropping bombs from the evening skies.

During the war years, Sam sadly lost his father, Richard. His dad died on the afternoon of 15 October 1943 at his home in Buchanan Street, Dalmuir. He had been a shipyard foreman before retiring from the yards, and was 75 when he passed away. It was a terribly sad moment for the family, but Sam, his youngest son, was very close to his father and was particularly affected by his death.

After the long and bitter conflict was over, Sam expressed an interest to get back into football, but realised it would have to be on the coaching staff of a club as Hartlepools still held his player registration. He was 37 years old when the bombs stopped falling and realistically his playing days were over, but he still felt that stranglehold the Victoria Ground club had over him. He had been asked to turn out in a number of charity matches, mainly at Yoker, and had happily accepted all invitations. Even approaching the ripe old age of 40, he still had fire in his boots. There was an annual Old Crocks charity match played at Holm Park, Yoker, and he was always happy to lead the line.

Just after his 37th birthday, in October 1945, he received a letter from Hartlepools United informing him that he was released and was now free to sign for another club. It was nothing more than an insult, and he scrunched up the letter and threw it straight in the bin.

When the position of trainer came up at Duntocher Hibs, it seemed tailor-made for him. He had a wealth of experience and had worked under some great coaches and managers during his time in the game. He applied for the position and successfully negotiated the interview process, being appointed just four days later at the beginning of July 1949. He was looking forward to getting started at Glenhead Park and would be responsible for making sure the players were fit and prepared for matches. In those days, the playing side at most Junior clubs was run by committee and a group of selectors on said committee would pick the team on a Saturday. The position of trainer was, in fact, almost like a head coach.

Sam had three weeks to whip his new charges into shape, before the Hibs made the short trip to Clydebank for their opening match. It was a grand occasion and after a tough 90 minutes, honours were shared with a 2-2 draw. Sam was delighted to be back involved at Junior level, almost two decades after he had left Yoker.

He enjoyed his time at Glenhead and after his first season at the club he recognised that Duntocher had a wonderfully talented group of players and realised that with one or two useful additions, they could perhaps press for success. He used the close season to organise a series of fundraising events, which brought some much-needed cash into the coffers, and when the 1950/51 season began the Hibs were in a much stronger position, both on and off the park.

They were soon playing great football and by the end of a long and tiring campaign they were crowned league champions after beating Benburb in the play-offs. A player called Bone had been a vital cog in the success, playing in every position for the team that season. There were celebrations in an ale house close to Glenhead Park into the wee small hours as the club toasted the success of the players in winning the Central League championship. Meanwhile, in a quiet corner of the pub, Sam sat nursing a beer, enjoying a chat with members of the committee and reflecting on this great triumph. It was a different feeling from that of winning trophies as a player, but Sam gleaned just as much satisfaction from being a part of the backroom team at Duntocher.

He stayed with the club for a couple of seasons, and enjoyed his time enormously at Glenhead Park, but eventually gave it up to spend more time at home with his wife, and out tending the garden he had grown to love, especially his prized roses.

Sadly, in November 1956, he lost his mum, Jane. She passed away at the age of 86, and one of his strong, guiding lights had been extinguished. His mum had been a massive influence on his life and was there for him every step of the way after the John Thomson tragedy; always ready to listen or talk.

It was just over six years after he lost his mum, in February 1963, that Sam felt the time was right to finally open up about his life and career. It had been 31 years since the accident at Ibrox and in the time that had passed, he had never courted publicity. In fact he had deliberately shied away from speaking about himself or his football career, and refused point blank to speak about the terrible events of 5 September 1931.

But the time seemed right and so he sat down with a journalist from the *Daily Express* to give a flavour of what life had been like for him in the intervening years. The interview gave a fascinating insight into what it was like to be Sam English, and he had decided to hold nothing back.

Rather interestingly, the interview took place in a house in Fife; the very house where young John Thomson had been born and raised in Cardenden, and still the home of John's brother, Jim. At the time, Sam was 54 years old and had decided to tell plainly and frankly what happened when he first came face to face with John Thomson, and also to describe what it was like to live a life 'less as a person than one half of an accident'.

There would be no raking over the cold ashes of bitterness and he had no desire to reopen any old wounds. The story of Sam English and John Thomson had been kept alive through the actions of others; it had never been allowed to fade through time. Not that Sam would ever, could ever, forget. But his name had been so cruelly sullied, and his life so heavily dominated by the events of a single moment, that he had readily agreed to talk. And by holding that interview at the home of Jim Thomson, perhaps there was a chance that meeting John's brother could finally give him some sort of closure.

On so many occasions Sam had been told of how he was 'the unluckiest player in Scotland'. He would put that right by answering, 'Not the unluckiest, but the second unluckiest.'

Sam recalled, 'Perhaps I have been silent too long. For the Sam English story has been twisted into a kind of hideous folk tale. One generation has warped it and passed it on to the next. Memories are long in football. Time and rumour have clouded my own.

'My father, a quiet, canny Irishman, warned, "You will never be allowed to forget it." He advised me to give up football. But I played on for seven years. Reluctantly leaving Ibrox two years after the accident I went to Liverpool. Then back to Queen of the South. Finally to lowly Hartlepools United. Aged 28, I gave up; after seven years in which I won two Irish international caps. Seven years of joyless sport.

'In Scotland at corner kicks the crowds shrieked, "Watch the keeper. Watch the killer." If ever I clashed with a player, opponents would run alongside and whisper, "That will be another man you have killed."

'In England they said bluntly, "Watch that murderer."'

Sam also told of how no one had ever defied the great Rangers manager, Bill Struth, but of how, following the accident, he decided against taking his advice. He explained, 'Manager Struth advised me to play with cotton wool in my ears. I declined. Cotton wool would have solved nothing.

'When there was a daring keeper playing against me that was the end of the game so far as I was concerned. Often I must have looked a non-trier. Yet abuse on the field was at least understandable. Speech-play is part of football. But I will never understand why the memory of it has so wilfully been kept so red and raw. Or why John Thomson's death has been embittered by lies.

'Still, I treasure a letter from John Thomson's mother. It is dated on the third anniversary of her son's funeral. It read:

> 'Dear Mr and Mrs English, received the beautiful floral tribute that you sent in memory of our beloved son John. His resting place was lovely with all the wreaths.
>
> The Celtic company were here with their tributes also.
>
> Our hearts are sad at this time, but nothing can bring our dear one back again.

I hope you are all well as this leaves us.

With kind regards. Yours sincerely, Mrs Thomson.'

Sam spoke of how he was almost overcome by nerves as he made the short walk up the path to the Thomsons' front door on the day of the interview. He said, 'It was not easy going up to the door of the Thomson house; not easy going back to a house I had last visited in the early 1930s. On that occasion, John's parents had invited me a week after the funeral. With Mr Thomson I visited the grave. We shook hands.

'Now John's parents are dead. The Thomson family, like mine, has dispersed. But John's older brother Jim, who was at Ibrox that day, still lives there, and was there to greet me as I knocked on his door. "Come in, Sam," he said easily. "We've often wondered what happened to you."

'Later, Jim offered me a sherry. I haven't had a drink for nine years, but I had one then. We sat together on the couch under the unfinished portrait of John Thomson and talked of the old days of my pal Neillie "Cleek" Dewar, and Davie Meiklejohn and Jimmy McStay ... and the Prince of Goalkeepers.

'As the shadows of late afternoon slowly filed into the room, Jim said quietly, "I never blamed you for what happened, Sam. Neither did my mother. Even when she was at her lowest she always spared a thought for you. I'm sorry you have been so troubled."

'It was as if he had given me the gift of a new life. I sipped the sherry. Here was peace.'

Sitting side by side in Jim Thomson's living room, they had discovered a mutual sympathy, as well as a shared understanding and friendship.

And to think that both Sam and John Thomson might have been playing for the same team, as Arsenal manager Herbert Chapman had made unsuccessful bids, at different times, to take both players to Highbury. That was not to be. Instead, the lives of these two young men were to cross suddenly and sadly before a crowd of 80,000 fervent supporters at Ibrox.

One of the greatest features of being a footballer for Sam was the opportunity to play in front of such big crowds. When he was out on the football field, he was free as a bird and keen to express himself in the most positive way possible. That remained the case wherever he played the game. Notwithstanding the negative side of the game, there had never been a greater feeling for the player than pulling on his boots and running out at Ibrox in front of a large crowd.

However, he recalled, 'Nowhere in the world are there teams like Rangers or Celtic. Probably what is known as the "hooligan element" is no greater a percentage of their support than of any other club. That there are many thousands of decent, warm-hearted Celtic followers I know well. I probably know it better than anybody else.'

But how different life might have been had the tragic events unfolded in a different way.

Sam recalled, 'In and around John Thomson's home in Fife there has been only kindness. True, on holiday at Kinghorn, I have overheard men say in the streets, "That's the laddie that killed Johnny Tamson." But they were merely identifying me. There was no harm in it.

'From my own neighbours around Dalmuir and Clydebank and Duntocher – men of all religions or no religion at all – I have enjoyed sympathy and understanding.

'Blind bigotry has bred elsewhere. In Glasgow, where after all these years I still wear a cap to hide my face.

'In the shipyards, where I meet young men, not alive at the time: they cannot remember the accident, but they cannot allow themselves to forget it either.

'In the un-surrendering hatred of the anonymous writers of letters to my home.'

But Sam revealed that not all letters he received were slanderous or negative. He explained, 'Some of the letters, ragged now from constant reading, I salvaged from the blitz of my home in the war. Like this one from a Glasgow man, "Personally, I come in contact daily with hundreds of people, mostly Celtic fans, and the opinion is expressed by each and every one – 'Sam English was not to blame. He is the same type of player as John Thomson, clean and appreciative of his opponent's ability.'"

'Now I am 54, still a sheet metal worker in the shipyards. We live alone, my wife and I, now that our daughters have married, in a four-room house high in Dalmuir. Sadie runs the kind of house where if you sit too long in one place you are liable to get polished along with the furniture. I have learned to love the garden.

'Three years ago I started going regularly enough to Senior football again, mingling with my friend Willie Thornton and other sportsmen at Firhill. Thanks to director George Brown and manager Scot Symon I also visit Ibrox occasionally.

'But the aching embarrassment of being some kind of grisly peepshow has not left me yet.

'At least the time has passed when I was afraid to look a stranger full in the face in case he would stare back at me and never stop staring. For something happened all those many years ago. I don't know what, and I understand even less.'

Sam's son-in-law Ronnie Cree was married to the youngest of the three English girls, Eleanor. Ronnie spent a lot of time with his father-in-law after he and Eleanor married, and knew the former Rangers striker like few others; describing him as quiet and reserved.

Ronnie said: 'Sam didn't get involved with many folk, because he didn't like being part of a big crowd. I tried for many years to get him to go back to the football, because I was in the Rangers Supporters' Club in Old Kilpatrick, but it was tough. He was back working in the shipyard and there was a guy there who ran the bus and he talked Sam into going to a game, but he wouldn't go without Eleanor. I think Eleanor and I were married at the time, but he took her everywhere.

'I was happy that we had persuaded Sam to go back to see Rangers, but he didn't go all that often. On one occasion, he took me to Ibrox one Saturday morning and big Jimmy Smith – the guy who had replaced Sam at centre-forward – was the trainer at the time. We were shown round the stadium and we saw the trophy room and went out on to the pitch. It was a fantastic experience.

'Sadly it was my wife who was told by another kid, "Your daddy killed somebody!" She was only five years old at the time and she told her mum and dad when she got home from school. That must have been hell for Sam. He just couldn't get away from it. It wasn't nice and every September he would sink into a deep depression, which was horrible to see.'

Ronnie added, 'Before I got involved with the family he was the trainer at Duntocher Hibs for a wee while, but after his time at Hartlepools, he stopped playing, period. I've heard stories of up to ten busloads of Celtic supporters heading down to Anfield to give him a hard time and boo him. And when he subsequently signed for both Queen of the South and Hartlepools they moved with him. He had a terrible time of it.

'After Hartlepools his father said to him, "Sam, you'd be as well giving up the football and going back to your trade," and that's exactly what he did. His dad told him that the baying mob would never leave him alone. He was right.

'It must have been really tough to go back to working in the shipyards after being a professional footballer, but he had no option. He had three girls and needs must.'

Ronnie insists his father-in-law never spoke about the incident. He said, 'He didn't ever speak about his career. I sometimes managed to get the odd word or two out of him and all he would say was, "I scored a few goals, but that's what I was there for."

'The only time he ever really opened up was when I would go up to help him with the garden. He was a keen gardener. He also liked a game of golf, so we would go to nearby Dalmuir Golf Club for a round and he would sometimes talk of some of the players who played during his time in the game. Of course, he knew everybody at the golf club as he'd stayed in the area most of his life.

'What a difference when Sam left Yoker to go to Rangers. It all changed for him then. One of the first things he did was visit a well-known tailor in Glasgow for a couple of new suits, Crombie coat, shirt and shoes. That was the Rangers way. He had to arrive at Ibrox on match day dressed like a tailor's dummy.

'But Sam was still very much a family man, even when he joined Rangers, because I recall my wife telling me once that her mother used to say, "I don't know how we ended up away down in Dalmuir as we were away looking at all these private bungalows."

'Sam was quiet and unassuming. It was just his way.'

Eighteen

GOALS, GOALS and more goals. That's what the majority of us crave when we pass through the turnstiles and make our way up to the stand. Of course, most are also there through loyalty to their club, but what makes them happiest during a game is a fantastic piece of skill, some robust defending, or the ball bulging the back of the net.

For many, the world of football revolves around the humble stat. There is an insatiable appetite to know who has won the most Premier League titles, or the player with the greatest number of international caps, or even the guy with the longest throw, who perhaps keeps a towel at the side of the park to clean the ball before throwing. The list is endless.

Sam English was a record breaker. His business was goals, and he scored lots of them. Sure, his blond hair got him noticed, but not nearly as much as his ability to stick the ball in the back of the net. A good, young defender or midfielder breaking into the Rangers team at a similar time would have been noticed for his ability to defend or create, but not nearly as much as someone scoring goals with the regularity of Mr English. A youngster who can score with such consistency is normally made for life. So who knows exactly what Sam could have achieved had his career path followed a smoother trajectory?

Of course, it's all ifs and buts. The only thing we know for sure is that in the 1931/32 season there were few defences who could hold back this boy wonder. Sam was a goal machine and his lightning quick bursts, intelligent movement and eye for an opportunity gave defences the length and breadth of the country endless nightmares. That season, at least, he was unstoppable. It was his debut campaign in the Seniors and he repaid boss Bill Struth with 44 league goals, and 53 overall, both of which broke existing club records. It's perhaps difficult to compare contemporary overall records with those of today, as the Scottish League Cup wasn't around in the 1930s, so Sam's tally included just league and Scottish Cup matches. But at the time of writing, 88 years after Sam set Rangers' record for league goals scored during a single season, it remains intact.

The great Ally McCoist is Rangers' all-time record scorer with an incredible 355 in all competitions. In all likelihood it's a record that will never be beaten. But even Super Ally couldn't get near Sam's 1931/32 league haul. In fact, the closest he got was ten shy, which he managed three times. McCoist had scored 34 league goals in 1992/93 when he suffered a broken leg while playing for Scotland in Portugal. He missed Rangers' last seven league games. Might that have been the year?

Of course, he scored goals consistently over a number of seasons, but that one record managed to evade arguably the greatest goalscorer the club has known. Mind you, McCoist seemed to break every other club record, so perhaps it's fitting that he left Sam's intact.

Fast forward to 1997/98 and it looked as though Italian striker Marco Negri would smash the figure – and then some. Negri scored 30 league goals prior to the New Year; half that amount from January to May would make him a record breaker. But one day after training he went for a friendly game of squash with team mate Sergio Porrini at a Glasgow city centre hotel. During the ensuing encounter he would almost lose an eye.

Following the accident, in which he copped a squash ball square in the face, Porrini drove him straight to hospital, although his knowledge of Glasgow being what it was, he steered them towards the maternity unit at Rottenrow. He was advised to head to Stobhill, where they had a specialist eye unit, and quick-thinking Porrini flagged down a black Hackney cab which they would follow to the Springburn hospital. Negri was eventually diagnosed with a detached retina as well as peripheral vision loss. While it wasn't quite the end of his season, he was out for a while and when he eventually returned, his focus was lost and he subsequently suffered a debilitating back injury.

Before McCoist and Negri, there was Jim Forrest, arguably one of the most naturally gifted finishers ever to play for Rangers. He signed for the Ibrox club as a schoolboy and was farmed out to Drumchapel Amateurs for a spell. But when he was unleashed into the first team in 1962, in place of the ageing Jimmy Millar, he proved a phenomenon. A couple of goals on his Old Firm debut marked him down as one to watch. He was just 17.

But it was in 1964/65 that the goals started to flow, almost effortlessly, and he was tipped to topple Sam's record, which had stood, at that time, for 33 years. Forrest was ruthless in front of goal, and it was felt that if anyone could break the record he was the man to do it. As the season progressed, his shot at glory grew arms and legs, and newspapers regularly gave over a growing number of column inches to the achievements of this arch marksman.

Between August and October 1964, he fired 18 League Cup goals in just ten matches, including both goals in the semi-final as

Rangers overcame Dundee United, a feat he repeated in the final as Rangers beat Celtic at Hampden. While league goals are the primary currency of a centre-forward, his League Cup exertions provide a sense of his capabilities.

On New Year's Day, he scored the only goal of the Old Firm game at Ibrox, his ninth league goal in five matches. Eight days later, he scored three times against Dundee at Ibrox, which took his tally for the season in all competitions to an incredible 40 goals. This saw him surpass, by one goal, the Ibrox post-war scoring record in all competitive matches held jointly by Max Murray, Jimmy Millar and himself.

But Forrest was still 13 goals short of the Rangers record held by Sam English, who had scored nine Scottish Cup goals to go with his tally of 44 in the league. Up to that point, the leading Ibrox marksmen for one season in all competitive matches were English with 53, Willie Reid with 48, Jimmy Fleming with 47, and Jimmy Smith with 46.

There were still 15 league games left to play, and a possible five Scottish Cup ties, so Forrest was in prime position to become Rangers' all-time record scorer in a single season. He also had his eye firmly trained on English's league record. Not that it bothered Sam, though, as he spoke freely of his desire to see the young centre-forward claim the record as his own.

Sam, who was 56 years old at the time, was interviewed by a journalist while being treated for muscular problems in a Glasgow hospital. He said, 'Jim can have my record with pleasure. I like this boy Forrest, he really has got it. The first match I saw him play I forecast that he would break my record.

'What impressed me most about him was the way he can shoot with both feet. The crowd have been a bit hard on Jim at times. He is just a boy and is gaining experience, so there will be a lot more goals from him in the years to come.

'I know how he feels. When I broke the record 33 years ago I got plenty of handshakes and congratulations. It is a wonderful feeling. I would also tip Forrest to become Scotland's regular centre-forward.

'Talking of the current team, I also like this boy Willie Johnston. He is so cool and calm I am sure he can go on and do great things.

'When I went to Rangers after scoring 293 goals in three seasons for Yoker Athletic I was put into the Ibrox first team straight away. And what a dream debut it was – to score two goals against Dundee.'

Jim Forrest wasn't likely to forget Dundee either, as his hat-trick against them saw him pass the post-war record of 39 goals. At the time, Forrest said, 'It was wonderful. The boys were all delighted that I was able to do it. It was a great feeling to score the goal that broke the record.

'But I would like the rest of the team to have their share of the praise. After all, they made the goals. And I cannot thank Jimmy Millar enough for the way he has helped me since I became the regular centre-forward.'

But he added, 'Beating the record is not the most important thing – it is winning the Scottish League championship. For me, that will always be the case over individual recognition.'

And he had a point, because when Sam English smashed Willie Reid's goalscoring record in 1932, Rangers finished only second in the league. Motherwell won the championship, and their centre-forward, the great Willie MacFadyen, scored 52 of his side's 119 league goals, a stunning haul which saw him eclipse Sam by eight during an incredible season. MacFadyen's haul also surpassed Celtic ace Jimmy McGrory's 40 league goals in 1926/27. In 1935/36, McGrory scored 50 league goals for Celtic.

In 1965, Rangers were chasing Kilmarnock for the league title and Forrest knew the value of being the number one club in the league, especially with qualification for the European Cup as an added incentive to that of being crowned a championship winner.

As the season moved into its final phase, there were five clubs still in with a realistic chance of winning the title. As well as Rangers and Kilmarnock, Dunfermline Athletic, Hearts and Hibs were all still there or thereabouts, and the ultimate prospects of all five remained in the balance.

The battles being waged by both Rangers and Forrest were naturally intertwined. Rangers were facing seven games in April, the final month of a long campaign, and the first of these was a home encounter with Falkirk, in which they prevailed 6-1. Forrest scored four times to edge closer to English's record of 53 in a single season (his cousin, Alec Willoughby, scored the other two). Included in the 21-year-old's four-goal salvo was his 50th of the season. Rangers were out of the Scottish Cup but Forrest still had five league games in which to score the four goals required.

In Scottish league fixtures, Forrest had scored 29 times, so unless he was to produce something incredible in the final five games, English's record of 44 was safe. Forrest had also scored six times in the European Cup, which was a mark of his individual class, especially as the half-dozen strikes included home and away goals against Inter Milan, and against the crack Yugoslavs, Red Star Belgrade. Of course, these goals didn't count towards English's record.

But the closing stages of the season would prove something of an anti-climax. Forrest would score just one more goal that season – against Morton at Cappielow in a 3-1 victory, in which Rangers were urged on by the vast majority of the 18,000 crowd.

As for Rangers' title challenge, the next two games, against Dunfermline Athletic at East End Park, and at home to Dundee

United, would make or break their season. Forrest played in both but Rangers lost 3-1 at Dunfermline, before going down 1-0 against United at Ibrox. It was so disappointing, and the title dream was all but over.

Forrest had hoped to give bride-to-be Margaret Hamilton an additional wedding present in the shape of a league medal, and Sam's long-held goalscoring record, but sadly he came up just a little short on both.

For the last two league games against Motherwell and Third Lanark (both away from home), Rangers manager Scot Symon dropped Forrest and replaced him with George McLean. The team won both, although it mattered little as the league was lost and Rangers finished fifth, six points behind champions, Kilmarnock, and also adrift of Hearts, Dunfermline and Hibs.

Still, Forrest finished the season with the stunning total of 57 competitive goals, which included a ratio of a goal a game in 30 league outings. He also had his 18 counters in ten League Cup matches, and three goals in three Scottish Cup ties – not to mention six in Europe.

As for Sam English, he was genuinely disappointed that Forrest hadn't been able to overtake either of his records, but was still able to fully appreciate the talents of the young Ranger. Like English, Forrest was a natural in front of goal, although perhaps, if anything, the latter's failure to grab the record in such a prolific season proved how good Sam had actually been. And, of course, it had been Sam's debut season in the Seniors.

Nineteen

THE FOOTBALL season was over and Sam turned dutifully to his garden. He was looking forward to another summer of planting, pruning and digging in his outdoor space at home in Dalmuir's Overtoun Road. It was rapidly becoming his sanctuary; the place where he felt most at home, and he would work away peacefully for hours, stopping only for a quick chat with passing neighbours or the postman. It was an oasis of calm, and after a couple of hours of lovingly tending his brightly coloured flowers, he would stop for a cuppa and a read of the morning paper.

Imagine his surprise, then, when he picked up the newspaper one day and the following headline was staring straight back at him, 'Famous ex-Rangers centre-forward Sam English rumoured to be dying'. He nearly choked on his tea, and no wonder. Sam did a double take, but it merely confirmed that the headline he'd read the first time was there before him in big bold letters. He sighed.

A few moments later, Sam noticed a friend striding purposefully towards his house; his usual laid-back gait more of a sprint. The man peered over the fence and saw Sam sitting enjoying his cup of tea. 'Thank God, you're alive,' he sighed.

Sam, who was 57 at the time, smiled, and replied, 'Believe me, I'm feeling absolutely fine.'

The pair sat down for a chat, and Sam told his worried friend: 'Like you I've just read in the newspaper that I was ill – but it's not true, and I have no idea how the rumour started.'

Throughout the day, a steady stream of friends and relatives called at his house for an update on the story. They were worried sick about it and wanted to make sure Sam was okay. Among the visitors was a newspaper reporter, looking for a follow-up on the original story. Sam decided it was probably best to put the record straight, so he told him, 'It's true that I've been off my work at the shipyard for more than a year with muscular trouble, but I'm not confined to bed or anything like that.

'There's plenty of life in me yet. I've been getting treatment at a hospital for my muscles so maybe that's how this silly story started.'

His wife, Sadie, added, 'When I went out shopping dozens of people came up and asked me how Sam was. I am very annoyed about the whole thing. Sam's not dying – in fact he's a lot better than he used to be.'

The former Ranger got on with his life and, although never one to court publicity, he would've raised a chuckle when the main newspaper in the Hartlepool area, the *Northern Daily Mail*, printed a letter from a supporter asking fellow fans who they believed was Pools' greatest ever player. The *NDM* embraced the topic. It was the close season and it was guaranteed to fill half a page, but the subject grew arms and legs and the feature became so popular that an array of names was soon being put forward, with many readers mentioning, in the main, two or three players. One name in particular kept cropping up: that of Sam English. There was no keeping a good man down.

Frank Barson, Billy Brown and Johnny Wigham also received many unofficial nominations, but after running with the theme for just over a fortnight, the *Mail* called a halt to the topic, and stopped short of saying that English was the best ever, announcing, 'There can be few better than Sammy!' That spoke volumes.

There was no doubt that Sam had made his mark on every club he played for. At Yoker, the sheer number of goals he scored in his three seasons with the Whe Ho assured him of legendary status at Holm Park, while at Ibrox his record haul of league goals in a single season and championship and Scottish Cup medals marked him down as a true champion.

When he moved to Liverpool, he was hailed as their saviour, and while the greatest centre-forward in the world could not have solved the Anfield club's problems on his own, English scored consistently well in the first half of his debut season before the constant fouling and incendiary remarks about John Thomson took a heavy toll on the player.

At Queen of the South, he lifted spirits and turned in some excellent performances on the pitch, but an inglorious end to his time at Palmerston Park meant that specific chapter in his career is better forgotten. At Hartlepools, he again scored regularly, but had slipped so deeply into a period of prolonged malaise that the football became less important to him. He found comfort in passing on the benefits of his experience to young kids hoping to make the grade, and was also well known for the time he made for supporters, and youngsters in particular.

One wonders just how far Sam could have progressed in the game had one of two different scenarios taken place. Completely hypothetical, I know, but had he decided to join Arsenal from Yoker, not only would the Holm Park side have received a healthy cash windfall, but Sam would have been joining a club with creative talents such as Cliff Bastin, David Jack and Alex James. With guys like that supplying the ammunition, Sam could have enjoyed a long and fruitful association with the Gunners. In the first five seasons of the 1930s, Arsenal won four league titles, and finished runner-up on the other occasion. Sam would have been joining arguably the best team in Europe.

Scenario number two plays out if Jimmy Smith hadn't been suffering from a heavy cold or flu on the morning of Saturday, 5 September 1931, and the injured Sam had watched the Old Firm game from the Ibrox stand. With his all-round talent and eye for goal, legendary status would surely have been there for the taking.

But Sam did play against Celtic, and he was involved in the accidental clash which led to John Thomson's death, and for that he suffered for the rest of his life. It simply wasn't fair.

On Wednesday, 12 April 1967, Sam died while a patient in the Vale of Leven Hospital. He was 58 years old, and passed away after a long illness. His family were by his side.

Sam, a sheet metal worker to trade, lived with his wife, daughter and son-in-law at Overtoun Road, in Dalmuir. He had been ill for some time with motor neurone disease, and eventually died of the condition. He was survived by his wife, Sarah, and three grown-up daughters.

Sam's son-in-law, Ronnie Cree, said, 'When Sam died, he'd had motor neurone for five or six years. It had been working on him all that time, and it more or less came to light because he was working on the tools. His hands would be shaking and he would struggle to hold them properly. They didn't know what it was then. It was years later before they came up with all the information about motor neurone, but it was on his death certificate. The worst bit for Sam was that he couldn't play golf. He would just sit there a lot of the time, and after a while he couldn't get up the stairs in his house. It was very tough to watch.'

Sam's funeral service took place in the Clydebank Co-operative Funeral Home on the following Friday, before the cortege moved on to Cardross Crematorium, just 12 miles from his home. More than 100 people attended the ceremony, including former team-mates and players, as well as friends from the golf club, who wanted to pay tribute to a footballer and friend of the highest calibre, and a man who lived only for his family.

Sam was finally at peace.

Twenty

ON A gable end in the Ravenhill district of East Belfast, a painting of Sam English stood 15 feet tall. It was part of a project called The Ulster Connection, and a celebration of all those from Northern Ireland who had played competitively for Rangers up until 2004.

The number of players remembered on the wall totalled 15: from James Macauley, who played just one game in 1910, to promising youngster Lee Feeney, who signed for Rangers from Linfield in 1999. In between, there were club legends such as Bert Manderson, Billy Simpson and Jimmy Nicholl; players who have amassed hundreds of first-team appearances between them and contributed greatly to the Ibrox club.

But one player stood out from the crowd. Sam English – with his shock of blond hair – adorning the classic footballer's pose; arms folded, chest puffed out and standing tall. Sam English: proud to be a Ranger.

The stunning mural was the brainchild of a group of local Rangers supporters, led by Ian McClean, Keith Bradshaw and David Rea. They were assisted in different ways by Colin Robinson and the local Bridge Community Association.

Sadly, the mural is no longer a part of the area following necessary safety work on the gable end. But the memories of such a tremendous work of art will never be lost to Ian McClean, who explained, 'The plan was always to feature a single player and build everything else around that player. We chose Sam English because we hoped his image would lead to local people asking about him, and then we could tell them all about his incredible goalscoring record. We wanted to make more folk aware of just how good a player he had been. Sam played for Rangers in a bygone era, and we felt there would be a great many Rangers fans who didn't know his story. He was a tremendously talented footballer and a great goal scorer. It was fitting that he was the centrepiece.'

Ian explained how the project started to take shape after a series of meetings. He said, 'Our local community association, The Bridge, on Ravenhill Road, received funding from a government source, and so Colin Robinson, director of the project, gave us £1,000 towards the cost of the mural. We organised a fundraising night in The Longfellow Bar, which was well patronised, and collected a further £500. Lagan Village Rangers Supporters' Club also made a donation, plus we got a really good deal on paint and scaffolding from local companies, which saved a few quid.

'Keith Bradshaw, David Rea, myself and a few others did most of the base work, whitewashing the wall with four coats. Keith and Davie then did the bulk of the painting. We projected the image of Sam English on to the wall late one night and a local artist, Mark Hutchinson, painted in the face. We were very pleased with the job Mark did.

'In all it took around three weeks as we were all in employment during the day and could only commit to the project at night. We received great support from local residents, perhaps because it was an original mural and not a paramilitary-style one. Most of the residents at that time would have been Rangers supporters, or they would at least have had a soft spot for the club.

'But after a few years, the wall started to show real signs of wear and tear. In fact, the mural actually protected the gable from water for a number of years as there were that many coats of paint on it.

'The old couple who lived in the house had given us permission to use the wall on the understanding that it could be painted over if any major structural work was needed. The painting stood for many years until the couple sadly passed away. The family wanted to sell the property and work was required so the mural had to go. It was disappointing, but it was part of the original agreement. Every now and again, if I'm passing the wall, someone will say to me, "Aw big man, fair miss the mural," and that always makes me smile.'

Ian, who was born and bred on Ravenhill Road, added, 'Working on the mural was a true labour of love for me. It was painted on the gable wall of a house which stood at the corner of Donard Street and Ravenhill Road. The grandmother of George Best lived on Donard Street at one time, so it was in a great location!'

In 2008, Sam was once again the subject of an art project, although this time the talented footballer was to be committed to canvas. Renowned Scottish artist Helen Runciman had worked on a wide range of subjects including iconic buildings, people and beaches, but her collection of Rangers greats was widely regarded as some of the finest sporting art around.

Based in Denny, Stirlingshire, Helen was approached regarding a commission which would be the centrepiece for a dinner to be held on the centenary of Sam's birth. As a huge Rangers fan, it was music to Helen's ears, and she started to collate as much information on the Irishman as she could.

She said: 'The Sam English painting was produced for a commemorative dinner in his honour. There are three images of

Sam in the painting and they represent his love of scoring hat-tricks, something he did six times during the 1931/32 season.

'The three images feature the things every world class centre-forward should have: a great shot, top-class header and, most importantly, a winner.

'Given the quality of photographs that were available from the 1930s, I was lucky that I was able to source some good quality images to work from. With a fine head of hair, a few curls and a winning smile I hope I was able to do justice to him.'

Helen added, 'The painting also includes the iconic Ibrox Main Stand frontage, a view of the main stand from the pitch and the words of another legendary Rangers front man, Bob McPhail, who described Sam as "the best centre-forward I ever played with".

'As a lifelong Rangers fan, creating paintings and sculptures of my heroes from more recent years is a labour of love. Making sure the memory of our players from past generations live on to allow today's fans to learn more about the history of our club, and the players and individuals who built the club up from the four boys who had a dream, is a great honour.'

From concept to finished article, the painting took around three months to complete, and the reaction when it was launched at the centenary dinner in the Thornton Suite was one of astonishment. In fact, the compliments keep coming.

The Rangers Supporters' Trust was keen to ensure the centenary of Sam English's birth be celebrated in a style befitting of the player's achievements, and decided to commission a unique piece of silver that would ensure the player would forever be a part of the football club.

They decided on a rose bowl, due to Sam's love of that particular flower, and immediately sought out a talented silversmith from Northern Ireland to bring their dreams to reality.

The idea was for the rose bowl to hold 44 silver balls, one for each goal scored by Sam in his record-breaking season. They wanted the bowl to be one of the most stunning pieces of artwork in the Ibrox trophy room, where it would sit all year round, only coming out at the end of each season to be presented to Rangers' highest league goalscorer.

It was a fantastic idea, and in Cara Murphy, they tracked down one of the best in the business.

Ms Murphy had just completed a desk set for the Silver Trust for Downing Street when she got the call, so 2008 was a busy year for her.

She said, 'I work mainly to commission and had made many other trophies so it was something I had done before. I hadn't long had an online presence when I was contacted by the Rangers supporters' group who wanted to give me the commission. They had found me by Googling "Northern Ireland Silversmith"! They wanted a silver award to commemorate the centenary of Sam English's birth and they liked the idea of having the piece designed and created in Northern Ireland.

'Obviously 44 goals is a huge achievement and one I wanted to represent in the design. I wanted to show the enormity of that through the silver and came up very quickly with the idea of the loose balls in the bowl. I explained my design through a bowl filled with 44 ping pong balls and was delighted they agreed, adding that it would be a different concept to many of the other trophies at Ibrox.'

Cara was sharing a workshop with her dad, Michael, in County Down, and it wouldn't be unusual for her to be working on several commissions at any one time, depending on the scale of the job.

The Sam English Rose Bowl, as she explained, was created from a large flat disc of silver. 'It was slowly hammered into its form. This process is known as raising and takes quite a while to complete. The silver is hammered over a steel former with steel hammers. This process is repeated and repeated until the required form is achieved. The outside of the bowl is hammered with a small hammer to create a surface of thousands of little polished hammer marks. I honestly can't remember exact timings but I know I only had a matter of months from initial contact until it was presented.

'With 44 balls I had to make 88 halves and then solder them together. I wanted the inside of the bowl and the balls to be highly polished to achieve the maximum reflection. There was a lot of work in the piece and the rim of the bowl is also engraved.'

When finished, the rose bowl was unveiled at a dinner held by the Garvagh Rangers Supporters' Club, in Northern Ireland, in June 2008. It was hailed as a thing of great beauty.

Cara added, 'I then took it across to Ibrox for the Sam English centenary match day in August. This was a wonderful day spent in the directors' box and meeting everyone. Some of Sam's family were also there, and it was lovely to meet them.

'Rangers were thrilled with the bowl when it was presented to them by the supporters. I was also really pleased with how the piece came together. The reflection of all the polished balls inside the bowl took on a kind of optical illusion which added to the story.

'I am from Northern Ireland although I studied silversmithing and jewellery at Glasgow School of Art from 1988 to 1992 so I was very aware of Rangers, especially getting the boat back and forward to Northern Ireland. I'd never been to a football match and hadn't known about Sam English but it was a special award to make because of his achievements, and I was genuinely delighted that he was getting the recognition he deserved. The centenary match was held in the August, as Sam's birthday was the 18th, which is also my birthday, so it was a nice coincidence!

'It was fantastic to see the rose bowl in the trophy room on the day it was handed over at Ibrox, but it's been a while and one day I hope I can get back to see it again as I'd love to see how the players react to it and to know if they see it as something special to be awarded.

'On a personal level, making something like this, where there is a narrative, is a challenge that I always enjoy. Including the six years that I studied in Glasgow and London, I have been a silversmith for 30 years. As you can imagine it's not a nine-to-five job but I really enjoy the making process. The hand-eye coordination of creating the work and the enjoyment of seeing the finished product being presented. It's also about the people you meet, the stories you hear and seeing the piece being used. Setanta Sports came to the workshop to film the rose bowl being created, so I knew the prestige attached to the piece.'

When Cara was at Ibrox to hand over the trophy, it was John Greig, voted the Greatest Ever Ranger in a poll by supporters, who was on hand to accept it on behalf of the club.

Sam's son-in-law Ronnie Cree insisted the family were proud of the record number of goals he scored in the 1931/32 season – and the silver trophy which was created to mark that achievement. He added, 'The Sam English Rose Bowl, which is awarded to the top league goalscorer each season, is a beautiful piece and something else which makes us all very proud.

'Marco Negri and Ally McCoist came very close to beating Sam's record during their careers, but they didn't quite get there, and with the way the modern game is now, who knows if the record will ever be beaten. In Sam's day a centre-forward was a centre-forward. Virtually his only job was to score goals. Sam once said to me that his job was made so much easier because his team-mates would always give the ball to him. Such a simple philosophy.'

Northern Ireland international Andy Little was a proud winner of the rose bowl in 2013, but insisted he didn't know he had won the trophy until the evening he collected the award. He said: 'I was so proud, but I must admit that it came as a big surprise. We were at the Player of the Year awards at the Hilton Hotel, in Glasgow, and as the season was finished I was enjoying quite a few rum and cokes. It was a great night and the lads were all having a good time.

'I was never one for counting goals, but Lee McCulloch and I had been having a bit of a race to see who could finish as top scorer, and I genuinely had no idea who had won. I knew it was close but as I was off on holiday to Thailand and the United States a few days later, I wasn't too bothered.

'Then there was a wee tap on the shoulder. "Eh, Andy, you're next up on stage!" I was shocked. I went up to collect the award, which was this absolutely stunning silver rose bowl and I was as proud as punch. At that time I hadn't realised the rose bowl was awarded on the basis of league goals only, so I was delighted. Ironically I scored 22 goals in 2012/13 – half the total Sam English managed.

'But I was really proud to win a trophy named after another Northern Ireland international centre-forward. The only disappointing aspect of it is that I didn't get my name on the trophy. That would have been just perfect. My mum and dad came over from Northern Ireland for the first game of the following season and I took them to the trophy room to see the rose bowl, and they were equally as impressed with it as I was, but mum asked why my name wasn't on it.

'We managed to get a nice photograph taken with it before it was put back in its glass cabinet. The winner didn't get to take it home, which was probably just as well as no doubt one or two of the wee silver balls might have got lost. Perhaps in the future the names of the winners might be engraved on it, or even a plinth.

'But to think that I'd won such a beautiful trophy at the club I've loved since I was a wee boy growing up in Enniskillen was just such a wonderful feeling.

'Some great players are also previous winners; guys like Kris Boyd, Kenny Miller and Nikica Jelavic, and of course the likes of Alfredo Morelos and Jermain Defoe have now been added. It's awesome to follow guys like that.'

Sam English Rose Bowl winners – league goals only
2009: Kris Boyd (27) Premier League
2010: Kris Boyd (23) Premier League
2011: Kenny Miller (21) Premier League
2012: Nikica Jelavic (14) Premier League
2013: Andy Little (22) Division Three
2014: Jon Daly (20) League One
2015: Nicky Law (10) Championship
2016: Martyn Waghorn (23) Championship
2017: Kenny Miller (11) Premier League
2018: Alfredo Morelos (14) Premier League
2019: Alfredo Morelos (18) Premier League
2020*: Jermain Defoe (13) Premier League
*Season unfinished

The Rangers Supporters' Trust played an integral part in organising a series of events to mark the centenary of Sam's birth, in August 2008. Mark Dingwall was on the board of the Trust at the time and explained how events unfolded. He said, 'We felt Sam's story was a great one, and many on the board felt it was sad how he had been treated. Sam had a lot of surviving family members who we knew would care greatly about how any event attached to his name would be perceived, so we knew we had to do it properly.

'After a few meetings, and a great deal of soul-searching, we decided to commission the rose bowl, the painting from Helen Runciman and put plans in place to hold a dinner in Sam's honour, which would take place in the Thornton Suite at Ibrox on the evening of Saturday, 16 August, after the Rangers v Hearts match. Sam was a great friend of Willie Thornton, so we liked the connection.

'The dinner was a complete sell-out and we were delighted to host several members of Sam's family. It was a great night and was topped off with a fantastic speech from future Rangers director John Gilligan, who finished his talk by saying, "A great wrong has been righted tonight." That summed it up for me, and when I looked across at Sam's youngest daughter, Eleanor, she had a big smile on her face.

'We had always hoped that we could lay to rest the ghost that Sam had somehow been responsible for John Thomson's death. This was about Sam English, nothing else. We wanted to mark the centenary of Sam's birth in style, but with a touch of class, and I think we achieved that. So many people on the Trust – like Simon Leslie, Stevie Tyrie, Christine Somerville, etc. – worked tirelessly to make it happen, but it was a real labour of love.

'When we were talking about commissioning the rose bowl, the Garvagh Rangers Supporters' Club organised a fundraising event, which was a big success. Gregory Campbell was one of the speakers that night. I'll be honest; when I first set eyes on Cara Murphy's finished creation, it was like Harry Potter's Goblet of Fire – it sent shivers cascading down my spine. Sam had loved his roses.'

The Rangers Supporters' Trust were also keen for the birthplace of Sam English to be marked by a plaque, and set out to find out exactly where he had been born. They were helped along the way by the Coleraine Historical Society, and once they had pinpointed exactly where Sam had made his entrance into the world, they contacted Coleraine Burgh Council, and they were only too happy to get involved. In February 2009, the former mayor of Coleraine, Maurice Bradley, invited members of Sam's family over to Northern Ireland for a ceremony to honour their talented relation. Deputy Mayor, Barney Fitzpatrick, was also very supportive.

Mark explained, 'We spoke to the council and they were fantastic. We got the plaques made and there were no problems with red tape. Dessie Monahan owned the land on which Sam's first house stood, and he was a joy to work with. We unveiled a plaque at the entrance to his house, and one on the actual property itself. It was a fantastic day.

'This was the perfect ending to the Sam English story. He had received the appropriate recognition in both Scotland and Northern Ireland. We felt our job was done.'

But there was one more task to perform, and it concerned the Rangers FC Hall of Fame.

At the top of Ibrox's famous marble staircase there is a large mahogany panel on the wall with a list of names. But this isn't just any list of names. As accurately as possible, it represents the greatest players to play for the club. It is a list of those fortunate enough to have been inducted into the Hall of Fame.

Everyone has a favourite player, and the chances are your choice will be up there on the panel, as it includes all the great names to have played for Rangers since the club's inception in 1872. So when chairman David Murray decided to mark the millennium by inaugurating a Hall of Fame, everyone had their own ideas of who should become members of such an exclusive club. It was a ground-breaking move by Murray, with Rangers the first club in Britain to come up with the idea for such a venture.

Of course, players such as John Greig, Davie Meiklejohn and Ally McCoist were almost a given. But of the thousand-plus players who have worn the Light Blue jersey with distinction, who would decide the incumbents, and what would be the criteria?

Rangers FC historian David Mason takes up the story, 'The chairman decided we should remember and honour the achievements and contribution made to the club by its finest players. A mahogany panel was fitted at the top of the staircase and it's one of the first things you see when you enter the stadium through the front door. The board displays the names of those players inducted into the Hall of Fame, and we hold an annual presentation ceremony to recognise their contribution.

'It's a great way to honour our former players, but it is also a commercial exercise, and allows us to stage a black tie dinner and bring funds into the club. I believe it serves both functions really well.

'Originally, the plan was for supporters to nominate former players through our website, and then a panel – consisting of Sandy Jardine, John Greig and myself – would sit down and discuss the merits of the players who had been nominated. After a year or two, it was down to Sandy, John and myself to put forward the players we thought should be in the Hall of Fame.'

The trio had to come up with criteria, which would need to be met before a player could be inducted. The five points of entry (each entrant would have to fulfil just one point) were that the player would have to have made in excess of 300 appearances for Rangers; he would have to have won a trophy while at Ibrox; be an international; served the club with dignity; or been an exceptional player.

David said: 'We wanted players from different eras, so each year we would nominate a couple from the 1920s and '30s, '40s and '50s and so on. The only time we ever inaugurated a block of players was to honour the Founding Fathers of the club.

'In 2008, there was a groundswell of opinion to get Sam English inducted. Apart from the Founding Fathers, Sam had made the least number of appearances of all 90 inductees, just one fewer than Graeme Souness, but he met other aspects of the criteria, like being an international or winning trophies while at the club. There is no doubt Sam was a player of exceptional quality, but that year we had been looking to induct Johnny Hubbard and Billy Simpson from that era. A major bonus for us was that both guys were still alive and would be able to attend the event. It wasn't a popular decision to omit Sam but we always knew he would be inducted in the near future.'

And Sam's time arrived 12 months later when his name was put forward by the panel, and unanimously passed. David said, 'We were delighted to induct Sam into the Hall of Fame in 2009. There was no doubt he could've been included on his goals alone, because his figures merited inclusion. But probably the only criteria he didn't meet was the number of appearances he made for the club. Everything else was a given.

'It's remarkable to think that Sam's record of 44 league goals in a season still stands to this day. Considering some of the great strikers we've had down the years, you would think someone might have beaten it, but I suppose it just goes to show how good a finisher he actually was. And to do it in his first season as a Senior player makes it all the more remarkable. He was definitely a special footballer.'

The late, great Sandy Jardine was also a fan of English, and felt that but for the events of September 1931, he could have gone on to become one of Rangers' greatest ever forwards: 'Unfortunately Sam didn't play for the club for a long time. He only played 82 games but still scored something like 71 goals. He is the record goalscorer in one season for Rangers and because of that we included him in the Hall of Fame. There's no doubt in my mind that if he hadn't been involved in the tragic accident with John Thomson, he would have stayed at Ibrox a lot longer. The unfortunate circumstances surrounding what happened led to his departure but we felt we had to recognise his achievement of scoring more goals than anyone in a single season.'

Rangers FC have arguably the richest history in the football world, and many of the club's players are known far and wide, but those from a bygone era are often victims of the passing of time; and their star is permitted to slowly regress into a vast universe. By committing Sam to a gable end or canvas, or creating a beautiful rose bowl, or inducting him into the Hall of Fame, the efforts of a great many people have ensured that Sam English will never be forgotten. For as long as our great footballing institution continues to function, the memory and achievements of 'Our Sammy' will live on. And that is exactly the way it should be.

Epilogue

THE CAR park was filled to capacity and the only space on an adjacent side street meant a tight squeeze between a Monday-to-Friday burger van and a mucky pick-up truck with the words 'wash me' written in the grime. On the approach to the Holm Park turnstiles, one is met with two murals which remind supporters that Yoker Athletic and Clydebank have entered into a ground-sharing pact these days. But once upon a time this walled stadium was the sole domain of the Whe Ho, founded 1886.

Venturing into the ground, around 80 or 90 supporters are present when the referee sounds his whistle to signal the beginning of this league encounter against St Anthony's, another Junior club with a long and illustrious history, and a side who play their football in the shadow of Ibrox Park.

It's a chilly afternoon, despite still apparently being officially summer, but there are plenty of hot drinks and snacks available to warm the cockles of one's heart.

But nothing gets rid of the chill for a real football man more than a goal, and the sides manage one each in the first five minutes. In the following quarter of an hour, Yoker and the Ants push hard to regain the advantage, and with 20 minutes on the clock, we are treated to a goal of real quality. A Yoker forward picks up the ball 18 yards out and lets fly. The goalkeeper hasn't an earthly of saving it. It's a goal all the way and even though the game is still in its relative infancy, it has all the hallmarks of a winner.

As the ball settles in the corner of the net, the scorer takes the acclaim of a small group of supporters behind the goal, just in front of the clubhouse, before high-fiving joyful team-mates on his way back to the centre circle. The beaten keeper lifts the net up with one hand, retrieves the ball with the other and kicks it in the direction of the centre circle. The teams play out the remaining 70 minutes without any further incidents of note. The goal would indeed prove to be the winner.

More points on the board for the Whe Ho, and Yoker supporters are once again hailing their favourites. The passion they have for this club is clear.

The goalscorer is Gregor Cree, a 25-year-old from Old Kilpatrick, and enjoying his third season in the blue of Yoker. And there is every chance that his uncanny knack for sticking the ball in the net is partly an ancestral hand-me-down. Yoker is his club. It was also his great-grandfather's club. And even more incredibly, exactly 90 years to the day have elapsed since his great-grandfather scored the winner for Yoker on this very ground; and at the same end.

And the name of his great-grandfather? Sam English. The same Sam English who prowled the opposition area at Holm Park with such distinction. In fact, once Sam became known in these parts for his goals, the very mention of his name was enough to strike fear into most visiting defenders.

Sure, the old ground has changed a bit since Sam's day. The well-worn green turf has been replaced by a 21st-century AstroTurf surface; the most radical of a number of improvements which have been made with the help of private investment and council assistance. The Holm Park makeover has met with the firm approval of all who frequent the place, and as crowds hover around the 100 mark for most games, there is plenty of space on the terracing for all who want to attend. The days of packing 10,000 hardy souls into Holm Park have gone, but those who come along nowadays are no less passionate about their team.

On the afternoon that Gregor's winner takes his side to the top of the table, there are parallels to be drawn with his great-grandfather's time at the club. Gregor's contribution helps his side gain three important league points, while 90 years ago to the day, his great-grandfather scored the winner against Petershill, and added another six. Yoker won the match 15-1 – but received just two points for their efforts, as was the law of the game back then.

After the match, Gregor told me, 'When I was growing up I was always aware of who my great-grandpa was and about his career. As a lifelong Rangers fan, I just thought it was amazing that he'd played for Rangers and scored a lot of goals! It wasn't until I was older and understood football properly that I fully appreciated what he had actually achieved.

'Once I began to realise the enormity of the records he still holds today and how he's remembered by both the club and fans, as well as some of the games he played in and the trophies he won; that's when I was really able to be proud and passionate about his legacy ... and I still am today.

'The things he'd achieved were all dreams of mine growing up too, and still are, so to know that he was good enough to achieve all of that gives me a lot of pride and satisfaction.

'I had also been aware that he'd played for Yoker but it really wasn't something I'd thought about too much when I was asked to sign for the club. It wasn't until I saw the satisfaction that my signing gave my grandpa that I recognised how coincidental, yet significant it was.

'When I learned that Sam's picture was still displayed proudly upstairs in the social club at Holm Park, after all these years, I made the Yoker chairman aware of our connection one day. It was his astonishment and that of other club officials which allowed me to fully acknowledge just how amazing it is.

'Since then, it really has felt like it was some sort of fate that I ended up playing for Yoker and I think that's why I now feel such a strong connection with the club; and Sam.'

It's time to leave Holm Park and as I walk through the gates on my way back to the car, I get the sense that the spirit of Sam English is still present at this great club. Holm Park is where Sam was happiest, and it's fitting that the club still has a member of the family on the playing staff. It's somehow prophetic, and comforting.

Acknowledgements

To the family of Sam English for their cooperation and help. Sam's son-in-law, Ronnie Cree snr, his grandson, Ronnie Cree and Gregor Cree, who has followed in his great-grandfather's footsteps by playing for, and scoring lots of goals for Yoker Athletic. A credit to their talented ancestor.

Murray Roxburgh, Helen Runciman, Mark Dingwall, Ian and David McClean, Stephen Miller, Lone Star Bankie, Peter Michael, Gill Watt, Michael Allan and Colin Poultney

Cara Murphy, silversmith, Northern Ireland

Colin Foster, Hartlepool United historian

Stephen Done, senior specialist, museum curator, Liverpool FC

Barbara Harding, Coleraine Historical Society

Katie McDonald, West Dunbartonshire Council archivist

Pauline Scotland, Liverpool Central Library

Sandra McKay, library officer, reference services, Hartlepool Central Library

Mary Frances McGlynn, reference and local studies assistant, Clydebank Heritage Library

Claire Daniel, Emma Yan, archives and special collections, University of Glasgow
Tom Miller, Andy Little and David Mason (Rangers FC)
Campbell Bissland (Yoker Athletic)
National Library of Scotland, The Inverclyde Heritage Trust, Watt Library (Greenock), McLean Museum (Greenock)
The residents of Crevolea

To the many contemporary reporters from Sam's era, for their colourful descriptions of play and the general information on Sam and his clubs. Invaluable.

Newspapers used for research included: *Daily Express, Daily Record, Sunday Mail, Liverpool Echo, Northern Daily Mail, Sunday Post, Port Glasgow Express and Observer, Glasgow Herald, Evening Times (Glasgow).*

Last but not least, to Jane Camillin and everyone else at Pitch Publishing, the number one sports book publisher in the United Kingdom.

To my mother-in-law May Gahagan, who passed away in January, 2020. Always 100 per cent behind everything I did, which was borne out by each of my books unashamedly taking pride of place on her bookshelf. Always in our hearts x

Also available at all good book stores

9781785314407

9781785314995

9781785316333

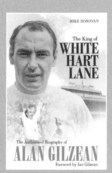

9781785315510

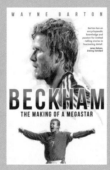

9781785316760

9781785312885

9781785315275

9781785312304

9781908051332